Father Mathew's Crusade

FATHER MATHEW'S CRUSADE

*Temperance in Nineteenth-Century
Ireland and Irish America*

JOHN F. QUINN

UNIVERSITY OF MASSACHUSETTS PRESS
· AMHERST AND BOSTON ·

Copyright © 2002 by University of Massachusetts Press
All rights reserved
Printed in the United States of America

LC 2001008662

ISBN 1-55849-339-5 (cloth); 340-9 (paper)

Designed by Dean Bornstein
Set in Adobe Garamond and Berthold Walbaum by Graphic Composition, Inc.
Printed and bound by The Maple-Vail Book Manufacturing Group

Library of Congress Cataloging-in-Publication Data

Quinn, John F., 1964–
Father Mathew's crusade : temperance in nineteenth-century Ireland and Irish America / John F. Quinn.
    p. cm.
Includes bibliographical references (p.   ) and index.
    ISBN 1-55849-339-5 (alk. paper) — ISBN 1-55849-340-9 (pbk. : alk. paper)
1. Mathew, Theobald, 1790–1856. 2. Temperance—Ireland—History—19th century. I. Title.
    HV5032 .M3 Q56 2002
    363.4'1'0941509034—dc21

2001008662

British Library Cataloguing in Publication data are available.

This book is published with the assistance of a grant from Salve Regina University.

Contents

Acknowledgments
vii

Introduction
1

CHAPTER ONE
Ireland in the 1830s
10

CHAPTER TWO
Drink and Temperance before Mathew's Crusade
40

CHAPTER THREE
Mathew's "Miracle," 1838–1840
57

CHAPTER FOUR
"Temperance Principles Are All but Universal," 1841–1844
86

CHAPTER FIVE
Temperance in Crisis, 1844–1845
116

CHAPTER SIX
The Famine Years, 1846–1849
129

CHAPTER SEVEN
Mathew's American Tour and Final Years, 1849–1856
154

CHAPTER EIGHT
Mathew's Legacy: Temperance after 1880
172

Notes
195

Bibliography
239

Index
257

Illustrations follow page 128

Acknowledgments

While writing this book, I accumulated a host of debts, which it gives me pleasure to acknowledge now. I thank my graduate advisers at the University of Notre Dame, Robert E. Burns, Father Marvin O'Connell, Thomas Kselman, and Philip Gleason, for their guidance and wise counsel. For help in gathering materials, I thank the staff of the Notre Dame Library and Archives, especially Laura Fuderer, Rita Erskine, and Sharon Sumpter. Christine McCullough of the Philadelphia Archdiocesan Archives provided me with several important documents. Christine Bagley, a research librarian at Salve Regina University, my present home, aided me on a number of occasions. I was also helped by the librarians at Sterling Memorial Library and the Beinecke Rare Book Library at Yale University, Drew University, the Special Collections Department of Georgetown University, Boston College, and the Boston Archdiocesan Archives.

Travel to Ireland and initial research on this project were made possible by the Zahm Travel Fund and the Department of History at the University of Notre Dame. In Ireland I was privileged to consult with Maurice O'Connell, formerly of Fordham University and now a Dublin resident, and with Jacqueline Hill of St. Patrick's College, Maynooth. I was greatly assisted in my work by the staffs of the National Library of Ireland, the Dublin Diocesan Archives, the Friends Library, Trinity College Library, the National Archives Office, and the Cork City Archives. Most of all, however, I want to express my sincere thanks to Father Pádraig Ó'Cuill, O.F.M. Cap., the former archivist of the Church Street Friary in Dublin. Father Ó'Cuill and the other friars provided me with every possible kindness as I waded through stack after stack of Father Mathew's correspondence. I wish also to thank Father Nessan Shaw, O.F.M. Cap., for giving me a tour of Cork and sharing his many insights on Father Mathew and the temperance movement.

Two grants from the National Endowment for the Humanities enabled me to spend summers at Yale University and Boston University, and to complete the project. Salve Regina University generously provided funding to help with publication costs.

Other people have helped as well. Three experts on Irish temperance movements—Elizabeth Malcolm, George Bretherton, and Colm Kerrigan—encouraged me and offered sound advice. Paul Wright and Carol Betsch, my editors at the University of Massachusetts Press, were supportive from the beginning. Other scholars and friends assisted me along my way: Charlotte Ames; John Buckley, F.S.C.; Thomas Day; Anthony DeBlasi; Jay Dolan; Joseph Durkin, S.J.; Robert France; Cristina Gillen; Patrick Gillen; the late Joseph Hamburger; Duane Jundt; Kathleen Kamper; Barbara Kathe; Bradley Lewis; Donald McLaughlin; Kevin McGrath, O.P.; Kerby Miller; John Raphael, S.S.J.; Paul Townend; Robert Wegs; Edmund Wehrle; my brother Peter; my sister, Maryann; and my wife, Marguerite. I would like to acknowledge specially my brother Bill, who offered insightful comments on each draft of the manuscript. Finally, the book is dedicated to my mother, Mary F. Quinn, and to the memory of my father, William J. Quinn. I so appreciate the support and encouragement they offered me year after year.

J. F. Q.

Father Mathew's Crusade

Introduction

THE IRISH ARE WELL KNOWN for their fondness for strong drink. Since at least the early nineteenth century, Irishmen have been stereotyped as "drunken Paddies" and intemperance described as the "Irish curse." Elizabeth Malcolm, a leading authority on Irish drinking habits, concedes that Ireland has had—and continues to have—more than its share of problem drinkers. Although the Irish government taxes alcohol more heavily than most of its European neighbors do, the policy seems to have little effect on its citizens' drinking behavior. The Irish people's response has simply been to spend considerable sums on alcohol. Indeed, they presently devote 12 percent of their income to alcohol, a higher proportion than any other Western people. In 1988 it was reported that the 3 million or so residents of the Irish Republic together shelled out more than $4 million a day on alcoholic beverages.[1]

Malcolm argues that the "drunken Paddy is but one side of the coin of Irish drinking habits; the other side features the teetotal Paddy—an important figure who is too often ignored."[2] Indeed, many of Ireland's leading figures have belonged to this minority tradition. Several of the most prominent nationalists of the nineteenth century were teetotalers: Charles Gavan Duffy of the Young Ireland movement, Charles Kickham and John Denvir of the Irish Republican Brotherhood, and Justin McCarthy of the Irish Parliamentary Party. In the twentieth century, both Patrick Pearse, the architect of the Easter Rising of 1916, and Jim Larkin, the radical labor leader, were total abstainers. Among church leaders,

Edmund Rice, the founder of the Christian Brothers, was probably the most noteworthy teetotaler.

Malcolm notes that Ireland presently has one of the highest proportions of teetotalers in the non-Islamic world. A 1982 survey of Irish drinking behavior showed that 10 percent of Irishmen and 25 percent of Irishwomen were total abstainers. A 1987 comparative study of Irish and American teenagers found that 17.3 percent of the Irish adolescents were teetotalers, as opposed to 11.3 percent of the Americans. And the editors of the 1999 *Encyclopedia of Understanding Alcohol and Drugs* write of the "high percentage of abstainers" in Ireland (but do not offer any statistical estimates).[3]

Mathew's "Miracle"

Having unusually high numbers of both heavy drinkers and teetotalers gives Ireland what researchers call a "bimodal distribution."[4] There are undoubtedly a number of factors responsible for this phenomenon, but it appears that this split over drinking dates back to the 1830s, when Ireland experienced its first temperance campaign. Its leader was Father Theobald Mathew, a Capuchin[5] friar, who was recruited in 1838 to lead the Cork Total Abstinence Society. After trying to promote the cause for several years without much success, local temperance leaders concluded that they needed a priest like Father Mathew to appeal to the Catholic masses. In some respects, he was uniquely qualified to head the movement. He had been in Cork since 1814 and gained an excellent reputation in the Catholic community for his unstinting work with the poor and his sympathetic manner in the confessional. At the same time, he was friendly with a number of the city's leading Protestants. He was also less of a nationalist and more of an anglophile than most of his fellow priests. These attitudes gained him a sympathetic hearing from British government officials and wealthy Protestants in Ireland and England.

Under Mathew's leadership, teetotalism increased dramatically in Cork and then spread through the province of Munster and eventually throughout Ireland. Initiates knelt down and swore before God they would never touch liquor again. Some people pledged because they accepted Mathew's claim that teetotalism would bring them prosperity and harmony at home. Others pledged because they thought he had the power to heal their ailments and infirmities. Whatever their motivation, at least 5 million Irish people—a majority of the population—had taken the pledge by the early 1840s, and Mathew had begun traveling abroad to enlist the Scots and English in his burgeoning movement. In 1839, the nationalist leader Daniel O'Connell hailed the temperance movement as Mathew's "mighty moral miracle."

In the mid-1840s, Mathew's movement began to fall apart. His health started to fail and his debts to accumulate, making it difficult for him to continue with his campaign. Certainly the Famine dealt a serious blow to the temperance movement; thousands of Mathew's followers died or emigrated during these years, and many of those who remained in Ireland broke their pledges at this time. With the Famine wreaking destruction throughout Ireland, temperance must have seemed a marginal concern to many Irish.

The Famine also contributed to the polarization of Irish society. Divisions between Catholics and Protestants, and nationalists and unionists, were hardening. Mathew's unusual attitudes became a liability for him and the temperance movement. Many Catholics began to wonder if Mathew was not too friendly with Protestants and the British government, especially after 1847, when he accepted a pension from Queen Victoria. Some considered him a "Castle" priest, a pawn of the authorities.[6]

With the movement unraveling around him in Ireland, Mathew summoned up his remaining energy and resources to make a trip to the United States to administer teetotal pledges there. Although he was ailing, his two-year sojourn in 1849–51 proved to be his most successful foreign trip ever. In Washington, D.C., he was invited to the White House and honored by Congress, and in every other city he visited he was well received by Protestants and Catholics alike, his only detractors being northern abolitionists and southern slaveholders irked by his noncommittal statements on slavery. During his visit, he pledged five hundred thousand Irish Americans, roughly one-third of the total Irish Catholic population in America.[7]

By the time Mathew returned to Ireland in 1851, his health had so deteriorated that he could no longer promote temperance actively. At his death in 1856, the temperance movement was weak and disorganized.

Branches of the once powerful movement still existed in a number of towns throughout the island, but no one attempted to continue Mathew's work. Teetotalism languished in Ireland until the 1880s, when Father James Cullen, S.J., took up the cause and eventually established the Pioneers, a Catholic total abstinence society, which is still in existence. Likewise in the United States, Irish American temperance organizations stalled in the 1850s and 1860s but gained momentum again in the 1870s, when the Irish-dominated Catholic Total Abstinence Union (CTAU) came into being.

The Forgotten Friar

While the teetotal movements in England and the United States have received considerable attention from scholars, the Irish movement—which was the most successful of the three in the 1830s and 1840s—has not been studied as closely. Elizabeth Malcolm's *"Ireland Sober, Ireland Free": Drink and Temperance in Nineteenth Century Ireland* and Diarmaid Ferriter's *A Nation of Extremes: The Pioneers in Twentieth Century Ireland* are the only major studies of temperance in Ireland.[8]

Father Mathew has not received his due, either. Statues of him have been erected in the centers of Dublin and Cork, and streets, bridges, and music halls have been named for him, but historians have tended to ignore him. F. S. L. Lyons did not once mention Mathew in his magisterial nine-hundred-page survey of modern Ireland, and Gearóid Ó'Tuathaigh made only a passing reference to Mathew in his study of pre-Famine Ireland. The same is true of R. F. Foster and T. W. Moody and F. X. Martin; Mathew is dispatched in a sentence in their detailed works. In 1979 Hugh Kearney, an expert on early modern Ireland, asserted that "Theobald Mathew is one of the most neglected figures in nineteenth-century Irish historiography. To his contemporaries he appeared to be leading a 'moral revolution' in its own way as important as the campaigns of O'Connell, but whereas O'Connell has continued to attract the attention of historians, Father Mathew's reputation remains embalmed within the tradition of the Irish Capuchins and remote from the concerns of Irish historians."[9]

Kearney was not especially interested in Mathew or the temperance movement and instead had more theoretical concerns. In his view,

Mathew was an overlooked agent of modernization in pre-Famine Ireland. He claimed that Mathew used temperance as a means of improving the Irish people, drawing them out of their folk beliefs and tradition-bound lifestyles. Kearney argued that Mathew's movement was middle-class, urban, and English speaking, intent on promoting literacy and thrift as well as sobriety among its members.

Kearney's depiction of Mathew as a modernizer provoked debate, but no one could dispute his claim that Mathew deserved more attention from scholars. Before Kearney's article, there had been only three serious biographies of Mathew, and each was flawed in one respect or another. John F. Maguire, a friend and supporter of Mathew, undertook the first biography in 1863. Although detailed and informative, it was short on detachment and long on inaccuracy.[10] In the 1940s, two more biographies appeared. In 1943 Father Patrick Rogers published a brief, laudatory study, and in 1947 Father Augustine, a Capuchin, followed with a much lengthier work.[11] Each book was valuable and pointed out some of the errors in Maguire's account. Augustine's thorough narrative was the most informative and reliable of the three studies. Still, like Maguire and Rogers, Augustine was an ardent defender of Mathew, and he slipped into hagiography in places; he excused his fellow Franciscan of all character flaws and regularly compared him to St. Francis of Assisi and on occasion to Christ.[12] Although he carefully chronicled much of Mathew's career, he did not adequately discuss the strained relationship that Mathew had with several members of the hierarchy.

Since Kearney's article appeared, three people have published substantive work relating to Father Mathew, though two of them are concerned more with temperance activities before and after him. Malcolm devoted one chapter in her book to Mathew and provided many insights. She remarked on Mathew's lifelong difficulties with money, alluded to his troubles with certain bishops, and made clear that she did not see Mathew as a modernizer. She pointed out that most of Mathew's adherents came from the countryside and contended that they were attracted to him for superstitious reasons.

Although Malcolm shed light on Mathew, she did not intend to offer a definitive analysis of him or the temperance movement in the 1830s and 1840s. Most of her book was concerned with events in the last half of the nineteenth century. George Bretherton completed a dissertation at Columbia University in 1978 on the Irish temperance movement from 1829 to 1847. Although this study was also helpful, much of it was devoted to the Protestant-dominated temperance societies that predated Mathew's entrance into the movement.[13]

Most recently, Colm Kerrigan published several articles on the Irish temperance movement and then a book, *Father Mathew and the Irish Temperance Movement, 1838–1849*, which synthesized the arguments presented in his essays.[14] The book took a thematic approach, focusing mostly on the social and economic aspects of Mathew's campaign, such as its impact on crime, alcohol consumption, and bank deposits. Mathew and other teetotal activists often boasted in the 1840s that the Irish people were drinking less, committing fewer crimes, and saving more money, but Kerrigan argued convincingly that the data were inconclusive. Nevertheless he acknowledged that Mathew had a significant impact on Irish society and paved the way for later temperance reformers.

Kerrigan also offered a brief but insightful consideration of the modernization question. He noted that both Kearney and Malcolm had made valid points. Mathew often used the language of thrift and improvement when trying to gain converts; at other times he played on people's superstitions and fears to cajole them into enrolling. In Kerrigan's view, Mathew was a pragmatist who was quite willing to tailor his argument to his listeners.

Kearney's depiction of Father Mathew as a neglected figure is no longer accurate, given the work these three scholars have completed. It is my hope that this book will complement the recent scholarship. I had access to the archives of the archdioceses of Philadelphia and Boston, the University of Notre Dame, and Georgetown University, which provided me with letters and diaries that none of the other scholars have seen. These materials allowed me to construct a detailed narrative of the progress of Mathew's campaign. They were particularly helpful to my chronicle of Mathew's American tour of 1849–1851 and exploration of Irish American teetotal activism in the late nineteenth century.

My focus is also somewhat different from that of Malcolm and Kerrigan. Although this book is not strictly a biography, I concentrate more closely on Mathew than they did. I show the ways in which Mathew's temperament and worldview helped and hindered the movement at different times. A gentle, compassionate man, Mathew could relate to people of all creeds, classes, and races, and he was a tireless worker, willing to wear himself out for the cause. But he could also be quick to anger and slow to forgive, was generous literally to a fault, and, convinced of his own indispensability in the movement, was unable to collaborate effectively with other temperance leaders.

As to the question of whether Mathew was a modernizer, I argue that in fact he should be seen as a man behind his times. Although Kearney was right to point out that Mathew saw temperance as a means of promoting literacy and economic advancement for the Irish people, Mathew was concerned more with using temperance to improve relations among Catholics and Protestants and among Irish and English. A dedicated anglophile and ecumenist, he resembled a cleric of the ancien régime in some respects. His views put him sharply at odds with the dominant political and religious leaders of Ireland and caused him one difficulty after another.

O'Connell, the Bishops, and Temperance

Whereas Mathew's assimilationist attitudes pleased all but the most hidebound Tories in the Ascendancy and Parliament, his outlook was bound to raise suspicions among Irish nationalists, both lay and clerical. Mathew's relationship with the nationalist leader Daniel O'Connell appears to have been complex. Although O'Connell has received considerable attention from scholars, most of his biographers fail to mention that he had an abiding interest in temperance from 1839 until his death in 1847 and was a pledged teetotaler from 1840 to 1842.[15] Even after his Repeal campaign had begun to flag,[16] he regularly hailed Mathew in his speeches and correspondence, and he spent much time and energy in 1844–45 trying to extricate Mathew from his financial difficulties. In contrast, Mathew generally avoided any public connection with O'Connell, fearing that any association with Repeal would bring the government's wrath upon him. Just what Mathew really thought of O'Connell is difficult to determine. He corresponded with O'Connell on occasion and even sought his help in obtaining positions for his friends, but in private he could be critical of him.

Lawrence McCaffrey is one O'Connell scholar who has explored the links between teetotalism and Repeal. He claims that O'Connell harnessed the temperance movement's resources—especially its reading rooms and musical bands—in the drive for Repeal and in fact co-opted the temperance movement despite Mathew's protestations.[17] Although it is undoubtedly true that many temperance activists were at times more concerned with the Repeal campaign, especially in 1843, when it reached its apex, Mathew's movement remained strong and was able to coexist with O'Connell's until the onset of the Famine.

O'Connell may have been intent on using temperance halls and bands to further the Repeal campaign, but he was also interested in linking temperance and nationalism at a theoretical level. Whereas Mathew saw the success of the temperance movement as a way to gain the goodwill of the British authorities and the Ascendancy, O'Connell saw it as clear evidence of the Irish people's essential virtuousness. By acting with such discipline, the Irish were demonstrating their capacity for self-government and the reasonableness of Repeal. Until the end of his life, O'Connell continued to champion temperance.

Although O'Connell and other lay nationalists probably did little damage to Mathew, several nationalists in the hierarchy were much more critical of him and ended up hurting him severely. Mathew has been largely ignored by church historians who write about the bishops and lower clergy in nineteenth-century Ireland,[18] and for one reason or another, the scholars who have studied Mathew have not explored his relationship with the hierarchy in any depth. Although most bishops were at least nominally supportive of him, two key prelates, Archbishop John MacHale and Bishop William Higgins, turned against him early and tried to keep him out of their dioceses. As the years passed, more bishops grew suspicious of him and undermined him at critical junctures. When Mathew found himself bankrupt in 1844, most members of the hierarchy made no effort to help him raise money. In 1847 several bishops intervened to block his appointment as bishop of Cork, dealing him a damaging blow at a time when his movement was struggling.

Mathew's Legacy: The Temperance Revival in Ireland and Irish America

In the late nineteenth century, both Ireland and Irish America experienced temperance revivals. In both countries, the leaders of the temperance movements established Catholic societies that had the full backing of the hierarchy. In other respects, the two movements were quite different. In Ireland, Father Cullen followed O'Connell's lead and tried to connect the Pioneers to the nationalist cause. In his speeches he regularly asserted that widespread temperance among the Irish would pave the way for Irish independence from England. In America, in contrast, leaders of the CTAU such as Archbishop John Ireland followed Mathew's example and promoted teetotalism as part of the effort to assimilate the Irish population. Like Mathew, Ireland sought the approval of his country's dominant Protestants and was willing to join hands with them to promote temperance. He hoped that teetotalism would undo the negative stereotypes that dogged the Irish community in America. For forty years— roughly 1880 to 1920—the Irish American temperance movement thrived. By 1930, it had petered out, largely because of the fallout from Prohibition. Cullen's Pioneers proved hardier and remained a vital force in Ireland until the mid-1960s and 1970s, when they found themselves unable to adapt to the dramatic political, cultural, and religious changes occurring in Ireland.

Although the CTAU no longer exists and the Pioneers are now only a small organization, it is fair to say that the movement Mathew initiated in 1838 left a deep impression on the people of Ireland and Irish America. Since Mathew's era, a sizable number of Irish and Irish American people have made the decision not to drink.

{ CHAPTER ONE }

Ireland in the 1830s: Politics and Religion

Unfortunately in this country politics and religion are one. If politics were separated we could easily manage the people.

Castlebar policeman quoted in
Alexis de Tocqueville's Journey in Ireland (1835)

WHEN ALEXIS DE TOCQUEVILLE and Gustave de Beaumont visited Ireland in the summer of 1835, they were struck above all by the impoverished state of the peasantry. Writing to his father shortly after his arrival, Tocqueville declared, "You cannot imagine what a complexity of miseries five centuries of oppression, civil disorders, and religious hostility have piled up on this poor people." After riding from Dublin to Carlow, he noted his impressions: "Pretty country. Land very fertile. Beautiful road.... Most of the dwellings of the country very poor looking. A very large number of them wretched to the last degree. Walls of mud, roofs of thatch, one room. No chimney, smoke goes out the door. The pig lies in the middle of the house. It is Sunday. Yet the population looks very wretched. Many wear clothes with holes or much patched. Most of them are bare-headed and barefoot."[1]

Beaumont, who returned to Ireland in 1837 for a second visit, produced a more detailed account of the poverty he encountered. Remarking that "misery covers the island," he noted that often as many as ten people lived together—with their requisite pig—in one-room cabins devoid of furniture. He estimated that one-third of the population were effectively paupers, entirely dependent on the potato for survival.[2]

Indeed, most Irish farmers were worse off in 1837 than they had been ten or twenty years earlier. The population was increasing steadily and grain prices had been slumping since 1815, when the Napoleonic Wars

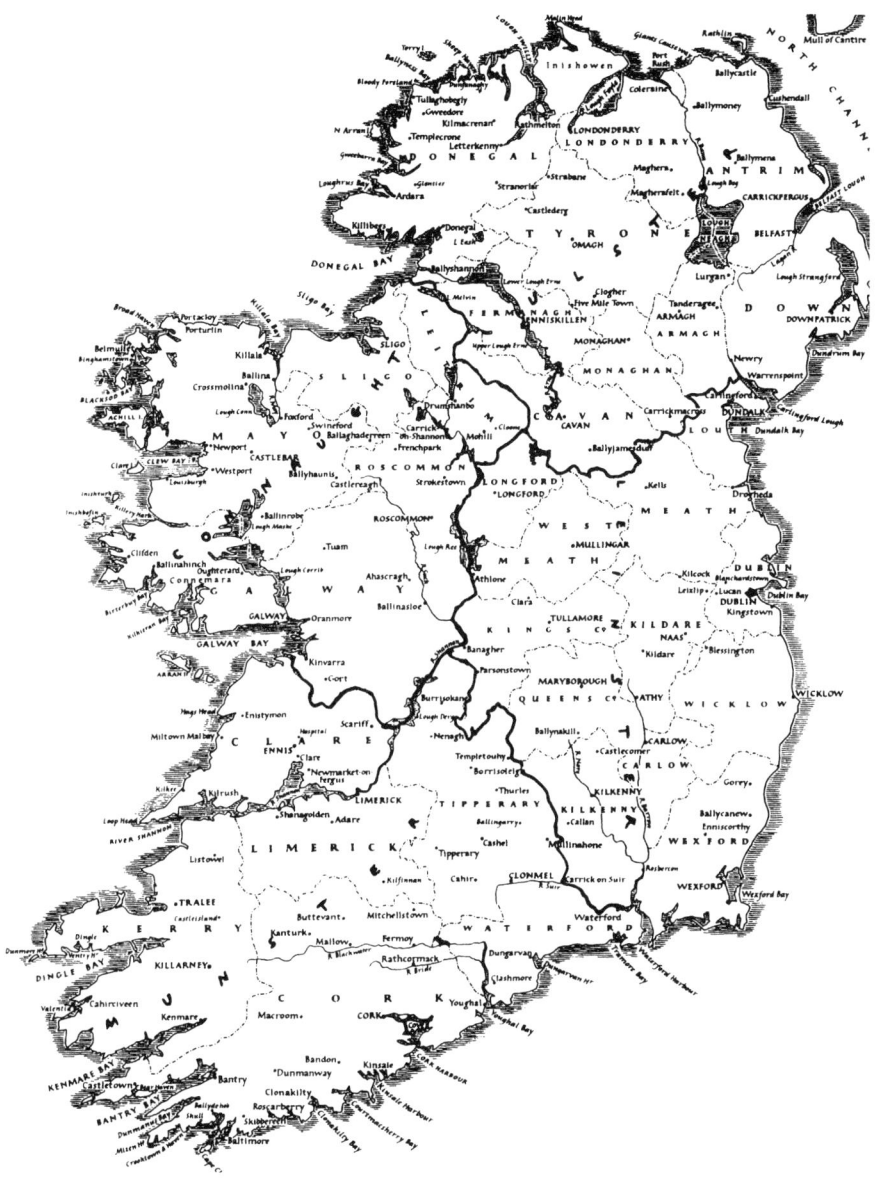

Political map of Ireland, mid-nineteenth century. Reprinted from Helen E. Hatton, *The Largest Amount of Good* (1993), by permission of the author and McGill-Queen's University Press.

had ended. As demand for grain fell, many landlords decided to shift to cattle raising, a less labor intensive undertaking than farming. In the face of these demographic and economic pressures, one-third or more of Ireland's farmers were barely scratching out a living.[3]

Nonetheless neither Tocqueville nor Beaumont witnessed any signs of despair among the people. Instead they found a deep and abiding faith among the Catholic majority. In one village, Tocqueville saw thirty men standing outside the priest's house, waiting their turn for confession; in another, he found the people fasting on Saturdays; and in a third town, he came across a large group of people praying the rosary in their church. When discussing the people's faith with two bishops, however, he received a more critical report. Although Bishop William Kinsella of Ossory acknowledged the piety and moral purity of the laity, he characterized many as "ignorant, intemperate and violent." Bishop William Nolan of Kildare and Leighlin offered a similar judgment: "They have many good qualities mixed with the faults that poverty brings. They are gentle, polite, hospitable. . . . But when the occasion of drinking to excess presents itself they do not know how to resist it. Then they become turbulent and often violent and disorderly."[4]

If the clergy had certain reservations about the Irish people, the reverse was not true as far as Tocqueville and Beaumont could determine. The laity had an almost worshipful attitude toward the clergy. Tocqueville claimed that an "unbelievable union" existed among priests and people. A Protestant lawyer in Dublin, John Prendergast, admitted as much to Tocqueville, saying, "[The Catholics'] only aristocracy is the clergy. For the Irish, religion has become not only a matter of faith, but a matter of patriotism. All Ireland is under the influence of Catholicism."[5]

The Catholic people also put great faith in Daniel O'Connell, a lawyer who for years had voiced their religious and political concerns. Although sixty-two years old at the time of Beaumont's second visit in 1837, O'Connell was still very much in charge of the nationalist movement in Ireland. Beaumont, evidently awestruck, described him as a "political genius" who "exercises a dictatorship over the people; his advice is obeyed as a command."[6]

Politics: O'Connell's Rise to Prominence

In the 1830s Daniel O'Connell was a power to be reckoned with in Ireland and England. In 1829 he had achieved a great triumph: the Duke of Wellington's Tory administration had at long last granted Catholic Emancipation. Catholics were henceforth eligible to sit in the British Parliament and serve as cabinet ministers, judges, generals, and admirals.[7] Emancipation had been Catholics' top political priority since the 1790s. O'Connell had finally gained it for them and thus freed them from the last vestiges of the Penal Laws.[8]

O'Connell had been prominent in Irish politics long before his victory of 1829. He was born in 1775 into one of the few Catholic families who had been able to hold on to much of their ancestral lands without having to conform to the Church of Ireland. As a member of the Catholic elite, he was able to take advantage of the opportunities that were gradually opening up for Irish Catholics and he was sent to France for his education. When the French Revolution turned bloody in 1793, he went to London, where he entered Lincoln's Inn for his legal apprenticeship (the Catholic Relief Act of 1792 had opened up the legal profession to Catholics). Since not much studying was required, he found himself a man of leisure from 1794 to 1796. While it appears that he drank to excess on occasion, he spent most of his days and nights reading philosophy, religion, and history.[9] Slowly but steadily, he worked his way through the key writers of the Enlightenment: Voltaire, Jean-Jacques Rousseau, William Godwin, Edward Gibbon, and Thomas Paine. His lifelong enthusiasm for democracy and utilitarianism and his commitment to nonviolent political action can be traced to his days in London.[10]

These deist philosophers also triggered a crisis of faith in O'Connell. He was mesmerized by Paine's *Age of Reason,* noting in his diary in 1796 that it had provided him with "a great deal of pleasure."[11] For the next decade or so, he remained estranged from the Church. Although he would attend Mass now and then, he would just as often wake up drunk on Sunday mornings and not bother to go to church.[12] In 1799 he enrolled in the Freemasons, and for the next few years he continued to read Enlightenment authors in his spare time. Finally, in 1809, responding to the entreaties of his devout wife, Mary, O'Connell began to attend Mass regularly and observe the Lenten fasts.[13] Gradually his faith would come back, and as the years passed he would become an increasingly articulate and committed defender of Catholicism. As his fervor intensified, he effectively turned away from his Enlightenment views on church-state relations. Although throughout his career O'Connell publicly championed church-state separation and religious liberty, his aggressive defense of Irish Catholic interests in the 1820s through 1840s was not really consistent with Enlightenment theories on the role of religion in politics. On most political questions, O'Connell espoused Enlightenment-influenced positions throughout his career, but on matters touching Catholicism he generally took a more militant line.[14]

O'Connell returned to Dublin to complete his legal studies in 1796 and was admitted to the bar in April 1798. In the weeks following, Ireland was rocked by rebellion. In May, Catholic nationalists launched a fierce sectarian revolt in the southeast counties and briefly triumphed at Wexford before being defeated by British troops at the battle of Vinegar Hill.[15] At the same time, the United Irishmen, a religiously mixed, Jacobin-oriented force, attempted a rising in Ulster but were dispatched quickly by the British forces. Two months later, a small French force landed in Connaught and caused more difficulties for the British before surrendering in September. By the time the fighting was over, thirty thousand lives had been lost.[16]

O'Connell had not participated in the various risings and had little sympathy for the United Irishmen. Although influenced by the Enlightenment, he was not a republican and was certainly not a Jacobin. Furthermore, he was fast becoming an insider in the elite legal, political, and social circles of Dublin. He was too much a part of the establishment to want to subvert it. Like most other patriotic members of the establishment, O'Connell had joined one of the militias formed to protect the country from the twin threats of French invasion and United Irishmen revolution.

Disturbed as he was by the risings of 1798, O'Connell was more troubled by the British government's reaction. Prime Minister William

Pitt decided that England and Ireland should henceforth be united. The semiautonomous Parliament in Dublin would be dismantled, and in return the Irish would receive seats in the Westminster Parliament. Pitt believed this measure would help secure and stabilize Ireland. When Pitt tacitly linked Catholic Emancipation to the proposed Union, the Catholic bishops and leading laymen supported him.[17] Most Catholics had little attachment to the exclusively Protestant Parliament in Dublin and were willing to support a new arrangement. O'Connell's voice was the only one absent from the chorus of Catholic support for the Union.[18] He condemned the proposed Union on nationalist grounds at a public meeting in Dublin in January 1800, but his protests were unavailing. In August 1800 the Irish Parliament dissolved itself, and in January 1801 the Act of Union took effect, making Ireland an integral part of Great Britain.

After a brief hiatus, O'Connell reentered the political fray in 1804, joining the Catholic Committee, a select group of Catholic aristocrats, gentry, and businessmen. The committee was concerned principally with obtaining Catholic Emancipation, since Pitt had not delivered on his promise after the Union. The leaders of the committee, John Keogh and the Earl of Fingall, were cautious men who were intent on demonstrating to the English government the unswerving loyalty of Irish Catholics. Although still a lapsed Catholic at this time, O'Connell was nonetheless more zealous about Catholic rights than the leaders of the committee. He saw Catholic Emancipation as a matter of simple justice and was not about to apologize for his advocacy.

THE VETO CONTROVERSY

In 1808 the Catholic Committee became embroiled in a protracted battle over whether the British government should be granted a veto over episcopal appointments in return for conceding Catholic Emancipation.[19] Under this plan, the British would be given a list of nominees for each vacant bishopric and the freedom to strike off any candidate they deemed disloyal. After approving or modifying the list, the government would send the names to Propaganda[20] for a final decision.

In May 1808, Henry Grattan, a liberal Irish M.P., proposed that Parliament consider a Catholic Emancipation bill linked with a veto, which he hoped would assuage the concerns of the more conservative members. However, this bill and a similar one that he proposed in 1813 were rejected by the House of Commons. After the second bill's defeat, the Irish bishops issued a pastoral address denouncing Grattan's proposal. This was a radical departure from the hierarchy's earlier statements, which had more or less supported a veto.[21] Two days after the bishops' meeting, the Catholic Board met to reflect on the bill and on the bishops' criticisms.[22] Since 1808, the lay Catholic leaders had been deeply divided over the propriety of a veto. Generally, the gentry and aristocrats were willing to accept a veto, and businessmen, lawyers, and other professionals were not. At this meeting, the tensions that had been simmering beneath the surface suddenly became public when O'Connell proposed a motion commending the hierarchy for its recent pronouncement on the veto question. This motion was offensive to the more cautious members of the board, who disagreed with the bishops' statement and revered Grattan. O'Connell's motion was ultimately approved, but it precipitated a split in the board. Twenty vetoists withdrew from the association, thus ceding the leadership to O'Connell.[23]

After gaining control of the Catholic Board in Ireland, O'Connell soon found himself in conflict with the English Catholic Board. The English Catholic leaders, vetoists almost to a man, had decided to consult Rome for a ruling on the question. In February 1814, the secretary of Propaganda, Monsignor Quarantotti, issued a rescript approving of the veto clauses in Grattan's bill. Quarantotti judged that the British wanted veto power only for public security reasons and had no interest in meddling in the Church's affairs.[24] This decision angered the Irish bishops, who decided to send Daniel Murray, coadjutor to the archbishop of Dublin, to remonstrate with the Roman officials. Through Murray's intercession, the rescript was withdrawn pending further review.

In 1815 Pope Pius VII, who was back in Rome after five years of imprisonment at Napoleon's hands, essentially reaffirmed Quarantotti's statement. The pope must have felt indebted to the British government for the role it had played in the defeat of Napoleon. Although Protestants, the British were perceived as bulwarks against the irreligious forces unleashed by the French revolutionaries.

The Irish bishops were in a quandary. They had taken a strong stand on a church-state issue, only to be contradicted by the pope. After some consideration they issued a letter that amounted to a polite but firm rejection of the Roman view. O'Connell took the same stand but was not nearly as diplomatic. Speaking at a public meeting in Dublin in January 1815, he remarked, "I am sincerely a Catholic but I am not a papist. I deny that the Pope has any temporal authority, directly or indirectly, in Ireland."[25] In the summer, Catholic lay leaders directed him to draft a remonstrance to the pope on the question. Although generally respectful, the letter included a warning "against the interference of your Holiness, or any other foreign prelate, state or potentate . . . in the arrangement of our political concerns."[26] Thus on church-state issues as well as other political questions, O'Connell was proving himself an aggressive Irish nationalist. In his view, substantive papal control over the Irish Church was almost as distasteful as British control over Irish domestic affairs.

THE CATHOLIC ASSOCIATION AND EMANCIPATION

By 1820 the veto controversy had faded, so O'Connell could devote himself to obtaining Catholic Emancipation without any strings attached. In February 1823 he founded a new organization, the Catholic Association, which would prove more formidable than its predecessors. Whereas the Catholic Committee and the Catholic Board had been elite organizations, the Catholic Association was decidedly egalitarian. O'Connell shrewdly chose to open the Catholic Association to the clergy and the lower classes. Committees were formed at the parish, town, and county levels, and reading rooms were established in even the remotest areas.

The response was overwhelming. Priests and bishops backed the group enthusiastically, as did many wealthy Catholics and more than a few Protestants. Yet it was the poor farmers, laborers, and tradesmen who joined in droves and formed the backbone of the association. Even many of those who had been active in secret societies were eager to join. O'Connell had repeatedly denounced secret societies for their violent tactics, but he had often been willing to represent Ribbonmen, Whiteboys, Rockites, and Threshers when they were brought to trial on charges of murder, rape, and pillage. Consequently, many members of secret societies saw him as an ally no matter what he might say.[27]

Money immediately began flowing into the association's coffers. Wealthier members were directed to contribute one guinea in dues annually, while lower-class members were expected to offer one penny per month.[28] Between 1823 and 1829, the dues—nicknamed the "Catholic Rent"—amounted to almost sixty thousand pounds.[29] O'Connell used most of this money to pay the association's legal and campaign expenses, but some funds were allocated to help build and maintain Catholic schools and churches. The Catholic Rent also served a psychological purpose: it helped convince the Catholic masses that they had an important role in the organization. By taxing them, O'Connell was trying to prove to them that they mattered.

In 1826 O'Connell and his associates set about harnessing the wealth and power of the Catholic Association in the general election. They chose several districts and campaigned for the Protestant candidate most sympathetic to Catholic Emancipation. They had several successes, most notably in Waterford, where they helped oust Lord George Beresford, an entrenched Tory incumbent, and replaced him with a young progressive landlord. The Beresfords were some of the largest landowners in County Waterford and had represented Waterford in Parliament continuously since the mid-eighteenth century.[30]

Two years later, the Catholic Association decided to run O'Connell for a seat in County Clare. Although the incumbent, Vesey Fitzgerald, was a strong supporter of Catholic Emancipation, O'Connell waged a fierce campaign against him. In his speech announcing his candidacy, O'Connell, ignoring Fitzgerald's liberal voting record, pronounced him an anti-Catholic bigot and "the sworn libeler of the Catholic faith" and presented himself as "one who has devoted his early life to your cause, who has consumed his manhood in a struggle for your liberties, and who has ever lived, and is ever ready to die, for the integrity, the honour, the purity of the Catholic faith, and the promotion of Irish freedom and happiness."[31]

O'Connell won the election by a more than 2 to 1 margin, which placed the Wellington administration in a difficult position. In March 1829, Sir Robert Peel, the home secretary, introduced a Catholic Emancipation bill. Matching O'Connell for mean-spiritedness, Peel attached a series of petty restrictions to the bill: Catholic bishops were not to assume their titles, Catholic mayors were not allowed to wear their robes of office at Catholic ceremonies, religious orders were limited in various ways, and so on.[32] He also attached one substantive wing to the bill: the forty-shilling freeholders would be disenfranchised. In April, King George IV signed Peel's Catholic Relief Bill into law. After twenty years of struggling, O'Connell had finally triumphed.

O'CONNELL IN PARLIAMENT

In February 1830 O'Connell took his seat at Westminster as the first Roman Catholic elected to Parliament since the Reformation. Perhaps spurred by his victory, he was soon agitating again on a grand scale—this time for the Repeal of the Union. He had never been enthusiastic about the Act of Union, and by 1830 many Irish Catholics were starting to share his view. In his addresses, O'Connell delineated the great economic and cultural benefits that would result from Repeal, but he never specified exactly what he meant by Repeal. Presumably, he envisioned an interdenominational body with powers and duties similar to those of the all-Protestant Dublin Parliament of the 1780s and 1790s.

When in Ireland, O'Connell campaigned tirelessly for Repeal, but at Westminster, he was almost a different man: more sedate and willing to work with British liberals and radicals to obtain meliorative legislation for Ireland and for Great Britain generally. O'Connell and most British progressives shared many of the same values: support for electoral reforms, such as expanded suffrage and a secret ballot, and opposition to slavery and capital punishment.

With Earl Grey's Whig administration replacing Wellington's Tory one in November 1830, electoral reform became a real possibility. In June 1832 the Whigs enacted a Reform Bill that effected modest changes in the English political landscape. Some district lines were redrawn to take account of demographic changes, and the franchise was expanded such that one in five Englishmen were now eligible to vote. The Irish were allotted five more seats in Parliament, but 95 percent of Irishmen—including the forty-shilling freeholders—were still not eligible to vote. O'Connell was disappointed but concluded that the bill was a step in the right direction.

The following year he again collaborated with British liberals, helping secure legislation that outlawed slavery in the West Indies, the lone outpost of slaveholding in the British Empire.[33]

These noble accomplishments did not impress the more zealous Repealers in Ireland. Among the hardliners was Feargus O'Connor, a newly elected M.P. for Cork, who began criticizing O'Connell for ignoring the issue. He threatened to bring Repeal before Parliament if O'Connell would not do it himself. O'Connell did not want to propose a Repeal bill, because he believed it did not stand a chance of passage and would only alienate his liberal allies in England. Still, O'Connor and others had left him no alternative. In April 1834 he dutifully brought before Parliament a Repeal proposal that was rejected overwhelmingly. This defeat was humiliating for O'Connell, but it was liberating as well. He had satisfied the militants' demand and could return to more productive parliamentary matters.[34]

Over the next few months, O'Connell's influence in Parliament increased dramatically. In January 1835 a general election was held that left neither the Whigs nor the Tories with a majority. O'Connell had thirty-four Repealers under his command and twenty-six Irish liberals loosely affiliated with him. This sixty-seat bloc amounted to almost 10 percent of the total seats. The Whigs knew that if they were going to unseat Peel—who had succeeded Grey in November 1834—they would need O'Connell's support. In February O'Connell went to Lichfield House at Westminster to meet with Lord John Russell and other leading Whigs. He promised to support the Whigs, who in turn agreed to enact more reforms for Ireland.

With O'Connell's assistance, the Whigs ousted Peel and formed a government under Viscount Melbourne. Although disdainful toward O'Connell and indifferent to Irish needs, Melbourne appointed Irish sympathizers to key positions in his administration. Russell became home secretary, and two progressive aristocrats, Lords Mulgrave and Morpeth, were respectively appointed lord lieutenant and chief secretary for Ireland. With Melbourne's administration in place and dependent on Irish support, O'Connell started pressing for further reforms. His top priority was to abolish the tax imposed on Irish farmers for the support of the Church of Ireland. He well knew that opposition to the tithe was intense in rural Ireland and secret societies were attacking landlords and maiming their livestock in an effort to resist it. He also wanted electoral reform to enable Catholics to participate more fully in local government and felt he should have a say in the appointment of judges, sheriffs, solicitors, and other officials in Ireland. He had more success in securing patronage than in obtaining the legislation he desired. Dozens of Catholics and liberal Protestants were appointed to important positions in Ireland. Michael O'Loghlen became Ireland's first Catholic attorney general in August 1835. Slowly but steadily O'Connell and the Whigs chipped away at the Tories' grip on Ireland's administration. By 1841 Catholics and liberal Protestants made up about 40 percent of the total appointments.[35]

At Westminster, O'Connell's progress was slower. Although Morpeth proposed tithe and municipal reform bills in 1835 and 1836, he was thwarted each time by the Tory-dominated House of Lords. In 1838 the Whigs finally secured some legislation for Ireland. In July, they extended England's New Poor Law of 1834 to Ireland, requiring the Irish to erect more than one hundred workhouses that would provide indoor relief to paupers,[36] and in August, the long-awaited tithe reform was enacted. This bill was more limited than the earlier proposals, however. Tithes were converted to a rent charge paid by the landlords rather than the tenants, and the tax rate was reduced 25 percent.[37] O'Connell was disappointed by the act but voted for it nevertheless. He would have to wait another two years for a municipal reform law to be enacted, and it too proved more modest than the earlier versions. The provisions of the bill were not nearly as democratic as O'Connell desired, but he saw them as steps in the right direction and offered his support.

O'Connell's willingness to accept these legislative half-measures and his reluctance to press for Repeal troubled intransigent nationalists at home. Among the disaffected was John MacHale, the archbishop of Tuam, who was a committed Repealer and an outspoken opponent of the tithe system. He was bitterly disappointed by O'Connell's support for the compromise legislation of 1838 and remained alienated from O'Connell for a couple of years after the passage of the tithe bill.[38]

What is striking about Irish politics in the first decades of the nineteenth century is the degree to which O'Connell dominated the scene. He was the de facto nationalist leader as early as 1813; twenty-five years

Ecclesiastical map of Ireland. © Donal A. Kerr 1982. Reprinted from *Peel, Priests, and Politics,* by Donal A. Kerr (1982) by permission of Oxford University Press.

later, he was still the undisputed political leader of Ireland's Catholics. In these years, he gained important reforms for Ireland and became a pivotal force at Westminster. Equally striking is the degree to which the political spectrum shifted in these decades. In 1810 O'Connell was, relatively speaking, a hardline nationalist, fighting with anglophile aristocrats over the veto issue. By 1838 he had become a relative moderate. Both Feargus O'Connor and John MacHale were more strongly nationalistic and anglophobic than O'Connell. Of course, O'Connell's position as leader was still secure in the 1830s. However, O'Connor and MacHale's discontent foreshadowed a more serious challenge that O'Connell would face from radical nationalists in the years following.

Catholicism: The Church Grows Militant

The Catholic Church was in the midst of a revival in the 1830s. New churches were being built, old ones were being refurbished, and new congregations of religious brothers and sisters thrived. As the Church grew in strength, many of its leaders became more self-assured and even aggressive. Some bishops and many priests were becoming more dogmatic in their theology and less interested in cooperating with Protestants. At the same time, many Protestants were engaged in a vigorous campaign to convert poor Catholics, and their proselytizing further deteriorated Catholic-Protestant relations. On political matters, the Catholic bishops espoused considerably more militant views than their predecessors had held at the time of the Act of Union. The bishops' political shift parallelled in many ways the changes in the laity's political attitudes. Still, the hierarchy as a whole was less nationalist than the lay Catholic leaders at this time.

THE CATHOLIC REVIVAL

The last decades of the eighteenth century were difficult for the Catholic Church in Ireland. As a result of the penal laws, there were not enough chapels for worship and the existing ones were often in disrepair. There were not enough priests to tend to the increasing Catholic population,[39] and some priests were lacking in virtue and zeal. The greed of some priests—or the appearance of it, at any rate—had sparked a violent response from the secret societies in several counties, such as Cork, where some priests suspected of avarice were assaulted by Whiteboys.[40]

Perhaps the best indicators of the troubled state of the Church were the actions taken by some of its prominent clerics. In the 1770s the primate, Archbishop Anthony Blake, refused to reside in his archdiocese, preferring to live with his relatives in Galway. In 1787 John Butler, the bishop of Cork, resigned his see so that he could inherit a title from one of his Protestant relatives. Butler gave up his office, conformed to the Church of Ireland, and married a distant cousin. (He returned to the Catholic Church later.) Another prominent cleric to depart the Church was Father Walter Blake Kirwan. A nephew of Anthony Blake, the absentee archbishop, Kirwan left the priesthood to become a Protestant preacher. Finally, at least ten priests from Wexford took an active part in the 1798 rising, and six of them were killed. Most were described by their bishop, James Caulfield, as "notorious for drinking and fighting," and several had been suspended from the priesthood before the rising. Clearly, the Church's difficulties were not simply a result of the Penal Laws. It had problems of its own, problems similar to those experienced by Anglicans at the time.[41] The legislation simply exacerbated them.

After 1800, though, there were signs of promise for the Church. In 1795 the British government had established a national seminary at Maynooth that provided its students with high-quality, affordable training. In 1802 Edmund Rice, a wealthy layman, established the Christian Brothers, a congregation dedicated to teaching. By 1808 two more men's religious communities had been founded: the Patrician Brothers and the Presentation Brothers.[42] These congregations grew rapidly and played important roles in Catholic education in the decades following.

Women's religious communities experienced similar growth in the first decades of the nineteenth century. Nano Nagle, a cousin of Edmund Burke, had established a new congregation, the Presentation Sisters, in 1776, but the order struggled initially and did not prosper until after 1800. In 1812 Mary Aikenhead founded the Sisters of Charity, a congregation who in mission and lifestyle resembled the French Daughters of Charity. In 1821 Frances Ball established the Loreto Sisters, and in 1828 Catherine McAuley set up the Sisters of Mercy. These four communities were involved in teaching and other apostolates rather than contemplation. By 1850 there were fifteen hundred sisters in Ireland, a thirteenfold increase over their numbers in 1800.[43]

The clergy, too, were more numerous and better disciplined after 1800. The major orders of friars—Franciscans, Dominicans, Augustinians, and Carmelites—had declined in number in the late eighteenth century,[44] and for this reason many friars lived alone or with only one or two other members of their community, staffing parishes. Their arrangements had been much like those of secular priests, except that the friars were virtually free from episcopal supervision. In the early 1800s, though, the two largest orders, the Dominicans and Franciscans, undertook important reforms.[45]

Change was equally evident in the hierarchy. By 1830 Ireland had four particularly distinguished bishops: James Doyle, Daniel Murray, John MacHale, and William Higgins. Doyle was appointed bishop of Kildare and Leighlin in 1819 and soon became the Church's leading apologist. Murray was appointed coadjutor to John Troy, the archbishop of Dublin, in 1809 and succeeded him fourteen years later. Murray was an articulate, conciliatory Catholic spokesman and an energetic church builder. MacHale was a theology professor at Maynooth College before being elevated to the see of Killala in 1825 and to the archbishopric of Tuam in 1834. MacHale was a zealous proponent of Catholic interests and hardline nationalism.[46] Higgins, a canon lawyer and Maynooth professor, was appointed to Ardagh in 1829.[47] Like his friend MacHale, Higgins was a tireless—and sometimes shrill—promoter of Catholic nationalism. Whatever their shortcomings, these men were a far cry from Butler and Blake of the previous decades.

Although the bishops did not see eye to eye on all political matters, most were committed to reforming and strengthening the churches in their dioceses. Perhaps the most eloquent testimony of a bishop's efforts to promote reform was furnished by a less prominent colleague of the aforementioned bishops, George Plunkett of Elphin. In 1826 Plunkett wrote a long letter to Cardinal Somaglia, the prefect of Propaganda, explaining and defending his policies:

> I found the Diocese of Elphin in a most disorderly state, not owing to the want of either vigilance or Zeal in my venerable and pious predecessor, but owing to the circumstances of the times. . . . I held general or Synodic

meetings of the Clergy of my diocese and with their concurrence I enacted regulations and framed statutes for the guidance of their conduct. Introducing a Clerical Dress and uniform which is and must be worn by every clergyman of my Diocese and I am proud to say that this distinctive dress is now adopted by all the clergy of the Province [Tuam]. Soutan[e]s, surplices and stoles were unknown until introduced by me. The clergy now never officiate without them. Drunken, immoral and disorderly clergymen have 'thanks be to God' been reclaimed. . . . The Conferences are regularly attended, and the priests of my Diocese go over the greater part of their theology in the course of the year. They are a respectable well-informed and enlightened body.[48]

Another indicator of the Catholic revival was the boom in church building that began in the early nineteenth century. In 1848 MacHale and Higgins claimed that two thousand chapels had been built in the preceding thirty years. That was an overestimate, but it is likely that almost that number of churches were built, expanded, or refurbished in that period. Ground was broken for cathedrals in several dioceses in the 1820s, including poor sees like Killala and Tuam. In 1829 Carlow Cathedral was completed after an expenditure of thirty thousand pounds. The most notable church to be built in this period was the Cathedral of the Immaculate Conception in Dublin, begun in 1815 and completed 1825. It was the most expensive and elaborate church constructed in England or Ireland since the completion of St. Paul's Cathedral in London in the seventeenth century. Always cautious, Murray located the cathedral on a side street so as not to excite Protestant anger.[49]

Regarding Catholics' attendance at Mass, a common method of assessing the Church's strength in a region, the statistics for pre-Famine Ireland are sketchy. Church historians and sociologists are unable to agree in their estimates. In 1972 Emmet Larkin argued in his now famous essay, "Devotional Revolution," that only about 33 percent of Catholics regularly attended Mass. He contended that wealthy farmers were the only Catholics to attend Mass consistently. One of Larkin's students, David Miller, modified Larkin's thesis, suggesting that 40 percent of Catholics attended Mass weekly. Miller contended that orthodox Catholicism was much stronger in English-speaking towns and cities than in Irish-speaking areas.[50]

More recently, three Irish scholars, Desmond Keenan, Patrick Corish, and Donal Kerr, concluded independently that Miller's estimate was still too low. Corish noted that the data Miller used were only from Masses celebrated in churches and not from those offered at Mass rocks and other outdoor sites.[51] Kerr claimed that there were groups of people who were not required to attend Mass—young children, the elderly and the sick—whom Miller lumped together with nonpracticing Catholics. These groups accounted for perhaps 25 percent of the Catholic population. Furthermore, some able-bodied Catholics did not attend Mass for valid reasons: the church may have been too far away, or they may not have had proper attire to wear.[52] Keenan offered similar criticisms and asked why the reforming bishops and priests made no allusions to Mass attendance problems. He noted that although Bishop Plunkett's list of difficulties in Elphin was detailed, it included no mention of low Mass attendance.[53] Finally, in his latest book, Kerr remarked that the bishops were concerned principally with whether the people were receiving their Easter Communion. He noted that Bishop Kinsella told Tocqueville that it was "nearly unknown" for a person in his diocese to fail to make Easter Communion. And the bishops' reports to Rome indicate they were satisfied on this point.[54] Clearly, there is no consensus on Mass attendance—or even on the propriety of using it in this period—and so other indicators must be examined to gauge the Church's influence in pre-Famine Ireland.

THE PERSISTENCE OF POPULAR RELIGION

Although Catholicism was resurgent in the early nineteenth century, many of the faithful subscribed to a variety of non-Christian beliefs side by side with their orthodox beliefs. Many people believed in the existence of fairies, banshees, and witches and feared the power of the "evil eye." Feast day celebrations (known as patterns), wakes, and pilgrimages to holy wells incorporated both orthodox Catholic and popular religious elements. These events generally included more drinking, dancing, and merrymaking than the clergy thought appropriate. From the late eighteenth century on, Church authorities had struggled to purge these activities of their pagan and decadent aspects, and by the 1830s, they had met with some success. However, popular religion retained some sway in much of rural Ireland until at least 1850.[55]

Irish Catholics were not unique in their syncretic belief system, but popular religion does seem to have been more deeply rooted in Ireland than in the rest of Europe. What distinguished Irish popular beliefs from continental varieties were their clericalist and sectarian orientations. Priests had remarkably high status in Irish popular religion: even the drunken ones were often thought to have powers to heal disease and overcome landlords, and certain priests were said to be able to bring the dead back to life.[56] Corish notes that Catholic priests were held in high esteem among Protestants as well. In cases of illness, some Presbyterians would consult a priest rather than a minister.[57]

Equally striking was the fiercely anti-Protestant slant of Catholic popular beliefs. In 1771 an English bishop, Charles Walmesley, O.S.B., writing under the pseudonym Signor Pastorini, had predicted that God would crush all heretics at some point in the 1820s. Basing his claims on the Book of Revelation, Walmesley declared that the destruction of the Protestants would usher in the final age of the Church. From 1810 through the 1820s, the prophecies were widely circulated in rural Ireland by peddlers, scholars, and beggars alike. The Colum Cille prophecies contained a similar message: Protestants would slaughter Ulster Catholics, but then Catholics of all nations would unite to crush Protestantism in both England and Ireland. Both prophecies were especially popular with many Ribbonmen and Rockites, who were eager to act as God's instruments in the war against the Protestants.[58]

TENSIONS BETWEEN CATHOLICS AND PROTESTANTS

In the late eighteenth and early nineteenth centuries, relations between prosperous Catholics and Protestants had been relatively friendly. Protestants helped build some of the Catholic churches of the period, including the Dublin Cathedral, and some Catholic and Protestant prelates were cordial with each other, notable examples being the bishops of Limerick, Charles Tuohy and John Jebb. In 1825, upon his consecration as bishop of Down and Connor, William Crolly held a party attended mostly by Protestants. After saluting various Protestant clergymen, he toasted Belfast, declaring it one of the most enlightened and tolerant cities in Europe.[59]

The most extraordinary ecumenical gesture of the period was Bishop Doyle's "Letter on the Union of Churches," published in the *Dublin*

Evening Post, in 1824. Doyle contended that there were no substantive disagreements between Rome and Canterbury: "On most of these [beliefs], it appears to me, there is no essential difference between the Catholics and the Protestants; the existing diversity arises, in most cases, from certain forms of words which admit of a satisfactory explanation, or from ignorance or misconception which ancient prejudices and ill-will produce and strengthen but which could be removed." To heal the Catholic-Anglican breach, Doyle believed, theologians from the two churches simply needed to meet to settle their differences, and then Parliament could enact the necessary legislation unifying the churches.[60] Doyle received support from Murray and a few other leading Catholics, but his proposal was never taken up by Parliament.[61]

Doyle's letter proved to be the high-water mark for ecumenism in Ireland. After 1825 Catholic-Protestant relations declined steadily. Although both sides were responsible for the growing tensions, a key catalyst was the Second Reformation launched in the 1820s by evangelical Protestants. The movement received its name from a statement made by Dr. William Magee, archbishop of Dublin in the Church of Ireland, in 1825: "In truth, with respect to Ireland, the Reformation may, strictly speaking, be truly said only now to have begun."[62] A fiery evangelical, Magee dispatched groups of Trinity College–trained ministers to the south and west of Ireland to convert the Catholic population. The Anglicans were joined in their crusade by Methodists, Presbyterians, and a few Baptists.

The campaign took several forms and continued on and off into the 1860s. Some evangelicals worked for Bible societies and helped to distribute not only Bibles but also anti-Catholic tracts. Others worked for the Kildare Place Society, a government-funded foundation that established elementary schools that taught poor children the basics of reading, writing, and Protestantism.[63] Finally, a number of Protestant ministers and laymen traveled around the countryside, preaching—sometimes in Irish as well as English.[64]

Despite substantial investments of money and manpower, the Second Reformation proved as much of a failure as the first. A few Protestant colonies were established in remote sections of Counties Kerry and Mayo, but they were short-lived. The Second Reformation only further estranged the Catholic and Protestant communities. Catholic bitterness escalated during the years of the Famine, when some evangelicals were accused of "souperism"—offering food and financial assistance to the starving poor on the condition that they convert to Protestantism. Corish notes that these missionary efforts were particularly upsetting to the Catholic poor and clergy: "What the campaign certainly achieved was to stir the long memories: the priest-hunter, the Mass-rocks, the lost lands."[65]

Religious tensions were heightened by the political battles of the 1820s. Many middle- and upper-class Catholics had been upset by the British government's stubborn refusal to grant Catholic Emancipation. Catholics had been promised Emancipation before the Act of Union, and many were running out of patience in the 1820s. Thousands of middle-class Catholics were attracted to O'Connell's Emancipation campaign, and many came to share his essentially sectarian outlook. At the same time, O'Connell's harsh rhetoric surely antagonized many moderate Protestants. One need only recall his characterization of Vesey Fitzgerald, his liberal Protestant opponent, as "a sworn libeller of the Catholic faith" to recognize the Emancipation campaign's chilling effect on Catholic-Protestant relations.

THE PRIEST'S STATUS IN SOCIETY

As Catholicism grew, the priests' standing in Irish society rose. To Tocqueville, who was used to French anticlericalism, the unity between priests and people in Ireland was striking. He watched people respectfully salute priests when passing them on the street in Carlow, and while accompanying a priest on his rounds in Tuam, he noticed even greater deference: "On seeing him the women curtseyed and crossed themselves devoutly, the men respectfully took off their hats. . . . 'What name will you give to your child?' he said to a poor woman who was taking a breath of air outside of her hovel. 'If your honour would care to choose himself,' said the woman, 'it would be a great joy to us.'"[66]

O'Connell revered the clergy in much the same way. Writing to a friend in 1837, he confided, "I believe that few men are less disposed than me to attack, by injury or calumny, the priests of God. I have often told you my secrets on the sentiments of veneration which a priest inspires in me. You will laugh at me, perhaps, when I add that I push this respect to superstition but the fact is I cannot defend myself from it. I have never known anyone, who has treated the ministers of the altar in a discourteous manner, to have prospered in the world. There is, even in this world, a curse on such people.[67]

Beaumont noted the same solidarity between priest and people in his travels through Ireland and contended that it stemmed in part from the Church's position as an unestablished body totally dependent on the people for support. In his view, this situation made Catholicism a much more formidable force in Ireland than on the Continent: "In Ireland, the clergy has complete authority over a people which recognises no authority but the clerical. . . . It is thus that a religious body, which we sometimes see the supporter of princes or the ally of privileged corporations, is in Ireland one of the most potent elements of liberty and democracy."[68]

Tocqueville offered some reasons for the close relationship between priests and people. Clerics tended to come from the same modest social background as the people, he argued, and they depended on the people rather than the state for their financial support.[69] Contemporary scholars generally accept Tocqueville's analysis, but offer additional explanations as well.[70] Kerr notes the importance of the priest in orthodox theology of the time: "The faithful . . . looked upon the priest as the 'Lord's Anointed'; and both they and the clergy themselves constantly referred to his 'sacred character.'" Kerr also remarks that the people respected the priests for their celibacy, their relatively high levels of education, and the prominent part many played in the struggle for Catholic Emancipation.[71]

THE CLERGY AND NATIONALISM

Like most of the Catholic laity, the bishops drifted away from unionism in favor of nationalism in the early nineteenth century. However, they were not fully committed to O'Connellite nationalism in the 1830s. Some were ardent nationalists, and a few, like Archbishop MacHale, were more militant than O'Connell. Still, a sizable number of bishops—probably the majority—adhered to the more conciliatory policies of Archbishop Daniel Murray.

Although moderate compared with MacHale, Murray represented a change from the generation that preceded him. His predecessor in Dublin, Archbishop Troy, was deferential to the English government.

Troy had been willing to accept an English veto on the appointment of bishops and parish priests in 1799 and remained open to the idea long after most of his fellow bishops had rejected it.[72] Murray had opposed the veto and been sent by his colleagues to Rome in 1814 to explain the Irish hierarchy's views on the issue. In 1824 he had been one of the first bishops to endorse O'Connell's Catholic Emancipation campaign. By the 1830s, however, he was the aging leader of the accommodationist faction in the hierarchy, a prelate who was willing to negotiate with the British and sit on government boards. Oliver MacDonagh provides an apt description of the archbishop's outlook: "Murray, although freed from the timorousness of the *ancien régime,* was still a pre-emancipation bishop, and bore to the end the very mark of his generation, deference to British power."[73]

Bishops MacHale and Higgins were a generation younger than Murray and a world apart from his mind-set. MacHale was educated at Maynooth, which had a strong nationalist orientation.[74] Higgins was trained on the Continent, just as Murray had been, but he taught at Maynooth before being consecrated a bishop. Maynooth was an important factor in the higher and lower clergy's drift toward nationalism. As early as 1825, John Foster, a conservative Irish M.P., tartly described the transformation that the seminary had worked on the clergy: "The students who enter it [Maynooth] are peasants. They leave it with as great an ignorance of the world as they brought into it, but they acquire in it an *esprit de corps,* which it is impossible to describe of which a taste for religious controversy and a keen anti-British feeling are the leading features."[75] Indeed, most of the bishops who shared MacHale's views had a Maynooth connection.[76]

Another factor that contributed to MacHale's and Higgins's views was the location of their dioceses. Tuam and Ardagh were far removed in every respect from cosmopolitan Dublin. These dioceses were more impoverished than Dublin and had been key targets of the evangelicals' campaign. Given these differences in age, training, and pastoral experience, it is not surprising that MacHale and his allies were often at odds with Murray and his supporters.

Murray and MacHale first quarreled over the national school issue. In 1831 the Whig government of Earl Grey had established a system of nondenominational elementary schools in Ireland. Despite some misgivings, the Catholic bishops supported the measure unanimously; O'Connell and other lay Catholic politicians endorsed the plan as well.[77] The bishops of course would have preferred to have their own schools and wanted more than two of the seven seats on the governing board.[78] Still, in practice, the national school system was denominational in most areas. In many districts, a priest served as the principal of an overwhelmingly—in some cases exclusively—Catholic student body. In the bishops' view, the national schools represented a substantial improvement over the Kildare Place Society and other Protestant-oriented educational foundations. Furthermore, since they did not have the resources to establish their own network of schools, this de facto Catholic system appeared to be the next best thing.

Trouble erupted on the subject at the bishops' annual meeting in February 1838. Higgins expressed his concern that the schools could spread indifferentism among Catholic youth. Most of the hierarchy disagreed, but MacHale shared Higgins's fears and promptly began a public campaign against the schools. Within a few months MacHale had persuaded his six suffragans and three other bishops of the dangers associated with the school system. Now ten of Ireland's twenty-six bishops were foes of the national schools.[79]

In response to MacHale, Murray launched a vigorous, public defense of the schools. The two prelates skirmished regularly in the pages of the *Dublin Evening Post*. In 1839 the bishops again took up the question at their annual meeting. MacHale wanted questions surrounding the schools referred to the pope for his judgment, but his proposal was rejected in a sixteen-to-ten vote. The minority proceeded to petition Rome anyway, claiming that certain texts used in the schools were heretical and the school system itself was a threat to the Church.

Characteristically hesitant to intervene, Rome hoped that the bishops could settle the question themselves. After Father Paul Cullen, the rector of the Irish College in Rome, visited Ireland and expressed his satisfaction with the schools, Rome was inclined to take Murray's side. In January 1841 the prefect of Propaganda issued a letter that neither approved nor disapproved of the schools. This was effectively a victory for Murray, because MacHale had sought Rome's condemnation.[80] MacHale pulled the schools in the Tuam archdiocese out of the system, but no other bishop followed his lead, so the system remained largely intact. Although Murray prevailed in this quarrel, MacHale must have felt that time was on his side, since he and most of his episcopal allies were considerably younger than Murray and his supporters. More conflicts would arise as the 1840s progressed and the MacHaleites would prove harder to vanquish.

Father Theobald Mathew: Out of Step

While lay and ecclesiastical leaders became increasingly militant in their political and religious attitudes, Father Theobald Mathew continued to advocate ecumenical, nonnationalist views. Mathew's upbringing was different from that of most Catholics and his seminary training different from that received by most of his fellow priests. These factors contributed to his distinctive outlook.

Mathew had a host of distinguished men and women among his forebears. The Mathews had arrived in Ireland only about a century and a half before Theobald's birth, but they had already provided Ireland with a viceroy, three Catholic archbishops, and several members of Parliament.[81] George Mathew came to Ireland from Wales and married a wealthy widow, Elizabeth Butler, the Viscountess Thurles, around 1620.[82] They had two sons, from whom three lines of Mathews descended.

From the early eighteenth century on, the bulk of the Mathew properties were located in Thomastown in County Tipperary. One of Mathew's biographers provides a description of the estate: "Containing nearly 2,000 acres of good land, it was abundantly supplied with timber.... Herds of red deer roamed at will through the woods; pleasure grounds invited the worried or the weary.... The main entrance was adorned with a noble heraldic gateway displaying the Mathew lions seated proudly on stone pillars; while a long avenue, finely lined with a triple row of large trees, swept up to the house which Maguire describes as 'an immense, long-winged, castellated pile, a noble mansion in the midst of a still nobler demesne.'"[83]

To maintain this property through the Penal Law period, the heads of the households conformed to the Church of Ireland. George Mathew conformed in 1709, and the successive owners throughout the eighteenth century took the same step. It does not appear that any of the Mathews became committed Protestants, however. They continued to marry Catholics, and the Mathews who served in Parliament consistently supported Catholic relief. Indeed, in the 1761 election, Sir Thomas Maude, Thomas Mathew's evangelical Protestant opponent, accused him of having undue Catholic sympathies. The tactic worked; confusion about Mathew's religious sympathies cost him the election.[84]

After Thomas's death in 1777, power passed on to his son, Francis, who inherited the family's three major estates: Thomastown, Thurles, and Annfield. Holding these three vast properties made Mathew one of the wealthiest men in the region. His lavish spending habits and inability to manage money, however, made him one of the most heavily indebted as well. By 1780, Francis Mathew was seventy thousand pounds in debt,[85] and trustees were appointed who sold off parcels of land to pay the creditors.

Theobald's father, James, was one of Francis's Catholic cousins. Orphaned as a child, James had been adopted by Francis and brought to Thomastown to live.[86] When he came of age, James was hired to work on the estate. He and his wife, Anne Whyte, were allowed to stay at Thomastown and raise their family. Theobald was born there on October 10, 1790, the fourth of twelve children.

By all accounts, Theobald was happy growing up in this unusual milieu. He and his Protestant cousins were the best of friends; he was the special favorite of Lady Elizabeth Mathew, the daughter of Francis (who after 1797 was known as the Earl of Llandaff). Lady Elizabeth knew and approved of Theobald's priestly ambitions and in 1800 furnished the money to pay for his education at St. Canice's, a Catholic boarding school in Kilkenny.[87] Theobald's warm relationship with his Protestant relatives undoubtedly contributed to the formation of his ecumenical outlook.

Mathew spent seven years at St. Canice's, performing well in his studies and gaining friends through his easygoing, conciliatory manner. In September 1807 he enrolled at Maynooth College for training as a secular priest. Shortly after his entrance, he broke the rules of the college by inviting several other seminarians to his room for a party. At the time, students were not allowed to visit their classmates in their rooms under any circumstances.[88] By throwing a party he had committed a serious offense. Believing that his expulsion was imminent, Mathew withdrew from the seminary.

He applied to join the Capuchins, who readily admitted him despite his record at Maynooth. The Capuchins, like most of the other religious orders in Ireland, were weak at this time—there were probably no more than twenty of them—and anxious for new recruits. In 1808 Mathew went to the Church Street Friary in Dublin to begin his novitiate.[89] Little is known about his training, but it is reasonable to assume that it was not especially demanding. Since he was probably the only novice at Church Street, in all likelihood he did not have to follow a standardized program of studies. On April 3, 1813, Mathew was ordained a deacon, and then on Holy Saturday, April 17, he was ordained a priest by Daniel Murray.[90]

Mathew's departure from Maynooth was a critical event. Had he stayed there, his worldview might have altered in several important respects. His ecumenical attitudes would certainly have been challenged and probably criticized as indifferentist by Maynooth professors. He would have received a rigorist training in doctrine and would have encountered many an Irish nationalist among his professors and fellow seminarians. Indeed, Maynooth might very well have transformed him. To recognize that the seminary had a strong Catholic nationalist orientation, one need only recall that John MacHale attended—and thrived at—Maynooth at this time.

After his ordination, Father Mathew was sent to Kilkenny to work with two other friars. Within a few months, he became embroiled in a conflict with the administrator of the diocese, Father Richard Mansfield, who accused him of distributing Holy Communion at Easter in the Capuchin church. At this time, the bishops strictly prohibited priests in religious orders from performing some functions, including the distribution of the paschal communion.[91] Father Mansfield suspended him without an inquiry into the truth of the charge. Later, upon learning of Mathew's innocence in the matter, Mansfield apologized profusely and offered to restore his faculties. Mathew, however, believed that his reputation had been tarnished and wished to leave the diocese and start anew elsewhere. In the autumn of 1814, the Capuchin provincial granted him a transfer to Cork.

In Cork, Mathew joined Father Daniel Donovan, a Capuchin who had been living alone in cramped quarters at Blackamoor Lane. The two friars became fast friends, and Mathew quickly became popular with the people of Cork. From Donovan he learned to speak Irish, a skill that proved invaluable to him in his later years.[92] As a preacher, he seems to have been good but not outstanding. Father M. B. O'Shea, a contemporary, claimed that Mathew's oratory suffered from technical flaws: his voice was weak and his gestures lacked substance. Nonetheless, O'Shea acknowledged that Mathew's emotional sermons were appealing: "We were not listening to his affectionate, earnest and pathetic exhortation more than ten minutes when our criticism, our bitterness, our self-importance left us; all that was in us unkind and harsh, was softened down; our heart beat only to kindlier emotions."[93]

Mathew gained more acclaim for his sympathetic manner in the confessional. Presumably, many of the parish clergy in Cork had been trained at Maynooth and thus had been taught to be strict confessors. Mathew's approach must have been a welcome contrast for many penitents. Daniel Madden, a contemporary writer, noted that Mathew was the preferred confessor of rich and poor alike. Father Patrick Rogers, one of Mathew's biographers, claims that even people from the neighboring towns gradually began to come to him for guidance and absolution. Eventually he took the unusual step of hearing confessions on weekdays as well as on Saturdays. Indeed, in a letter to a fellow Capuchin, he noted the "numberless confessions" that he had to hear as one reason he could not leave Cork for even a single day.[94]

When not administering the sacraments, Mathew was involved in various projects to assist the people of Cork. For indigent girls, he established an elementary school that also provided training in needlework and other crafts. For boys, he set up a night school at the same site. In 1819 he founded the Josephian Society, a confraternity for young men, whose members visited the sick, taught in his schools, and conducted catechism classes.

Although Mathew was committed to a wide variety of activities for the betterment of the poor, one issue he never concerned himself with was temperance. He drank moderate amounts of whiskey as well as wine and, when entertaining, generally offered his guests wine and whiskey punch. During the cholera epidemic of 1832, he sent bottles of whiskey to the hospitals for the treatment of the sick.[95]

In 1821 Father Donovan died, leaving Mathew alone to run the friary. Since 1816, Donovan had been the provincial, and upon his death, Mathew was elected his successor. The Capuchins were certainly demonstrating their confidence in the thirty-two-year-old friar, but the election also signified the Capuchins' continuing shortage of personnel.

In the 1830s Mathew became involved in the Catholic building boom, purchasing the Botanical Gardens in Cork with his own money and converting the land into a cemetery for Catholics. Until this time, all of the cemeteries had been controlled by Protestants, and Catholics often had difficulty arranging proper burials. At Mathew's cemetery, priests were welcome to preside at graveside services, and the poor were provided free interment. In keeping with Mathew's ecumenical attitudes, the cemetery was open to Protestants as well. Mathew also broke ground on a church in the center of the city. The blueprints called for an elaborate Gothic design that he believed would cost ten thousand pounds. However, he seriously underestimated the expenses involved. By 1840, fourteen thousand pounds—including four thousand pounds of Mathew's own funds—had been spent, and the church was still nowhere near complete.[96]

Unlike most of his clerical brethren, Mathew seems to have remained aloof from the political controversies of the period. Given his many pastoral and social activities, he probably did not have much time to spare for political activism. He did, however, join the Catholic Association in 1824. To a fellow Capuchin in Dublin, he wrote, "You would confer an additional obligation on me by handing a guinea to the Catholic Association as my subscription, that I may have the honour of being a member." Beyond this modest gesture, there is no evidence of political activities on his part. Although Cork was a center of O'Connellite activity in the 1820s and 1830s, he participated in no political controversies and often boasted that he had never voted in any election. While other clergy were adopting more sectarian attitudes, Mathew remained on friendly terms with Protestant leaders in Cork and received substantial financial support from them for the maintenance of his schools and the building of his church.[97] Mathew's ecumenism and detachment from O'Connellite politics indicate that his views were more or less in line with those of Daniel Murray and his allies, a strong but declining force in 1838. Thus

Mathew's views were out of step with both the bulk of the laity, who were strongly O'Connellite, and the increasingly confident and strident faction of the clergy led by Archbishop MacHale. As the 1840s progressed, most priests and laymen would become still more nationalistic and Mathew's views would become even less fashionable.

{ CHAPTER TWO }

Drink and Temperance before Mathew's Crusade

To picture an Irishman truly, either by words or on canvas, or to represent him accurately on the stage, it was considered indispensable that he should be drunk.

S. C. Hall and A. M. Hall, *Ireland, Its Scenery* (1841)

VISITORS TO IRELAND in the early part of the nineteenth century differed about some features of Irish life, but all were in agreement about the centrality of drink in the lives of most people. Traveling through Ireland in 1805, Sir John Carr was appalled by the amount of whiskey drinking he witnessed: "The excessive use of whisky in Dublin cannot fail of attracting the attention of a stranger, where this deleterious liquor is now, by act of Parliament, distilled from raw oats; . . . The number of shops where this liquid poison and other drams, almost equally hostile to morals and life, are sold, is truly shockingly great. In Thomas-street every other house seemed to be a dram-shop. . . . [I]n this street alone, composed of one hundred and ninety houses . . . I believe there are no less than fifty-two houses licensed to vend raw spirits." Seven years later, Edward Wakefield noticed similar problems. He ascribed the people's fondness for whiskey to Ireland's harsh climate.[1]

Some Irish observers shared these concerns about the widespread drunkenness in their country. In 1795 Henry Grattan warned his colleagues that drunkenness was increasing at a dangerous rate and was a major factor in the crime and faction fighting of the time.[2] Twenty-five years later, the Anglo-Irish novelist Maria Edgeworth noted that the more affluent Irish had lately reduced their drinking: "Those desperately tiresome, long, formal dinners" in which the guests typically consumed "more than they could eat and twenty times more than they should drink were no longer commonplace." The Halls, a wealthy Irish Protestant couple, had similar memories: "We are ourselves old enough to recollect when a host would have been scouted as mean and inhospitable, who had suffered one of his guests to leave his table sober. . . . If a guest were able to mount his horse without assistance, in the 'good old times,' he was presented with a . . . glass, which he was forced, seldom against his will, to 'drink at the door.' This glass usually held a quart: it was terminated by a globe, which . . . contained a 'drop' sufficient to complete the business of the night. The degradation was looked upon as a distinction; an Irishman drunk was an Irishman 'all in his glory.'"[3] Not everyone was as happy as Edgeworth and the Halls about the changes. Historian Marianne Elliott notes that in the early years of the nineteenth century, many Dublin lawyers "reflected nostalgically back on 'the morning of whiskey, the noon of duelling, and the nights of claret' which characterised the Irish legal system at the end of the eighteenth century."[4]

While many in the upper classes were moving—albeit hesitantly—toward sobriety, no one witnessed any comparable improvement in the drinking habits of the working classes. Indeed, in 1825 when an Ulster minister organized a temperance society for the butchers of his town, limiting them to three glasses of whiskey per day, most found the rule too burdensome and quickly dropped out.[5]

In 1834 Parliament created the Select Committee on Inquiry into Drunkenness to investigate the drinking customs of the working classes throughout the United Kingdom. Headed by James S. Buckingham, a radical M.P. and temperance advocate, the committee conducted a six-month inquiry. In its report, several witnesses, who admittedly were temperance proponents, argued that drunkenness was a problem throughout the United Kingdom. George Carr, a Congregationalist minister from County Wexford, claimed that drunkenness had taken a heavy toll on Irish society: "I have the common experience of every Irish, perhaps I might add, of every British family. For where is the family that has not mourned over some member, a victim to drunkenness?" John Edgar, a Presbyterian minister from Belfast, echoed Carr's sentiments and claimed that intemperance among the working classes was damaging the Irish economy. He asserted that in Belfast some tradesmen regularly missed work on Monday—and occasionally Tuesday—because of drunkenness.[6]

John Finch, an English temperance advocate who had traveled widely in Ireland, argued that drinking pervaded Irish life: "In Ireland, I think, upon a moderate calculation, one shop out of four is a whiskey shop. . . . The principal manufactories there are breweries and distilleries; some of the finest homes and mansions are those belonging to brewers and distillers, and the poverty of the people is beyond description." Finch concluded with a suggestion that Parliament forbid Irish pubs from opening before 8 or 9 A.M., "for there is a great deal of dram drinking by five or six in the morning in most large towns."[7]

On the basis of the testimonies of Carr, Edgar, Finch, and others, the committee concluded that drunkenness was a serious problem among laboring men, women, and children in England, Scotland, and Ireland. The committee cited the poor example formerly set by the upper classes, the excessive number of pubs and spirit sellers, and the low price of whiskey as factors contributing to the problem. They asserted that intemperance had had a devastating effect on the peoples of the United Kingdom. Drunkenness had destroyed the health of many and caused idiocy and madness in some; had hurt the economy; had weakened the armed forces; and had contributed to pauperism, crime, theft, and prostitution.[8]

Beverages of Choice: Parliament Whiskey, Poteen, and Porter

Whiskey and beer were the favorite alcoholic beverages of the Irish in the first decades of the nineteenth century. Some of the gentry preferred brandy and wine, but distillers and brewers held the lion's share of the liquor market. The whiskey and beer consumed were generally produced in Ireland. Distilleries were centered in the south and east of the island, and most breweries were located in or around Dublin and Cork.[9]

When considering Irish whiskey, it is important to distinguish between whiskey produced by the distillers and poteen (sometimes spelled *potheen* or *potin*), the illicit whiskey produced in rural stills. Legally produced whiskey was dubbed "Parliament whiskey," because distillers were obliged to pay the government a duty on each gallon produced. Of course, no taxes were paid on poteen, so it was much cheaper than Parliament whiskey. Depending on the rate of duty, a gallon of poteen sold for one-third to one-half the price of a gallon of Parliament whiskey. (A gallon of poteen sold for as little as two and a half shillings, and a gallon of Parliament whiskey for six to nine shillings.) Poteen had a different taste as well. John Edgar described it as a "peat flavour" that some people found appealing.[10]

Along with whiskey, several types of beer were brewed in this period. Porter was a dark brown mixture of beer and ale that gained its name through its popularity with porters and other manual laborers.[11] Stout, a stronger drink, also had some appeal. Brewing beer required more time and ingredients than were needed for distilling whiskey. For this reason, established brewers did not have to worry about illicit competition. They were also freed from paying duties on their product after 1795. Nevertheless, in the 1830s, beer was popular only in the urban areas. Outside Dublin and Cork, whiskey was the Irishman's beverage of choice.

Determining just how much whiskey and beer were being produced and consumed in this period is quite difficult. For whiskey, one can begin with the excise reports. In 1784, duty was paid on 1,760,000 gallons of whiskey; in 1807, that number had more than tripled to 5,700, 000; by 1829, it had increased to 9,240, 000. The number of taxed gallons continued to increase throughout the 1830s, peaking at 12,500,000 in 1836. George Bretherton notes that excise figures are not as helpful as one might expect. First, because the whiskey sent to retailers was often over proof, retailers would dilute their products with water and other additives. These alterations added perhaps 20 percent to the volume of the whiskey. Thus if 10 million gallons were taxed, then probably 12 million gallons were distributed. Furthermore, one must also consider the nontaxed whiskey that licensed distilleries produced. In some cases the revenue officers were bribed, and it was a common practice to smuggle small amounts of whiskey—a gallon or so—out of the plants. Estimating with any precision the amount of distillery whiskey that escaped duty is impossible. Bretherton suggests that for every two gallons of whiskey that were taxed, another gallon was not taxed, though he admits this estimate may be too high.[12] With these modifications, 10 million gallons of taxed whiskey become 18 million gallons of consumed whiskey.

Finally, one must take into account poteen production for a true estimate of whiskey consumption. Estimates of the amount of whiskey made in these stills is mere conjecture. Bretherton tentatively offers 8 million gallons as an estimate of annual poteen production in the 1830s, though this estimate could be low, because he assumes that whiskey consumption rates were uniform throughout Ireland.[13] Experts agree that poteen was much more common in the rural parts of the north and west than the other parts of the island.

It is much easier to estimate beer production levels. In 1800, about 100,000 barrels of beer were produced annually; by 1832, production had increased to 770,000 barrels; and in 1837, the brewers' production surpassed 1,000,000 barrels, a level it would not reach again for several years. Virtually all this beer was consumed in Ireland; about 1 percent was exported. Given that these figures are for barrels and the barrels held thirty-six gallons, it is clear that more beer than whiskey was produced and consumed in Ireland in the early nineteenth century. Elizabeth Malcolm contends that per capita consumption of beer and whiskey was 3.5 and 1.12 gallons, respectively. Her estimate for beer consumption seems fair, but her figures for whiskey consumption appear to be based on the excise reports alone and thus seriously underestimate the per capita whiskey consumption. Assuming that Bretherton's figures for whiskey production are accurate, the per capita consumption of whiskey would approach that of beer.[14]

The Centrality of Drink to Irish Lives

To understand why the Irish consumed such large quantities of whiskey and beer, it is necessary to recognize the many functions that alcoholic beverages served in Irish daily life. The Irish word for whiskey, *usquebaugh*, literally means "water of life." The Select Committee on Inquiry into Drunkenness concluded that the working classes throughout the United Kingdom used "intoxicating drinks with almost every important event in life, such as the celebration of baptisms, funerals, anniversaries, holidays and festivities, as well as in the daily interchange of convivial entertainments and even in the commercial transactions of purchase and sale."[15] This testimony suggests that whiskey had a symbolic importance in the lives of the Irish people, conferring significance and perhaps solemnity to rites of passage and other important events.[16] On the other hand, it could just as easily be viewed as a sign that the Irish lower classes were dependent on alcohol and used any occasion, be it mourning or celebrating, as an excuse for heavy drinking.

Whether or not whiskey had any symbolic meaning in the personal lives of most Irish, it certainly played a significant role in many business transactions. When purchasing livestock or produce, the buyer was expected to treat the seller to at least one drink. As one of Mathew's correspondents noted, "No bargain was considered lucky unless it was consecrated and cemented by a libation."[17] The drink was a sign of good will and an indication by both parties that they were willing to conduct business with each other in the future.

Whiskey was also believed to be an elixir for almost every ailment. During the cholera epidemic of 1832, it was often dispensed to the sick—recall that Father Mathew himself helped restock cholera hospitals with whiskey. Some people took whiskey in the morning to help themselves wake up, and others drank it before going to bed to ensure a good night's sleep. Some parents gave their children whiskey to pacify them when they were crying and reward them when they were well behaved. Pregnant women and nursing mothers also took whiskey. And whiskey was sometimes given out to cure hangovers. The morning after having had too much to drink, an Irishman was likely to be given a "hair of the dog that bit him" to sober him up. Although it might not have helped cure illnesses or hangovers, whiskey at least was effective as a painkiller, which was more than could be said about some other medicines of the day.[18]

Pubs, and their unlicensed equivalents, shebeens, also had a variety of functions in Irish life. They served as meeting places for Irishmen who felt their homes were too poor to allow them to entertain, and as James Barrett notes, they were a welcome refuge to young married men who lived in close quarters with their wives, children, and in-laws. Pubs also provided some banking functions in smaller towns, with publicans changing large bank notes into coins and occasionally providing loans to patrons.[19]

Thus the role of drink and taverns in Irish life was more complex than it might initially appear. Whiskey and taverns were central elements in many Irishmen's leisure activities. Whiskey helped the Irish mark joyful events in life and helped console them in their grief. It was also the drug given for every ailment, from colic to cholera. At the same time, however, whiskey and beer helped many men—and some women—simply get drunk. Many men went to pubs not so much to see old friends as to become inebriated. Thus although many Irish used alcohol in moderate quantities for social, economic, and medicinal purposes, many others were heavy drinkers.

The Stirrings of Temperance

The movement to limit alcohol consumption began in the first decade of the nineteenth century in the United States. It is fitting that temperance originated in America rather than Europe because intemperance appears to have been a more serious problem there than in Ireland or England.[20] At first reformers were concerned only with drunkenness and did not object to people's drinking alcoholic beverages in moderation, but gradually the movement's leaders became opposed to any consumption of spirits. By the mid-1830s anti-spirits men found themselves being disparaged as "moderationists" by a new, more militant group, the total abstainers. The progression of the movement helps explain why teetotalers were described as temperance advocates.[21] Of course, total abstainers opposed even the temperate use of any alcoholic beverages, but their predecessors had been proponents of temperance. The label remained even after the movement's goals had shifted.

Although in Ireland and the United States the temperance leaders' increasing hostility to drink can be charted easily, their attitudes toward government intervention are more difficult to characterize. Their views on government intervention, for example, ranged from strict voluntarism to limited government intervention to prohibitionism, though in Ireland—unlike in the United States and United Kingdom—a strong prohibitionist movement never developed. To complicate matters further, there were no obvious correlations between temperance proponents' views on alcohol and their views on governmental action. For example, a moderationist might favor strict controls on whiskey production, whereas a total abstainer might have no interest whatever in government intervention.

The first known temperance society was established in Saratoga County, New York, in 1808, and similar associations sprang up throughout New England in the years following. These groups were opposed to drunkenness but not to spirits or beer per se.[22] The movement gained momentum in the 1820s, when the Reverend Lyman Beecher, a prominent Congregationalist minister with evangelical leanings, delivered his Six Sermons on intemperance. Beecher argued forcefully that it was not sufficient for temperance advocates to discountenance drunkenness. He reminded his audience that the moderate intake of spirits was often the first step on the road to habitual drunkenness. If temperance advocates were serious about their cause, they must give up spirits altogether. (He did not call for abstinence from beer or wine, however.) Beecher's sermons were influential and helped shift the outlook of many temperance leaders.

Beecher also called for the establishment of a nationwide temperance organization to oversee the growing movement, and in 1826 the American Temperance Society (ATS) was established in Boston. With the strong support of lay and clerical members of the Presbyterian, Congregational, and Methodist Churches, the society expanded its membership dramatically. In 1831 the ATS claimed 170,000 members and by the mid-1830s, more than one million.[23]

In 1829 the activities of the ATS were made known in Ireland through the work of the Reverend Joseph Penney, a minister who belonged to a branch of the Presbyterians known as Seceders.[24] A native of County Down, Penney had emigrated to New York State in 1819. In the 1820s he became active in the temperance movement, and in 1829 he returned to his native Ulster to spread the temperance message. He persuaded his friend and fellow Seceder, John Edgar, to take up the cause, and in September of that year, Edgar, together with four ministers and one layman, founded the Ulster Temperance Society (UTS) in Belfast. The UTS resembled the ATS in many respects, for example, in requiring that its members take a pledge to abstain from the consumption of spirits.

At about the same time, another temperance society was set up in southeastern Ireland by George Carr.[25] Technically Carr's New Ross Temperance Society predated the UTS by a couple of weeks, but he was encouraged to found his group by Edgar.[26] Like the ATS and UTS, the New

Ross Temperance Society opposed the consumption of spirits but not fermented beverages.

Although Carr and Edgar were both ministers and were acquainted with each other, they had different outlooks, and each society reflected its founder's vision. Edgar was a theology professor at the Belfast Academical Institution and hewed to a strict Calvinist line in all doctrinal matters. He took a dim view of Catholics and liberal Protestants alike. Carr was just the sort of Protestant whom Edgar distrusted. A liberal Congregationalist, Carr brought a number of Quakers, Unitarians, and even Catholics into his group.[27] In fact, he tried to enlist Bishop Doyle, the most prominent Catholic prelate of the time. Doyle wrote two letters to Carr in which he offered qualified support for the anti-spirits movement.[28]

The UTS and New Ross Temperance Society can be seen as representative of two very different strains of Protestantism. Throughout the nineteenth century and in the first decades of the twentieth, temperance was one of the few issues on which evangelicals agreed with liberal Protestants, and these two branches of Protestantism favored temperance for very different reasons. For liberals, it was a social justice concern. Temperate habits coupled with government regulation of taverns would lessen crime and poverty and improve the quality of life of the poor. For evangelicals, drunkenness was a serious sin against God that was leading many souls to eternal damnation.[29] Outside Ulster, the Protestants who involved themselves in the temperance movement were generally of a liberal bent; most were ecumenists who were interested in a variety of social justice causes.

After 1829 the temperance movement proliferated throughout Ireland. It was especially successful in Ulster, where in 1833 the *Belfast Temperance Advocate*, the UTS newspaper, claimed the group had fifteen thousand members.[30] Edgar and his co-workers had attracted a number of businessmen and landlords and dozens of evangelical ministers from all denominations. In addition to its own newspaper, the UTS had a couple of articulate, prolific spokesmen. Edgar, for one, penned numerous tracts and pamphlets on the temperance question that helped earn him recognition across the Irish Sea. He toured both Scotland and England, giving lectures and words of encouragement to the fledgling societies.

Despite its reach, the UTS was a parochial organization. It was exclusively evangelical Protestant—no Catholics, Quakers, or Unitarians were recruited—and had links to the Orange Order, the secret, quasi-Masonic, Protestant organization.[31] One of the key Orange leaders was Colonel William Blacker, a prosperous landowner. When the Orange Order dissolved itself in 1836, Blacker, a temperance enthusiast, urged the ex-Orangemen to join the new temperance associations. He believed that the Orange Lodges, when functioning properly, fostered discipline, self-control, and other virtues among the members and the temperance societies could exercise a similar influence. Many former Orangemen evidently took Blacker's advice. George Bretherton notes that Ulster temperance societies expanded dramatically in the months after the Orange Order closed and believes this was no coincidence.[32] Given the overlap between the UTS and the Orange Order, the UTS may be described as not merely Protestant dominated but sectarian. For this reason, it was destined not to exert any influence outside of Ulster.

In the south of Ireland, temperance societies initially grew at a slower pace, but their diverse makeup gave them more potential to expand than the UTS. In October 1829 two Quaker doctors, Joshua Harvey and John Cheyne, helped found the Dublin Temperance Society (DTS), which attracted men from a variety of denominations, including the Church of Ireland, the Unitarian Church, and the Society of Friends. The DTS was also much more lay dominated than the UTS. Although a few ministers joined the society, doctors, lawyers, and businessmen controlled it.[33] Other founding members were Richard Webb, an affluent Quaker printer, and Philip Crampton, a prominent attorney and Whig politico. With Webb's assistance, the DTS leaders were able to circulate a series of temperance pamphlets. In some, Dr. Cheyne tried to disabuse people of the belief that alcohol helped prevent or cure diseases. His tracts had a scholarly tone and were filled with citations to medical works.[34]

In April 1830 the Dublin Temperance Society was replaced by the Hibernian Temperance Society (HTS). As the name change indicates, the Dublin leaders had become more ambitious and were intent on spreading temperance throughout the island. The HTS had an even broader social and religious base than its predecessor. In 1832 the organization counted among its directors Bishop Doyle and another Catholic clergyman, several ministers, a couple of military officers, and some businessmen and professionals.[35]

Side by side with the HTS, a number of local temperance societies sprang up throughout Ireland in the early 1830s. Several auxiliary societies were founded in Dublin, including the St. Peter's District Society, the St. Kevin's District Society, and the Cuffe Street Society. In the area surrounding Dublin, societies were functioning in Maynooth, Kingstown, and Leixlip. In the southeast, Waterford and Wexford had established societies, and the New Ross Temperance Society was still flourishing. Generally the societies in rural areas attracted proportionately more people than the urban societies.

Cork and its environs were particular strongholds for the temperance movement. In fact, outside of Ulster, Cork was the leading center of temperance in the early 1830s. The city had three groups, and its surrounding towns and villages boasted twenty.[36] Two of the societies in the Cork vicinity were particularly noteworthy for their ties to Robert Owen, the English visionary socialist.[37] An Owenite community existed at Ralahine in County Clare from 1831 to 1833, and it proscribed the consumption of spirits in its regulations.[38] At Glandore, James Redmond Barry, a wealthy landowner and disciple of Owen and William Thompson, tried to establish an ideal community.[39] He closed all but two of the taverns in the town and left the remaining pubs with only one entrance so that passersby would be able to see who was frequenting them. At the same time, Barry promoted the work of the local temperance society and tried to persuade the priests of the area to join the cause.

The existence of the two Owen-affiliated societies suggests that there was a secularist element in the temperance movement. Brian Harrison, an expert on temperance in England, notes that many skeptics and atheists were active in the early years of the temperance movement there. He contends that Charles Bradlaugh became an atheist while attending temperance meetings and notes that John Henry Newman's brother, Frank, was both a skeptic and an ardent prohibitionist.[40] Harrison also claims that John Finch was an atheist.[41] Secularists were never a major force in the English temperance movement and were even less prominent in the Irish movement, but their presence gave unsympathetic clergy an excuse to shun the cause. The charge that temperance was a godless crusade cropped up periodically throughout the 1830s. When Father Mathew took the helm of the movement, he was careful to stress its Christian nature.

Clearly, temperance principles appealed to a wide variety of people in the early 1830s. Rigid Ulster Calvinists, various reform-minded Quakers, some Catholic clerics, and even a few utopian socialists marched under the banner of temperance. Nevertheless, it had not yet captured the Irish masses. With the possible exception of the UTS, temperance societies were elite operations. Changes were needed if temperance advocates hoped to gain a mass following.

The Rise of Teetotalism

During the 1830s temperance leaders made a decision that greatly increased their popularity among the Irish poor: they moved from opposition to spirits to teetotalism. It may seem odd that by taking a more extreme position, temperance advocates were able to gain more adherents, yet a total abstinence policy had several advantages over a moderationist course. It was more consistent and more easily understood by people. More important, the moderationist view had paternalistic overtones and many moderationists were affluent people who had never drunk spirits in the first place. Critics could justifiably argue that moderationists were determined to rid the lower orders of their addiction to spirits but had no intention of altering their own drinking habits.[42] By agreeing to banish wine and port from their dinner tables, middle-class temperance advocates gained a certain legitimacy in the eyes of the Irish poor.

Teetotalism also offered a plausible strategy for the reclamation of habitual drunkards. Moderationists had never had any notion of how to treat habitual drunkenness, a common problem among the Irish poor. Generally they viewed drunkards as lost causes and instead concerned themselves with preventing drunkenness. In the mid-1830s, various reclaimed drunkards began speaking to working-class audiences. Most prominent among them was John Hockings, an English blacksmith who traveled across Ireland proclaiming the wonders of teetotalism and distributing temperance medals.[43]

Whatever its doctrinal attractions, teetotalism was also aided by the kind treatment it received from the moderationists. The *Irish Temperance and Literary Gazette,* a newspaper founded by moderationists in 1836, gave teetotalers a sympathetic hearing. Moderationists were rarely critical, in public at least, of their more militant brethren. On the other hand, teetotalers were often scathing in their criticism of moderationists, depicting them as lukewarm and ineffectual. George Bretherton rightly labels the conflict between teetotalers and moderationists as a "one-sided struggle."[44] Total abstainers persistently exhorted and cajoled their moderationist colleagues and gradually came to dominate the temperance movement.

The first major total abstinence society was established in Preston, England, in 1832. This society, in contrast to the more patrician moderationist societies in England and Ireland, was organized by artisans and unskilled laborers and included several reformed drunkards among its ranks. The Preston society and other English total abstinence groups provided the impetus for teetotalism's rise in Ireland. Whereas the anti-spirits movement reached England by way of Ireland, total abstinence came to Ireland by way of England. John Finch was one of the activists who toured Ireland championing total abstinence. An iron merchant from Liverpool, Finch visited Ireland several times between 1833 and 1836 and established at least seventeen teetotal societies throughout the island.[45] Equally successful was Hockings, who spent most of 1838 touring Ireland. He was a charismatic speaker who appealed to crowds in Ulster and southern Ireland alike.

Some Irish natives also vigorously promoted teetotalism. William Martin, an elderly Quaker reformer, embraced the movement in the early 1830s and established a small total abstinence society in Cork in 1835. Many of the leaders of the anti-spirits agitation also switched over to total abstinence. George Carr, the Quaker activist Richard Webb and Unitarian James Haughton, and Father John Spratt, a Carmelite friar, discarded their moderationist policies for teetotalism in the mid-1830s.

John Edgar was the only major figure from the anti-spirits campaign who refused to embrace total abstinence. Edgar argued that teetotalism was opposed to Scripture. Since Christ drank wine on numerous occasions and even transformed water into wine at the wedding feast of Cana, Edgar felt compelled to defend the moderate intake of wine and beer.

Teetotalism, in his view, not only lacked a biblical basis, but was a revival of the Manichean heresy.[46] Because of Edgar's steadfast opposition, the total abstinence movement did not progress as rapidly in Ulster as in the other provinces. Eventually Edgar grew weary of battling against both tavern keepers and teetotalers, and in 1841 he withdrew completely from temperance work, devoting himself to the Second Reformation campaign in the Connaught region.

Edgar's opposition notwithstanding, the total abstinence movement was full of momentum. By 1838 teetotalism had become the dominant force in the temperance movement. What the teetotalers lacked was an effective leader and an efficient organization that could draw the Irish poor into the movement without alienating more affluent sympathizers. None of the prominent Irish teetotalers was capable of reaching the Catholic masses. Finch and Hockings, both Englishmen, had more success with the Irish poor than any native temperance spokesman had. William Martin knew that the movement would have to recruit someone for this task. When Father Mathew joined the cause in 1838, the movement found its leader.

The Catholic Church and Temperance

Father Mathew is depicted by many historians as an unusual man, that lone Catholic priest involved in the Protestant crusade against drink.[47] It is true that Mathew was exceptional in some respects. He had a much more genteel upbringing than most of his clerical colleagues; he was an ecumenist and anglophile at a time when most of his Catholic brethren were militantly Catholic and nationalistic. However, his support for temperance was not all that extraordinary. Many Catholics, lay and clerical alike, had joined the temperance movement before Mathew, even though there was considerable opposition on theological and practical grounds to teetotalism in some Catholic circles. The Catholic hierarchy, too, demonstrated concern about drunkenness and support for temperance long before 1838.

Irish bishops had been condemning drunkenness since at least 1614, when the bishops of Armagh issued regulations forbidding drunkenness at wakes and funerals.[48] In 1761 the diocese of Armagh went one step further and banned all drinking at wakes and funerals. In 1789 the bishop of Clogher adopted an even stricter policy: priests were forbidden from offering Mass at funerals where drink had been served, and the laity were warned not to distribute drink at funerals. Priests who knowingly violated this rule were to be suspended from the ministry, and laymen who offered drinks at funerals were to be denied the sacraments until they apologized publicly and paid a fine. The Clogher statutes also prohibited drinking on Sundays and holy days, and violation of this rule was deemed a mortal sin.[49] The Tuam statutes of 1817 forbade priests from entering a tavern on any occasion and stated that if a priest was seen drunk on three occasions, he was to be suspended from the priesthood.[50]

These rules and similar ones in other dioceses are signs that the bishops were concerned about drunkenness and in some cases willing to take stern measures to combat it. Drunkenness at funerals and wakes was a particular concern, but the Clogher and Tuam statutes indicate that at least some bishops were troubled by excessive drinking on other occasions as well. Of course, these fragmentary statements and regulations do not amount to a groundswell of episcopal support for either the moderationist or the total abstinence position, but they do bespeak an anxiety about excessive drinking in Ireland and a willingness to take concrete measures to address the problem.

Individual priests and laymen were even more active in the campaign for temperance. John Carr, who toured Ireland in 1805, noted that people occasionally took temperance pledges from priests: "In Dublin . . . the priest has been more effective than the legislature: his prohibitions against the consumption of liquors for one, two or three months are seldom, if ever, violated."[51] These pledges were thus temporary and applied only to spirits. Carr did not specify whether those taking the pledge were habitual or moderate drinkers.

In 1817 Jeffrey Sedwards, a nailer, established a small teetotal society composed mostly of artisans in Skibbereen, County Cork. He and most of the other members were probably Catholics, because Skibbereen was an overwhelmingly Catholic area. Furthermore, few of the Protestants in the area would have been artisans. Most telling, though, is the first rule of the society: "No person can take malt or spirituous liquors, or distilled waters, except prescribed by a priest or doctor."[52] Sedwards's society had support from priests from its early days. Father Michael Collins, the parish priest of Skibbereen, was affiliated with the teetotal group, and in the 1830s two priests from the area, both named Jeremiah Moloney, worked on its behalf.

In the same year that Sedwards was establishing his group, two Dublin priests, Fathers Michael Blake and Henry Young, formed a men's confraternity, the Purgatorian Society, that was affiliated with Blake's parish, Saints Michael and John. Members were encouraged to occupy themselves with a variety of charitable works, but Blake and Young were concerned especially with improving the laity's behavior at wakes. Consequently, members were urged to attend wakes and read spiritual books to increase the solemnity of these ceremonies. Members of the confraternity were not allowed to enter public houses on Sundays or paydays, and any member seen drunk was subject to fines for the first two offenses and expulsion for the third.

The Purgatorian Society was thus neither a teetotal nor an anti-spirits organization. Still, by focusing the members' pastoral activities on wakes and regulating their drinking habits, Blake and Young were demonstrating a concern for temperance. In the years following, both Blake and Young became teetotalers. Young and two of his brothers, Fathers William and James, spent much of their time and energy preaching against intemperance.[53]

In 1829 Bishop James Doyle wrote his famous letters on drunkenness, in which he expressed sympathy for the anti-spirits movement but did not endorse total abstinence. Instead he wanted to promote beer consumption through favorable licensing regulations: "The great and insurmountable obstacle to the progress of Temperance Societies . . . is found in the *revenue laws*. . . . I have no hesitation in stating that if malting and brewing were exempted from tax, and the impost on whiskey raised, drunkenness in a little time would almost disappear from the country."[54] Doyle was joined in the anti-spirits campaign by some other Catholics, including Stephen Woulfe, who became attorney general in 1837.[55]

By the mid-1830s the number of priests and Catholic laymen involved in the temperance movement had increased dramatically. Father James Maher, an uncle of Paul Cullen and friend of Daniel O' Connell, had already established a teetotal society in Carlow by 1830. Most parish teetotal societies were founded later in the decade, however. In 1837 Bishop George Browne of Galway and Bishop Patrick Kennedy of Killaloe became patrons of their local temperance societies. In the same year, Father John Kenyon—later famous for his support for extreme nationalism—became engaged in temperance work in Tipperary.[56] In 1838, the year of Mathew's entrance into the movement, Dublin already had a couple of priest-led temperance societies. Aside from the Young brothers, Father John Spratt had been the most prominent temperance priest in the Dublin area.[57] The city of Cork had at least four priests involved in temperance work before Mathew's advent: Fathers Eager, Coppinger, Scannell, and O'Sullivan. In Youghal, a town near Cork, Father Foley was a longtime teetotal advocate, and in Tuam Father Lyons had been promoting the cause for several years.[58]

Clearly, a significant number of priests and a handful of bishops were actively promoting temperance before Father Mathew entered the scene. Considering the priests involved, it is striking how many held influential positions in the Church. Two temperance priests, Michael Collins and Michael Blake, were later appointed bishops. Others, such as James Maher and Michael O'Sullivan of Cork, were never elevated to the episcopate but were influential with many bishops. These men were part of the Church's establishment; they were not gadflies by any means.

Given the stature of the priests and laity involved in temperance, it is fair to say that temperance was a mainstream Catholic concern. Temperance advocates just needed an articulate spokesman to unify the movement. Father Mathew was the right priest at the right time for the temperance cause. He had all the necessary attributes, and he signed on just as the movement was starting to spread.

{ CHAPTER THREE }

Mathew's "Miracle," 1838–1840

A reformation [has occurred], which, for the rapidity of its progress, and the excellence of its immediate results, is unexampled in history. The consistency of [Father Mathew's] practice, the previous benevolence of his life, and the confidence with which he is regarded, [is the cause for the] large number of the Irish people now pledged to the total disuse of all intoxicating drinks.

Irish Temperance Union Annual Report (1840)

IN CORK, most temperance advocates had become teetotalers by the mid-1830s. Men such as William Martin, a Quaker reformer, Richard Dowden, a Unitarian merchant, and the Reverend Nicholas Dunscombe, a Church of Ireland minister, were filled with zeal for the total abstinence cause but were unable to draw many people into the movement. Martin recognized that the cause needed a Catholic spokesman if it hoped to appeal to the city's largely Catholic population. Martin decided to recruit his friend, Father Theobald Mathew, who served with him as a director of the Cork House of Industry, a nonsectarian home for the sick and elderly poor. Upon seeing Mathew at the home, Martin would regularly point out one or more unfortunates to him and attribute their condition to excessive drinking. He would then implore Mathew to join the total abstinence movement: "Oh, Theobald Mathew, if *thou* would but take the cause in hand!"[1] Martin's persistent appeals probably had some effect on Mathew, but in the beginning of 1838 he still had not committed himself to the temperance movement. In March, the need for a Catholic leader was again demonstrated to him when a lay Catholic teetotaler, John O'Connell, alerted him to some anti-Catholic remarks expressed by a Protestant minister at a recent temperance meeting.² O'Connell did not ask Mathew to join the movement. Instead, he wanted Mathew to furnish him with a letter of introduction to Father Michael O'Sullivan, who, as vicar general of the diocese, was the most prominent teetotal priest in the region. Yet when Mathew heard O'Connell's account, he promised to do more than merely write a letter; he would seriously consider joining the movement himself. Mathew called for a meeting of the Cork teetotal leaders on the night of March 10. At the meeting, Martin, O'Connell, James McKenna, a Catholic ex-soldier from Liverpool, and other teetotalers waited expectantly for Mathew to declare himself a total abstainer, but to their disappointment he said that he needed another month to think it over. On April 10 he would announce his decision.

Mathew had compelling reasons for not plunging into the temperance campaign. First, he had no experience in the new teetotal movement and had not been a part of the moderationists' campaign against spirits in the early 1830s. Furthermore, he knew that temperance was a controversial cause and that his decision to join would be greeted with anger and scorn by many influential men and women of Cork, including, perhaps, his own bishop, John Murphy, whose family owned a major brewery. By joining he might also alienate his own family members, since two of his brothers and one of his brothers-in-law owned distilleries.

Mathew decided to join the movement nevertheless. At the April 10 meeting, he announced, "These gentlemen [Martin, McKenna, and O'Connell] are good enough to say that I could be useful in promoting the great virtue of temperance, and arresting the spread of drunkenness. . . . [Thus] I feel I am bound, as a minister of the gospel, to throw all personal considerations aside and try and give a helping hand to gentlemen who have afforded me so excellent an example. . . . After much reflection on the subject, I have come to the conviction that there is no necessity for [liquor] for anyone in good health; and I advise you all to follow my example. I will be the first to sign my name on the table, and I hope we shall soon have it full." As he signed the book of the new Cork Total Abstinence Society (CTAS), Mathew exclaimed, "Here goes, in the name of God!"³ After him, thirty-five other people at the meeting signed. Although he had agonized before committing himself, Mathew would never question the decision he announced that night. His crusade had begun, and from this point on he would work unceasingly to bring about the triumph of temperance.

Cork temperance advocates now had a new leader. In place of Martin, who was almost seventy and considered eccentric by many, they would be led by Father Mathew, who at forty-seven was in the prime of his life. Mathew had an impressive appearance that seemed refined without being snobbish. Father James Birmingham, one of Mathew's earliest allies in the temperance movement, provided a detailed description of Mathew's physical appearance at the beginning of 1840: "Mr. Mathew is . . . well built for strength and . . . straight and erect as any man may be at five-and-twenty. His complexion is sanguine, and indicative of health. . . . His hair is black; thinly, if at all, interspersed with the blossoms of age. His forehead is sufficiently extended to mark him a person of clear and strong understanding—his nose is Roman—his well-chiselled mouth and chin denote undeviating determination. . . . His manners are very prepossessing, being remarkable at once for their simplicity and urbanity. . . . His dress is plain and scrupulously neat—nothing *à la mode,* and nothing ultra-clerical." Father Augustine provides an equally revealing description of Mathew's home in Cork, which was elegant and spartan at the same time, just what one might expect from a Franciscan with an aristocratic lineage. Mathew's living room contained "a side-board, a side-table, a centre-table, some chairs, and a writing desk. A fine bust of Lord Morpeth, the popular [Chief] Secretary for Ireland and a friend of [Mathew's], was flanked by two very large volumes of the Sacred Scriptures on the side-table. A portrait of Cardinal Micara, the General of the Capuchins, hung on the wall opposite the fire-place."[4] Mathew lived alone in this modest but comfortable apartment, but had a valet and a cook working for him.

With Mathew the temperance movement gained not simply an impressive-looking priest but an articulate spokesman. Whereas Martin had been a high-strung speaker prone to making extreme statements, Mathew was persuasive and nuanced. Whereas Martin regularly denounced spirits in the harshest terms, often calling them "poisons," Mathew was careful to avoid such Manichean-sounding statements and instead limited himself to denouncing drunkenness.[5] Generally he stressed the practical advantages of teetotalism rather than the horrors of drunkenness. He emphasized that husbands and wives would get along better and have more money at their disposal if they were to take the pledge.[6]

Under the direction of this charismatic and attractive priest, the CTAS grew rapidly. In Mathew's first week as president of the society, more than three hundred people enrolled.[7] After a few weeks, he had to move his meetings from a schoolhouse near his home to the Cork Horse Bazaar, a cavernous building with a capacity of four thousand. There he held meetings every Sunday, giving the pledge to new teetotalers and offering encouragement to those who had already taken it. Mathew also administered the pledge at his home at virtually any hour of the day or night.

By fall 1838 Mathew's name was becoming widely known in temperance circles throughout Ireland. In November, the *Dublin Weekly Herald*, Ireland's leading temperance newspaper, included a tribute to him in which the editors remarked that as a result of Mathew's labors, "Cork bids fair to rival Preston" as a temperance stronghold. This was a colossal understatement. By the end of the year, he had enrolled six thousand people, which made the CTAS the largest temperance organization in the United Kingdom. By the beginning of 1839 he was attracting visitors from all parts of the Munster province—Kerry, Limerick, Waterford, and beyond. James McKenna, who had been named secretary of the society and was serving as Mathew's own secretary, claimed in early 1839 that people were coming "sixty and eighty miles from Cork, without any other business but enrolling themselves in this society."[8]

In some respects, the trip to see Mathew was a pilgrimage. The Irish had a long tradition of walking great distances to visit shrines and other holy places, where they normally made a vow or promise to God. In return, the pilgrims hoped for a material reward, such as improved health or a better job.[9] Since those who trekked to Cork were planning to make a promise before God and were hoping that a material gain would result, they were pilgrims of a sort.

While the people went to Mathew, other temperance advocates went to the people. McKenna spent some time touring Ulster, promoting temperance, and the Irish Temperance Union (ITU), a teetotal society based in Dublin and led by Quakers, hired agents who criss-crossed the island in search of converts to the cause. Although these men were credible promoters of temperance, none had much success in attracting new members. Generally, McKenna and the ITU agents attracted twenty or, at most, thirty new members at their meetings.[10] It seems most prospective teetotalers preferred to walk miles to Cork to receive the pledge from Mathew than receive it in their own towns from McKenna or an ITU representative.

In August 1839 the CTAS claimed twenty-four thousand members, a fourfold increase over its membership at the beginning of the year.[11] The society also boasted eight reading rooms in the city of Cork. These rooms were meant to serve as social centers where teetotalers could meet their friends, read newspapers, and drink tea and coffee. Mathew recognized that many members, especially those from the working class, needed a place to go to relax and socialize. The reading rooms were meant to serve the same social functions as the taverns.

In September Mathew abruptly changed his course of action and decided to start traveling. He made a brief trip to County Tipperary, visiting Cahir and Golden and enrolling seven thousand people. Upon returning to Cork, Mathew found more pilgrims than ever waiting to enlist in his society. Elizabeth Malcolm notes that in September and October 1839, approximately forty-eight hundred persons were enrolling each week. This was a massive increase over the enrollment figure for 1838, when at most four hundred persons joined weekly. Suddenly, temperance had caught fire. In October, the *Dublin Weekly Herald,* the *Nenagh Chronicle,* and the *Waterford Chronicle* were all in agreement that the CTAS had topped fifty thousand, a twofold increase from August. As the society expanded, Mathew received more notice from influential persons. F. W. Conway, the editor of the Liberal *Dublin Evening Post,* discovered Mathew in September and immediately started giving him favorable coverage. (Kerrigan claims Conway took the pledge in 1839.) At about the same time, the *Freeman's Journal,* a Repeal newspaper, began including sympathetic reports on Mathew's society. And at a banquet in Cork in October, Daniel O'Connell paid homage to Mathew, describing temperance as a "moral and majestic miracle." Mother Catherine McAuley, the foundress of the Sisters of Mercy, was similarly excited. From Dublin she wrote to a sister in Cork, "The walls of Dublin are covered with placards proclaiming the good he has accomplished. It is no longer a laughing matter. All description of persons speak most seriously of his extraordinary success, and all wish he could extend his influence to every place."[12]

Mathew's Followers

The meetings of the CTAS were headed by Mathew, Martin, McKenna, and two younger men: John F. Maguire, a journalist, and Frank Walsh, a lawyer. With this group directing the society, all the leaders except Martin were now Catholic. The society's rank and file was even more heavily Catholic. Data exist showing the religious affiliations of CTAS members in many towns throughout Ireland. A constable in Macroom, a town west of Cork, claimed in early 1840 that of the 878 people in his district who had joined the CTAS, only one was a Protestant. Macroom was 2 percent Protestant, so theoretically there should have been seventeen or eighteen Protestants in the temperance society. In Kinsale, a coastal town southwest of Cork, the subinspector estimated that only 40 of the 640 teetotalers in the town were Protestants. Kinsale's population was 10 percent Protestant, so theoretically the CTAS should have included sixty-four Protestants. In other counties, constables reported similarly lopsided figures. The subinspector for Oulart in County Wexford estimated that thirty-five hundred people had taken the pledge in his district and all but one were Catholic. Protestants comprised about 10 percent of the town's population. In Waterford, which was 15 percent Protestant, only two Protestants were among the six thousand residents enrolled in the CTAS. Wherever Mathew's society had gained a foothold, the story was the same. In 1846 Mathew wrote to one of his Unitarian allies, James Haughton, ruefully admitting that his movement had never caught on among Protestants: "The teetotalers of Ireland are a Roman Catholic body. There are not fifty Protestants united with us, though I have made every effort to induce them to associate with us."[13]

The transformation of the CTAS into a de facto Catholic organization in the months after Mathew took over as president is rather puzzling at first glance. Mathew was a thoroughgoing ecumenist—an indifferentist in the eyes of some Catholic critics—and took pains to keep the movement from taking on a sectarian hue. For example, during the first years of his campaign, he refused to administer the pledge inside Catholic churches.[14] At the same time, he took certain actions, discussed later in this chapter, that undoubtedly antagonized Protestants. However, the tenor of the country provides the best explanation for the religious composition of the movement. Since Ireland was polarized along religious lines at this time, most Irish Protestants probably dismissed Mathew's ecumenical statements as rhetoric. The large majority were unwilling to join any organization headed by a Catholic priest, regardless of his outlook. And most Catholics, lay and clerical alike, probably made little effort to welcome Protestants into the local societies.

The Pledge

The ritual surrounding the pledge ceremony also contributed to the sectarian nature of the society. Normally, people who took the pledge from Mathew got on their knees before him. The wording of the pledge changed somewhat over time, but at the start prospective members recited, "I promise, while I belong to the Teetotal Abstinence Society, to abstain from all kinds of intoxicating drinks, unless used medicinally, and that I will discountenance, by advice and example, the causes of intemperance in others." By March 1840 the pledge had been lengthened to include a petition for God's assistance and an exemption for the use of alcohol in sacramental functions. The latter insertion was intended to satisfy members of the Church of Ireland who received communion under both species. In 1841, though, Mathew decided to tighten up the wording of the pledge. First he deleted the phrase "while I belong to the Teetotal Abstinence Society." A few weeks later, he removed the clauses allowing members to drink alcohol for medical or sacramental purposes. By fall 1841, new members were pledging not to consume any alcohol for any reason for the rest of their lives.[15]

After the new member had recited the pledge, Mathew made the Sign of the Cross over the person's head and bestowed his blessing. At first, the benediction was brief: "God bless you, and enable you to keep the promise you have given." By 1841 the blessing had been expanded and solemnized: "May God give you grace and strength to keep your promise, and I now mark you with the Sign of the Cross that you may put your trust in Christ crucified and in him alone and that you may always bear in mind that you have sealed your promise with this symbol of our Redemption and, should anyone tempt you to violate your pledge, that you may be able to say to the tempter with the apostle Paul: 'Let no man molest me for I bear the stigmas of My Lord and Saviour Jesus Christ in my body.'"[16]

Upon enrolling, initiates received a membership card and a temperance medal. One side of the medal showed an image of a lamb—symbolizing Christ—below a cross. Above the cross were the words "In Hoc Signo Vinces."[17] On the reverse side of the medal the words of the pledge appeared in the shape of a cross. Clearly, the pledging ceremony was a religious ritual and the medal—the identity badge for most members—a religious symbol. Although all the language and imagery of the pledge and the medal were generically Christian rather than Catholic, several parts of the ceremony certainly must have troubled many Protestants. Kneeling before Mathew, having the Sign of the Cross made upon one's head, and receiving Mathew's benediction would disconcert most Protestants. The imagery of the medal may well have struck some Protestants as idolatrous, and the medal itself may have borne too close a resemblance to a Catholic medal or scapular for many Protestants.

In some respects, it is surprising that an ecumenist like Mathew would have designed the pledge ceremony and the medal in this fashion. On the other hand, the ritual would have lost much of its power if these elements were omitted and would not have had nearly the same effect on most Catholics. Furthermore, deleting religious references from the ceremony and the medal would have left Mathew open to the charge of secularism.

Other aspects of the pledge were controversial as well. On the critical question of the nature of the pledge, Mathew never clearly stated whether the pledge was akin to a solemn vow or merely a promise. However, the solemnity with which he administered it led many to consider it a vow. A Maynooth seminarian recalled his experience taking the pledge from Mathew: "Folding my arms in deep deliberation, I knelt amongst the crowd, I registered in heaven my solemn promise of total and perpetual abstinence, and got the benediction of Father Mathew." A police inspector in Skibbereen, writing about the teetotalers in his district, remarked that the pledge was "a voluntary act—a solemn vow made before God and the world—and the solemnity of that vow resembles the solemnity of an oath." The editors of the *Dublin Evening Mail,* a Protestant and Tory journal hostile to Mathew, reported that violations of the pledge were considered "reserved cases" from which "not even any vicars can absolve." Presumably, they believed that only bishops could forgive lapsed teetotalers for breaking their pledges. Some of Mathew's fellow priests wondered as well if the pledge were not a vow. In July 1840, Father James Dowling, a curate from the diocese of Meath, asked Mathew to clarify his position on this question:

> I have been requested by a very considerable number of the priests of this and the other districts of this diocese to ask you if you have made any change latterly in the constitution of your society. Until lately it was understood that every member was free, as far as the *obligation of the pledge* was in question, to withdraw whenever he chose; but now some doubts are beginning to be raised.... The question therefore arises: do you now *require* all persons entering the society to have *an intention of binding themselves for life?* There is also a great anxiety to know whether you regard the obligation of the pledge as a mere *obligation of honour* or whether you regard it as *binding in conscience* ... and if so whether you regard it as so *binding sub gravi [under pain of grave sin]* or not?[18]

Unfortunately, Mathew's answer to Dowling's letter is not extant. The issue did not go away, however. In all likelihood, he did not give Dowling a clear answer, because the issue was raised again and again in the years following.

Never Too Young

Whether the pledge was a vow or only a promise, it was clearly a serious act, so Mathew should have taken care to ensure that potential members were in a position to make a commitment of this type. Instead, he eagerly administered the pledge to virtually every person who came before him: children as well as adults, intoxicated people, and even people who were hesitant to pledge. Indeed, there was scarcely anyone to whom Mathew was unwilling to administer the pledge.

It is impossible to know for certain how many children were included among Mathew's membership rolls. There are a host of references in police reports to children being among the pledged, so a considerable number were probably involved. A subinspector from Queens County (now known as County Laois) claimed that some "children under the age of ten" had taken the pledge from Mathew. Several men who were politically prominent in the last years of the nineteenth century took the pledge from Mathew as children, including John Denvir, a revolutionary nationalist, and Justin McCarthy, a leader of the Home Rule movement.[19] John Ireland, who as archbishop of St. Paul, Minnesota, was a champion of temperance, recalled taking the pledge at Mathew's hands as a youngster: "When I was a very young boy, Father Mathew came to my native town to administer the pledge. I served his mass, and he asked me to attend him. He went about everywhere, giving the pledge, and everywhere he administered it, I took the pledge. He used to sometimes introduce me as his little teetotaller; I was not then seven years old." Mrs. Asenath Nicholson, an American Protestant evangelist who visited Ireland in 1844–45, reported that Mathew administered the pledge to toddlers and even babies: "Some of the little ones he took in his arms; on all heads he put his hand. . . . A large circle was formed [around Mathew with] the children, kneeling down, clasping their hands, and lisping the pledge. Those who could not speak were carried in the arms of their mothers, and they, kneeling, repeated the pledge for them. . . . A few moments before four, the assembly broke up, and mothers and children ran after the good man, the mothers crying, 'The baby, plase, wants the pledge.'"[20]

Mathew was not alone in the effort to enroll children in the temperance movement. Ann Carlile, a friend of his, founded a children's temperance society in England called the Band of Hope,[21] and the temperance activists who preceded Mathew were also interested in recruiting young people. In 1837 the moderationist leaders of the Hibernian Temperance Society established the Dublin Juvenile Temperance Society. It was perfectly understandable that Mathew and other temperance leaders would want to involve young people in their movement before they had any experience drinking. Even so, Mathew's willingness to administer the pledge to small children and babies is difficult to fathom.

More problematic for Mathew were the countless cases of prospective teetotalers who came to take the pledge in an intoxicated state. Having decided to take the pledge, many men would have a "farewell drop" of whiskey—"farewell quart" is perhaps a more accurate description—before the ceremony. A subinspector in County Wexford noted that he "saw numbers take the pledge in a beastly state of intoxication." Another Wexford policeman concurred: "Numbers have I am told and have little doubt took it in a state of intoxication and returned to take it again having forgotten they took it. They also drank to very great excess before they took it for days and nights." One inspector in County Galway reported that the poorer people in his town had initially thought they had to take the pledge drunk "to render it useful," but no longer subscribed to that view. Most police inspectors in other counties observed similar practices. Mathew must have had some reservations about giving teetotal pledges to intoxicated people, but in many cases he inducted them nonetheless.[22]

Finally, there were at least a few instances in which Mathew administered the pledge to people who were unsure about taking the pledge. These people typically were heavy drinkers who had come before Mathew at the behest of their relatives or employers. Father Augustine describes how Mathew dealt with them:

> Just as many a turbulent poor fellow who would not "demane himself by taking their durty pledge" was about to effect his escape, Father Mathew would appear on the scene and, quickly divining the situation, bid him a warm welcome, take him affectionately by the hand, tell him he was delighted to see him, and that it was so good of him to have come of his own free will too. "You are doing a good day's work for yourself and your family," he would add. "You will have God's blessing on your head".... Then before the poor captive could recover from the confusion wrought by this caressing language, he felt a strong tightening on his left arm, and a gentle pressure on his right shoulder, as Father Mathew uttered the final words... "Kneel down now, my dear, and I'll give you the pledge."

This practice of Mathew's—pressuring reluctant people to take the pledge—was even more questionable than his other tactics. Yet it appears that only a small number of people entered the society in this manner; most seemed to have joined willingly.[23]

At first, administering the pledge to all comers and hedging on its meaning worked to Mathew's advantage. More people took the pledge and few broke it, since most people believed they had sworn a solemn oath not to drink. As the years passed, however, these issues would reappear and serve to weaken the movement.

Touring for Temperance

After a brief but fruitful trip to Tipperary in September, Mathew determined to increase his traveling. In late September he received a letter from G. H. Fitzgerald, the acting mayor of Limerick, that outlined the dramatic improvements that had occurred in Limerick since a branch of Mathew's society had been established in July. Fitzgerald was also coroner and so was able to compare the death rates and crime statistics before and after the establishment of the local temperance society:

> I have held about 140 inquests since the 1st of last October, and I can safely affirm that half that number were caused, either directly or indirectly, by intoxicating liquors. There were eight cases of death by drowning while in a state of intoxication; several by burning while ditto; many from apoplexy while ditto; and, within a short period from each other, four persons committed suicide while under its hellish influence. But, thank God, a bright prospect is now dawning. Your unparalleled exertions in the cause of temperance have been, under God, crowned with the most signal success and, I believe, in no place more than in Limerick. A moral regeneration has taken place among the people of this city, which is really most astonishing. . . . Our police reports are much lessened. . . . Our streets and places of public resort are regular and quiet.[24]

In November, Mathew had an opportunity to see for himself the salutary effects his society was having on the people of Limerick, when he was invited to preach a charity sermon on behalf of a school there run by the Presentation Sisters.[25] Charity sermons were common at this time throughout Ireland. Popular priests were regularly invited to preach on behalf of the many new schools, churches, orphanages, and other institutions that had been established. Tickets were sold for the sermon, and a collection was often taken up after it to raise funds for the fledgling institution. Being invited to preach in Limerick indicated that Mathew's reputation as a churchman and orator was spreading.

He agreed to give the charity sermon and promised to spend a day administering the pledge in Limerick. As news of his planned trip spread through Limerick and the surrounding towns, thousands of visitors converged on the city. By November 30, the date of his arrival, about forty thousand visitors had arrived in Limerick, whose residents numbered fifty thousand and many visitors were unable to obtain suitable shelter.[26] Some were forced to stay in cellars in rundown neighborhoods, while others slept outside in the unseasonably warm temperatures.

On Sunday after delivering the charity sermon, Mathew went to the courthouse to administer the pledge; he also administered it inside his brother-in-law's house. For the next forty-eight hours, he gave the pledge almost without respite to group after group. Because of the size and fervor of the crowd and the limited space, several mishaps occurred. An iron fence and a staircase outside the house of Mathew's brother-in-law were broken, and a balustrade overlooking the Shannon River came apart. Several people fell in the river, a few were hurt seriously enough to require hospitalization, and at least one person—a pregnant woman— died from her injuries.[27] Some of Mathew's friends thought he might be in danger as well, so they persuaded the mayor to call out troops to maintain order.

On Tuesday afternoon an exhausted Mathew boarded a coach for Cork. Apart from the injuries and death caused by the crowding, this sojourn had been a remarkable success. Mathew had brought two thousand medals and cards with him to Limerick, not having had the faintest intimation that he would pledge more than one hundred thousand people during his short stay. Estimates varied widely about how many people really pledged, and since cards were not distributed to most new members, there was no way to be certain about the number. The staid London *Times* offered 120,000 as an estimate, while the *Dublin Evening Post*, which promoted teetotalism, claimed that 200, 000 had enrolled. Father Augustine adopted the Limerick *Reporter*'s figure of 150,000 in his account. If this last estimate is accurate, Mathew had enrolled three times more people in three days in Limerick than in the first nineteen months of his campaign. The editors of the *Dublin Weekly Herald* could not believe the reports they heard: "[the Limerick *Reporter*'s estimate of 150,000 pledges] we think must be greatly overstated."[28] If true, Mathew's labors in Limerick had completely eclipsed the combined efforts of all the other

Irish temperance activists in Ireland in the previous decade. The *Dublin Weekly Herald*'s staff was, understandably, not yet ready to face the fact that temperance was now Mathew's movement and all other actors were marginal.

A week after leaving Limerick, Mathew arrived in Waterford at the invitation of the bishop, Nicholas Foran. Waterford could be considered a teetotal stronghold, since Foran, Father John Sheehan, who was a prominent O'Connell ally, and the leaders of the Christian Brothers were all teetotal enthusiasts. Edmund Rice, the founder of the Christian Brothers, and Patrick Joseph Murphy, his successor as superior, were both actively involved in the temperance movement.[29] After resigning the leadership of the congregation in 1838, Rice devoted all of his energies to temperance work. Murphy founded a juvenile temperance society in 1838, and in the summer of 1839 Foran established a branch of the CTAS in Waterford. In November, Foran extended a gracious invitation to Mathew: "Anxious to cooperate with your zealous and, under God, successful undertaking of bringing the people of this country to habits of temperance and sobriety, I and the clergy of this city are doing what we can to induce our flocks here to enrol themselves in your Society. A great number of habitual drunkards have willingly come forward and expressed their ardent desire to become members of your Temperance Society, but many of them, from their extreme poverty, are unable to defray the cost of a trip to Cork. If you would make it your convenience to come here . . . you would, I have no doubt, do incalculable good. While you are here my house shall be yours."[30]

Mathew's trip to Waterford was almost as successful as his visit to Limerick. When the newspapers announced the impending trip, many thousands of visitors pressed into Waterford, a town with a population of twenty-five thousand.[31] Starting early on the morning of December 11, Mathew administered the pledge all day long and well into the night, breaking only for meals. The following day he again started early in the morning and continued almost without pause until 8:00 P.M., when his coach departed for Cork. Because of the size of the crowds, Mathew directed the people to approach him in groups of two hundred or more. The local newspapers concluded that Mathew added eighty thousand to ninety thousand to his rolls during his two-day visit. The newspapers also noted that this time there were no deaths from overcrowding, although several people had suffered injuries.

The editors of the *Dublin Weekly Herald* were just as enthusiastic about Mathew's visit as the Waterford-area newspapers. This second triumph of Mathew's erased any lingering skepticism about his Limerick tour. The *Herald's* editors offered a higher estimate of the pledges in Waterford—one hundred thousand—than the other newspapers. They also remarked that more women than men took the pledge this time, which was unusual since men normally composed the large majority of those pledging.[32] Because women were much less likely than men to be heavy drinkers, most were generally interested more in persuading their husbands and sons to enroll than in taking the pledge themselves. Furthermore, since some of the women pledging were prostitutes, there must have been a stigma attached to pledging for many Irish women.[33]

After leaving Waterford, Mathew returned to Cork for a few days before visiting Clonmel, the leading city in Tipperary, on December 17. This trip was also successful but did not receive as much attention from the newspapers. During his two days there, Mathew enrolled almost sixty thousand people. Considering that Clonmel's population was slightly less than fifteen thousand, this was quite an achievement.[34] Thousands must have streamed in from neighboring towns and villages, just as they had in Limerick and Waterford.

After Clonmel, Mathew stopped touring for a few weeks and enjoyed a relatively quiet Christmas and New Year's Day at his home in Cork. His brief break gave the newspaper reporters a chance to consider what he had achieved in 1839. The *Dublin Weekly Herald* editors estimated that more than 340,000 people had taken the pledge from him and that at least 130 taverns had closed down that year. They also noted that a large number of bakeries had opened in the preceding months. Presumably, not spending money on liquor gave many people more money to spend on bread and other foodstuffs. The editorial concluded triumphantly, "Drunkenness has ceased to be a fashionable vice, or even tolerated by the lower orders."[35]

In the middle of January 1840, Mathew again set off, touring the south of Ireland. He went first to Kilkenny, where he was warmly greeted by his fellow Capuchin, Father Jeremiah O'Reilly, and the bishop, William Kinsella. Compared with earlier tours, this visit was mildly disappointing: only ten thousand people enrolled.[36] From Kilkenny he traveled to several small towns and villages in the south-central region.

In early February, Mathew ventured to Cashel, hoping to hold a meeting at the Rock of Cashel, a historic mount where St. Patrick had once preached. Like many sites of historic religious significance, the rock and the church ruins atop it had been controlled by the Church of Ireland since the Reformation. Through an intermediary, Mathew requested permission to use the site, and the rector, Dr. Whitty, refused him. Whitty asserted that teetotalism was unscriptural and, in fact, the handiwork of the devil. Although Whitty was certainly more extreme in his attitudes than most of his clerical brethren in the Church of Ireland, some ministers—especially those with evangelical leanings—shared his suspicions of this friar-led movement. This experience must have demonstrated to Mathew that at least certain members of the establishment had their misgivings about him and his movement.

Despite Whitty's rebuff, Mathew held a successful meeting in Cashel. Using a site adjacent to the rock, he was able to enroll several thousand people. From Cashel, he proceeded west to Limerick and then north into Ennis and Tulla in County Clare. The police inspector in Ennis reported that "an immense number of the peasantry—perhaps two-thirds of the population of the district pledged."[37]

In March, Mathew's schedule became even more hectic. On the first, he was in Birr in King's Country (now known as County Offaly) at the request of his friend, Father John Spain, who was struggling against a popular renegade priest in the town. Mathew preached a charity sermon on behalf of the Sisters of Mercy, who had just established themselves there at his behest, and then occupied himself with administering the pledge. Again he was supremely successful: about eighty-five thousand people took the pledge from him during his two-day visit. Mathew was then prevailed on to stop at Borrisokane, a small town in Tipperary, by Father James Birmingham, an outspoken teetotal enthusiast. Birmingham recalled Mathew's stopover:

I asked Mr. Mathew to do me the honour of spending the day with me. He expressed his regret that time did not permit him. . . . Each moment Mr. Mathew was on the point of moving away; but each moment brought numbers from the surrounding parishes, who, having heard that the Rev. Gentleman had been in Borrisokane, threw aside their various implements of industry, and hurried in to enlist themselves under the standard of temperance, and receive the good man's benediction. Fatigued and breathless, men, women and children rushed forward indiscriminately to take the pledge. Mr. Mathew could not bring himself to disappoint such eagerness, or damp such ardour. He was consequently obliged to remain; . . . he received in this small town, without any previous notice having been given, seven or eight thousand souls.

From Borrisokane, Mathew went on to his original destination, Nenagh, one of the larger towns in Tipperary, where he pledged twenty thousand people in one day.[38]

The following week, Mathew arrived in Galway, the largest town in the province of Connaught. He had been invited by the bishop, George Browne, who had been one of the first prelates to join the temperance movement. By coincidence, Daniel O'Connell was also in Galway at this time, making a rare court appearance on behalf of a priest accused of libel. This was also a campaign stop for O'Connell, who was about to renew his agitation for Repeal and was anxious to rekindle the nationalist spirit of his supporters in the west. Shortly after their arrival, O'Connell and Mathew had the opportunity to meet for the first time at a private party at the local college.[39] Mathew was careful not to appear in public with O'Connell, however, for fear of seeming partisan.

The Miracle Worker

After delivering a charity sermon for the benefit of the Presentation Sisters in Galway, Mathew set about his usual task. Here the masses were as difficult to control as they had been in Limerick, Waterford, and elsewhere. They pressed around him with what Father Birmingham euphemistically described as "holy violence." More detached observers probably would have admitted that a variety of factors were responsible for the unruly state of the crowd. First, a vast throng was pressed into a very small area. Second, at least some of the prospective members were drunk, having taken their "parting drop" en route. Probably the most important cause of unrest among Mathew's followers, however, was the desire of many people to touch or be touched by him. Much of the peasantry believed that Mathew had extraordinary healing powers. S. J. Connolly claims that in pre-Famine Ireland, priests were often thought to be able to cure the sick, but he singles out Mathew and a handful of others as being more widely venerated as healers than other members of the clergy. Therefore, some of those pressing in on Mathew at Galway and his other stops were interested less in teetotalism than in being cured of blindness or another disability. They were intent on making physical contact with him. Some wanted him to lay his hands on them, and others wanted to touch and perhaps tear the hem of his garment.[40]

The issue of miraculous healings, like the question of the nature and duration of the pledge, was potentially volatile for Mathew. He certainly did not want to banish the halt and the lame from his sight, but neither did he want to encourage the peasantry to view him as a miracle worker. He responded by bestowing his blessing on all who asked for it while at the same time reminding the assembled throngs that he had no special powers.[41]

Despite problems with the crowd's behavior, Mathew's days in Galway were a success. He enrolled at least fifty thousand people into his society and witnessed a sober, peaceable St. Patrick's Day there.[42] For as long as most people could remember, St. Patrick's Day had been marked by drunkenness and carousing throughout most towns in Ireland. From Galway, Mathew went east to Loughrea, where he was welcomed by the local bishop, Thomas Coen, who, like Browne, was a longtime teetotal advocate. While many thousands of people came to Loughrea to take the pledge, hundreds, perhaps thousands, of others came to Mathew in search of a cure. The local police inspector noted with dismay this dimension of Mathew's visit:

> It was melancholy and distressing in the extreme to witness the credulity and the superstition evinced by persons of every rank and station professing the Roman Catholic religion, who were present at the ceremony, in believing that the Rev'd Gentleman was possessed of supernatural power, and was able to cure disease, to restore sight to the blind, strength to persons who had been cripples from their childhood, in fact of performing cures, which were nothing short of miracles; gentlemen of rank and station in the country, who are magistrates and

grand jurors, and who are in the habit of taking a leading part in every publick action, assured me that they had seen Mr. M[athew] perform cures which were absolutely miraculous. . . . There is scarcely a single person amongst the lower orders, who is not firmly persuaded that he has the power of working miracles. Mr. M[athew] did not appear to openly encourage this erroneous supposition, and at the same time, he took scarcely any pains to disabuse the persons who had conceived this idea. It is likely he rather encouraged this opinion, knowing that it would be a good means of keeping the pledge inviolate.

The inspector added a postscript that demonstrated that Catholics were not the only ones who thought Mathew could work miracles: "A Mr. Lister of Listerfield, a protestant gentleman of independent fortune, came to him . . . from the Co. Roscommon, where he resides. . . . I am told Mr. L came to him with a view to benefit his health, which has been in a very bad state for three or four years."[43] After pledging forty thousand at Loughrea and blessing thousands more, Mathew traveled further east to Portumna and then to Roscrea. After brief stops in these towns, he finally returned home to Cork for a few days of rest.

On March 28, Mathew set off on a long-awaited trip to Dublin. He had been invited by Archbishop Daniel Murray to preach a charity sermon in his church, the Pro-Cathedral, which was the most prominent and ornate Catholic church in the city.[44] The day after he arrived, Mathew preached to a crowd of six thousand that included the lord lieutenant's son and several other notables. The sermon, which was later published, emphasized the need for ecumenism: "Disciples of Christ, engaged in the same glorious pursuit—heaven and immortality—'by this shall all men know that you are my disciples, that you love one another' [Jn. 13:34–35]. We are all children of the same father; the same blood flows in our veins; we are all believers in the same Saviour; redeemed at one price—followers of the same gospel of love. Oh! that its sweet and beneficent spirit would diffuse from pole to pole, uniting all mankind as one family, and making a world happy."[45] Mathew had long held these liberal sentiments, but this may have been the first time that many Irish people outside of Cork learned of them.

Mathew launched a weeklong temperance mission. Initially, he was flanked by three priests and two laymen: Dr. John Yore, vicar general of the archdiocese; Father Andrew O'Connell, pastor of one of the most important parishes in the city; Father John Delany, a Capuchin; Charles Bianconi, an Italian-born entrepreneur; and W. J. Battersby, a Catholic publisher and pamphleteer.[46] Aside from Archbishop Murray, these five men were perhaps the most distinguished Catholics in Dublin. Both Yore and O'Connell had founded temperance societies that were independent of Mathew's organization.[47] Before beginning the pledge ceremonies, Mathew gave an address that dealt with his reputed healing powers, a now much-discussed issue. He noted that some people "imagined that [I] could heal diseases. Nothing could possibly be more mistaken than such a notion as that. It [is] . . . a source of much trouble, and serves no other purpose than to give an air of superstition to [our] meetings."[48] It was wise of him to offer this disclaimer, since much of his audience in Dublin was more affluent and cosmopolitan than his followers in other parts of Ireland.

After speaking, Mathew began administering the pledge. At the end of the first day, he had added forty-six hundred people to his ranks, a disappointing tally by his standards. Over the next seven days, he enrolled another sixty-five thousand people. Considering that Dublin's population was 230,000, Mathew's grand total of 70,000 pledges was relatively low.[49] It is true that several temperance societies had been active before Mathew's visit, so Dubliners had had previous opportunities if they so desired. Still, if Mathew could enroll eighty-five thousand during a two-day visit to Birr, it would stand to reason that he could have added well over one hundred thousand to the movement during his maiden tour of Dublin.

Before departing from Dublin, Mathew again demonstrated his liberal sentiments toward Protestants by attending a tea party at Trinity College, the bastion of the Ascendancy.[50] He had been invited to a soirée by several young teetotalers at the college. At the party, nine students took the pledge, which so thrilled him that he promised to send each of them a silver temperance medal in lieu of the standard bronze version.

From Dublin, Mathew traveled south to Enniscorthy, Wexford, and New Ross, the last being the hometown of G. W. Carr, who had founded the New Ross Temperance Society in 1829. At Enniscorthy he was the guest of the bishop, James Keating. After spending four days in County Wexford and adding eighty thousand people to his rolls, Mathew headed home for a few days.[51] Over the next several weeks, he traveled to counties Tipperary, Limerick, Waterford, and Kerry, delivering sermons and temperance lectures and pledging still more people. In mid-June he visited Maynooth College at the invitation of the president, Michael Montague. This was apparently Mathew's first visit to Maynooth since his unhappy departure from there in 1807, and he stayed at the home of the Duke of Leinster rather than at the college. The duke, a progressive landlord who lived on his estate, had been an early promoter of temperance.[52] Mathew went into the town of Maynooth and met with temperance leaders and preached at the dedication of a new church; however, he spent the bulk of his time at the college. By the end of his visit, 250 seminarians—a majority of the student body—and eight professors—almost half the faculty—had taken the pledge. The Maynooth seminarians represented most of Ireland's future priests, and Maynooth professors were frequently appointed bishops. So this was quite an achievement for Mathew and the temperance movement.[53]

For the rest of the year Mathew maintained the same grueling schedule. He traveled extensively through the southern half of the island and ventured several times into the western province of Tuam. Only Protestant-dominated Ulster remained outside of his ambit. He returned twice to Dublin, each time at the request of the archbishop. In late September he was back in the pulpit of the Pro-Cathedral, preaching another charity sermon. His audience was again filled with notables from the establishment, including the chief secretary, Lord Morpeth. Six weeks later, Mathew returned once more to preach in the Pro-Cathedral. Each time he stayed in Dublin for a couple days to administer the pledge. He may have enrolled as many as one hundred thousand people during these two visits.[54]

After further travel, Mathew finally returned to Cork for the Christmas holiday. He'd had a truly remarkable string of triumphs. Two-and-a half years since he had committed himself to the teetotal movement, Mathew had drawn close to 2.5 million Irish people into his movement, or about 30 percent of the total population of Ireland.[55] The last thirteen months had been particularly momentous, however. From the time of the Limerick trip till Christmas 1840, he had toiled unceasingly for temperance, and the movement had grown almost exponentially. As one might expect, the liquor industry was beginning to feel the effects: the number of gallons of legal whiskey consumed had fallen from 12,296,342 in 1838 to 7,401,051 in 1840; beer production had fallen from 1,017,230 barrels in 1837 to 639,733 in 1840; and the number of retailers of spirits had dropped from 20,399 in 1838 to 15,253 in 1840.[56]

Observers were astounded by the dramatic changes they witnessed in Irish behavior and attitudes. W. J. Battersby declared that a "moral revolution" had occurred and asked, "Who could have imagined that *two millions and a half of persons in Ireland alone,* would have joined in the glorious cause?" The Halls, who spent most of their time in England, took a tour of Ireland in 1840 and were amazed by what they saw:

> In reference to the extent to which sobriety has spread, it will be almost sufficient to state that during our recent stay in Ireland, from the 10th of June to the 6th of September 1840, we saw but six persons intoxicated; and that for the first thirty days we had not encountered one. In the course of that month we had traveled from Cork to Killarney—round the coast; returning by the inland route; not along mail-coach roads, but on a "jaunting car," through byways as well as highways; visiting small villages and populous towns; driving through fairs; attending wakes and funerals . . . in short, wherever crowds were assembled and we considered it likely we might gather information as to the state of the country and the character of its people. We repeat, we did not meet a single individual who appeared to have tasted spirits; and we do not hesitate to express our conviction, that two years ago, . . . we should have encountered many thousand drunken men. From first to last, we employed, perhaps, fifty car-drivers: we never found one to accept a drink; the boatmen at Killarney, proverbial for drunkenness . . . declined the whiskey we had taken with us . . . and after hours of hard labour, dipped a can into the lake and refreshed themselves from its waters. . . . Of the extent of the change, therefore, we have had ample experience: and it is borne out by the assurances of so many who live in towns as well as in the country, that we can have no hesitation in describing sobriety to be almost universal throughout Ireland.[57]

Dangers from Church and State

Mathew's first two-and-a-half years promoting temperance had been a tremendous success. It is not surprising that, as the movement expanded and Mathew's fame spread, opposition began to develop. One might expect that distillers, brewers, and publicans would oppose Mathew's work in an effort to protect their livelihoods, but they did virtually nothing to thwart him. Many probably cursed him in private, but scarcely any dared criticize him publicly. Instead, Mathew faced opposition from two other sources and danger from a third. Certain government officials were wary of him, viewing his movement as nationalist and potentially seditious. Certain members of the hierarchy were opposed to him for the opposite reasons. They deemed him insufficiently nationalist and too friendly with Protestants. Finally, Daniel O'Connell and the Repeal movement were threatening to him in two respects. First, if O'Connell were too outspoken in his praise for Mathew and teetotalism, the government might consider the total abstinence movement an appendage of the Repealers. Second, O'Connell, being an astute politician, might try to exploit the temperance movement for his own ends. Mathew and his aides had built a complex infrastructure: many local affiliates had reading rooms and musical bands complete with uniforms and instruments. Such attractions would be of great help in the campaign for Repeal. The opposition of any one of these three forces—the government, the bishops, or O'Connell—could conceivably cripple the temperance movement. The government could suppress the society, the bishops could divide the Catholic masses from Mathew, and O'Connell could possibly transform the temperance movement into an arm of his Repeal machine.

Of the three forces, the British government probably presented the least threat to Mathew. In 1840 the indolent, vaguely progressive Viscount Melbourne was lingering on as prime minister. Having little interest in Irish affairs, he delegated all responsibilities to the lord lieutenant and the chief secretary. Viscount Ebrington, appointed lord lieutenant in 1839, and Lord Morpeth, who had been chief secretary since 1835, were more liberal than the prime minister. They and most of the other officials at Dublin Castle—especially Thomas Drummond, the undersecretary—were more sympathetic to the Catholic majority than previous administrators had been. Morpeth, too, was a friend of Mathew's. The administration thus was predisposed to support or at least tolerate Mathew's campaign. By promoting sobriety and respect for the law, Mathew was simplifying the task of governing Ireland.

Nevertheless, some officials at Dublin Castle must have had reservations about Mathew's movement. In March 1840 the inspector general,

Duncan McGregor, distributed a confidential circular to police officials in the twelve southern and western counties where temperance was thriving. The questionnaire was detailed: McGregor wanted to know the numbers who had pledged; the religion, gender, and economic status of those who had pledged; how the pledge ceremony proceeded; and whether temperance led to either a decrease in crime rates or an increase in deposits at savings banks. Most important, he wanted to know whether the temperance movement had a hidden political agenda.

On some points, the inspectors were in full agreement. Almost all respondents—forty-five out of forty-seven—claimed that the bulk of the people pledging held to superstitious beliefs about Mathew and the pledge. Many people believed that Mathew or the medal could heal their infirmities, and some even thought that pledging would guarantee their salvation. Most teetotalers seemed equally convinced that terrible chastisements awaited pledge breakers. The subinspector for Waterford City reported, "There are many here who think that if they were to break the pledge—some great misfortune, insanity or sudden death would certainly be the consequence. There were very many who thought also that Rev'd. Mr. Mathew had power to cure diseases and infirmity and actually brought the unfortunate beings . . . to this city to be relieved by his merely laying his hands upon them." An officer from Ennis, County Clare, wrote, "Stories are told confidently of persons becoming deranged who broke the Pledge, and of the whiskey they were about to drink [which upon] approaching their lips, turned into blood." A subinspector from Dunmore, County Galway, described the medal's reputed power: "The medal I understand is looked upon with a degree of reverential awe and considered by some that while they possess it, no evil can happen." The medal could even ward off the bullets of policemen and soldiers, or so thought some of the teetotalers of Abbeyleix in Queens County.[58]

On the question of the political aims of the temperance movement, the inspectors were divided. A minority saw temperance as a front for O'Connell or secret societies such as the Ribbonmen.[59] An officer from Kenmare, County Kerry, complained about the local society's meetings: "The worst characters are most frequently in attendance; where they remain, instead of being industriously employed, up to late hours, ranting politics. . . . Temperance is certainly an amiable virtue, . . . but it does not stand in need of medals, banners, committees and parades."⁶⁰ An officer from Charleville, County Cork, took an even darker view, convinced that the temperance society in his district was fomenting revolution: "A number of workmen were overheard [saying,] 'We lost the battles of Vinegar Hill and Ross by drunkenness, but we are more secure and united now [and] when the battle comes, no whiskey, no tattlers.' . . . On another occasion it was said to a Protestant clergyman in an unguarded moment, 'Father Mathew will soon pull down your churches and put you all under our feet.'" The officer added a postcript: "On Patrick's Day an inflammatory speech was made here . . . the following being part of the substance: 'That they should prepare for war against their enemies, and that they would have to wade up to their knees in Protestant blood, and that the poor house . . . would be made prisons for them, and that they would have no English laws here.'"⁶¹

Most inspectors, however, saw no grand political designs in the temperance movement and reported something along the lines of the reply from the officer in Skibbereen: "There does not appear to me to be any thing of a sectarian or political object or bearing, influencing those who take the pledge. The motive seems to me to be a sincere desire to overcome the great cause which has long obstructed their moral and physical advancement."⁶²

The officials at Dublin Castle took no immediate action after reading these reports. In all likelihood, they shared the view that Mathew's movement was not politically threatening. In July the lord lieutenant issued a public statement that politely cautioned the temperance societies not to allow their processions to include any political banners or symbols. Lord Ebrington first noted the good effects that temperance had conferred on the Irish people and then asked the temperance societies to be "particularly studious to avoid any demonstrations which can possibly be construed into Party Exhibitions, or can give reasonable cause of offence or alarm to any of their countrymen." Although the statement was hardly a rebuke, Mathew saw it as confirming his belief that his movement must remain absolutely separate from O'Connell and the Repeal campaign.⁶³

While Mathew did his utmost to evade O'Connell, O'Connell made repeated efforts to associate himself with Mathew. At a meeting in Bandon, County Cork, in early December 1839, O'Connell devoted much of his speech to praising the temperance movement.⁶⁴ He closed by noting that he was watching to see how the movement fared before deciding whether to reactivate the Repeal campaign.⁶⁵ Why he would base his actions on the success or failure of the temperance movement is not entirely clear, but the remark served to link the two movements in the minds of many.

In the months following, O'Connell took up his newfound cause enthusiastically. In July 1840, he spoke at a temperance meeting in London. At the rally was William Lloyd Garrison, the young American abolitionist, who was deeply moved by what he heard: "That sturdy champion of Irish liberty, . . . Daniel O'Connell, made a powerful speech in favor of the doctrine of total abstinence. He was received with a storm of applause that almost shook the building to its foundations. The spectacle was sublime and heart-stirring beyond all power of description on my part."⁶⁶

In October 1840, O'Connell took the next logical step: he became a teetotaler.⁶⁷ Once he took the pledge, he had a perfectly legitimate justification for wanting to appear with Mathew at temperance rallies or tea parties. By this time, too, he was promoting Repeal: he had established a Loyal National Repeal Association in July and begun speaking at Repeal rallies in the southern and western counties. O'Connell's words and actions complicated matters for Mathew considerably. Still, the situation was not as perilous for Mathew as it initially appeared, for O'Connell was still backing the Liberal administration in hopes of obtaining more concessions for Irish Catholics. As long as the Liberals held power, O'Connell would campaign for Repeal only half-heartedly. Repeal had the potential to become a mass movement were O'Connell to devote his peerless political skills to it, but at the end of 1840, it remained just a potentially powerful force and Mathew did not have to worry that it would overwhelm the temperance movement.

The final threat to Mathew at this time came from the bishops. Since, despite Mathew's rhetoric, the movement was overwhelmingly Catholic, Mathew was dependent on the good graces of the bishops. Initially, he received nothing but praise from the hierarchy. He had been welcomed and feted by the bishops of Limerick, Waterford, Galway, Clonfert, Ossory, and Ferns and the archbishops of Dublin and Cashel. But in the summer of 1840 he began to encounter difficulties with two of the key nationalist bishops, William Higgins and John MacHale. In August, Mathew received a long, unfriendly letter from Father Richard Davys, Higgins's vicar general. Davys reminded Mathew of the encounter they had had the previous month. At that meeting Davys had informed Mathew that Higgins would allow him into Ardagh only if he remitted all proceeds from his tour to the diocese to help pay for the cathedral that Higgins was building. Mathew's "repeated refusals to acquiesce" in this policy had

> so surprised Dr. Higgins and all the Clergy of his Lordship's Diocese that he has at length yielded to their pressing and repeated solicitations to administer himself the Temperance pledge in the Diocese of Ardagh—he has already commenced with very signal success in one of his own parishes at Moate and while I write is busily engaged in his Lordship's Chapel in this town [Athlone] administering the pledge to thousands who have thronged round him and to whom he has just promised that he will give their friends and neighbors a public opportunity at last Mass on next Saturday of being also enrolled in the good cause of Temperance—I am instructed by his Lordship to convey to you his determination of giving the pledge himself in even the humblest local city in his Diocese that your conceiving yourself bound to visit this diocese . . . may not interfere with your future arrangements in visiting other parts of the country.

While Davys concluded his letter on a warmer note, assuring Mathew of the "great value Dr Higgins sets on your unparallelled labours in this holy cause," he had nonetheless made clear that Mathew was not needed in Ardagh and not particularly welcome there.[68]

The same week, Mathew received a cryptic note from Father Martin Browne, parish priest of Balla in the Tuam archdiocese, informing him that "circumstances beyond the reach of [his] control" had forced him to postpone Mathew's upcoming trip to his parish. Browne had been pressured by MacHale to cancel the visit. In September, Father Joseph Burke, a teetotal priest from Ballinrobe, County Mayo, wrote Mathew a letter lamenting MacHale's actions: "It was universally known that you were to visit Balla . . . and thousands were anxiously expecting your visit. But when it was said that you were not to come the disappointment was great indeed and the most mischievous rumours were spread amongst the people by our enemies. I have been endeavouring to remove them but [the] facts speak too strongly. The clergy almost to a man condemn the proceeding but the Bishop is not to be shaken out of his resolve." Burke also helped clarify Higgins's and MacHale's rationale for opposing Mathew's campaign: "Of course you are aware that Doctor Higgins has been giving the pledge in his own diocese and has deigned to distribute medals and cards purely Catholic so that the protestants who are very edifying members of our society cannot wear them; our Bishop . . . has adopted the same plan. The motive is as I have heard the other day from Dr. MacHale, *the great sums of money* brought by you out of the country to the serious injury of the people. . . . The Bishop seems to think that he will be able to amass large sums of money for the cathedral by the temperance movement, but the people will have no other medals than those with your name . . . upon them."[69]

Thus the bishops had no theological or practical objections to teetotalism. They would not have administered the pledge if they had misgivings about it. Instead, as Burke suggested, they had two other motives for opposing Mathew's work. Both bishops were anxious about money. Ardagh and Tuam were two of the poorest dioceses in Ireland, and both bishops were worried about finding adequate funds to support their extensive building projects. Both prelates were also vehemently opposed to Protestantism. Since the 1820s, their dioceses had been besieged by well-financed Protestant missionaries who were striving to bring about the Second Reformation. Consequently, Mathew's determination to attract Protestants to the temperance movement and his close association with various Quakers and Unitarians angered MacHale and Higgins and led them to suspect Mathew of indifferentism.

These confrontations with Higgins and MacHale were certainly unpleasant for Mathew, but they probably did little damage to the temperance movement at this time. As a result of the bishops' opposition, Mathew decided to put off any trips to towns in either Tuam or Ardagh (he returned to Tuam the following year, as discussed in Chapter 4). Since these dioceses were remote and sparsely populated, being banned from Balla did not matter terribly much. Furthermore, Higgins's and MacHale's hostility to Mathew was not widely known; neither bishop criticized Mathew in public.[70] Still, MacHale and Higgins were a formidable duo: if they remained hostile to Mathew, they could create considerable difficulties for him.

Thus several potential dangers loomed on the horizon for Mathew and the temperance campaign. If the Tories took power, they might suppress the temperance campaign. If O'Connell's Repeal movement became powerful, it could swallow up the campaign. If more bishops became alienated, they might undermine it. Then again, these were all "ifs" that might never materialize. At the end of 1840 Mathew's movement was vast and still expanding at a remarkable rate. Mathew himself was brimming with confidence and starting to think about traveling abroad to promote the cause.

{ CHAPTER FOUR }

"Temperance Principles Are All but Universal," 1841–1844

The man who would now boldly avow hostility to the cause, and recommend the people to desist from the practice of that which has become national, and almost universal, would be regard[ed] as one strangely stultified, stupidly foolish, or determinedly wicked.

Nation, February 25, 1843

Early in January 1841 Mathew was again in Limerick. Before administering the pledge to his assembled followers, he took stock of the movement's achievements over the preceding two-and-a-half years: "The cause is progressing. . . . Thank God, we are no longer known as a nation of drunkards. The eyes of the whole world are fixed on our society, and the members of it are the most moral, peaceable and well-conducted people on the face of the earth. It is now composed of 3,400,000, all with improved condition, all animated with a spirit of self-respect."[1]

Although proud of his accomplishments, Mathew was far from complacent. He was determined to maintain his grueling travel schedule. In 1841 he would not only return to many of the towns and villages he had visited in 1839 and 1840, but also venture for the first time into Protestant-dominated Ulster. Sectarian tensions had been steadily increasing in the north in the previous decade. O'Connell hoped to have a triumphal tour of Belfast in the spring of 1841 as part of his Repeal campaign, but the Protestant population in the city was so upset about the prospect of his visit that he had to travel to Belfast using an assumed name and taking the back roads. And when he finally arrived in Belfast, he was not well received. One evening he appeared at a Repeal meeting, a dinner, and a temperance soirée arranged by 450 of his female supporters. The ladies' party did not last long; Orangemen broke up the gathering by tossing paving stones through the windows of the building.[2]

Mathew's friends warned him that he, too, would face hostile and perhaps even violent crowds if he visited the north, but he was determined to go.³ His plans were complicated by the attitudes of two of the Ulster bishops, William Crolly, archbishop of Armagh and Primate, and Cornelius Denvir, bishop of Down and Connor. Both men made it clear to Mathew that he was not welcome in their dioceses. Crolly claimed to sympathize with teetotalism but was said to worry that Mathew's presence would upset local Protestants—even though Protestants were among those who had entreated him to allow Mathew into the diocese. An old-fashioned gallican like Archbishop Murray, Crolly was always concerned about maintaining good relations with the Protestant establishment and the British authorities. Denvir held similar views and objected to Mathew's visit for the same reason.⁴ Unfortunately for Mathew, Crolly and Denvir presided over substantial sections of Ulster; Crolly's archdiocese included the historic city of Armagh, which St. Patrick had established as the ecclesiastical center of Ireland, and both Belfast and Lisburn were under Denvir's domain.

Mathew had some benefactors, too, among the northern bishops. His supporters included Edward Kernan of Clogher, James Browne of Kilmore, Patrick McGettigan of Raphoe, and Michael Blake, bishop of Dromore, who was a longtime teetotaler and ally of Mathew. As a pastor in Dublin in the 1810s, Blake had established the Purgatorian Society, a confraternity that encouraged temperance. This meant that Mathew was welcome in counties Monaghan, Fermanagh, Cavan, and Donegal and in portions of counties Down and Tyrone.

Mathew first visited the north on St. Patrick's Day. He pledged thirty thousand people in the town of Monaghan and then accompanied Bishop Kernan further north to Clogher, County Tyrone. Meanwhile in Dublin, teetotalers were marking St. Patrick's Day in regal fashion. All the Dublin temperance societies marched in a massive procession through the center of the city. Fathers Andrew O'Connell, John Spratt, John Yore, and J. J. F. Murphy (a Capuchin who served as Mathew's representative in Dublin) appeared in horse-drawn carriages, as did James Haughton, the Unitarian reformer. Thousands of rank-and-file teetotalers followed them, each wearing a scarf. They marched to the music of several temperance bands.⁵

In late May Mathew made his first in-depth tour of the north, visiting counties Monaghan and Cavan. Bishop Browne warmly welcomed him and appeared with him in several towns. At each stop, Mathew encountered large crowds that often included Protestants. From County Cavan Mathew traveled farther west to Letterkenny in County Donegal. There he met Bishop McGettigan, who took the pledge at his hands. In mid-June Mathew left Ulster to attend to business in Dublin. During his three-week visit, Mathew had pledged at least eighty thousand people and had not met any resistance from the Protestant communities.[6] Indeed, some Protestants had listened to his speeches with interest, and a few had even taken the pledge from him.

In August Mathew was back in the north. This time he visited Newry, a city in County Down. The guest of Bishop Blake, Mathew preached at the consecration of one of the new churches in the diocese on August 15. At the end of the month, after having visited several more towns, Mathew returned to Newry to attend a soirée in his honor at the local Temperance Hall. In his toast, Mathew first praised Blake and then expressed his gratitude to the many Ulster Protestants who had shown him kindness in the previous weeks. He made special mention of his pleasant meeting with Colonel William Blacker, a former leader of the Orange Order. Blacker, an ardent teetotaler, had presented Mathew with a poem commemorating his visit to Ulster.

Mathew's remarks were followed by a speech from Charles Gavan Duffy, a young Catholic journalist who would soon achieve political prominence. Duffy stressed the need for the temperance movement to offer constructive activities for those who pledged. He said more reading rooms should be established and more night classes and public lectures offered. Mathew had long been a promoter of reading rooms and musical bands for the rank-and-file teetotalers and was delighted to learn that Duffy shared his concerns. He was so taken with Duffy's address that he had thirty thousand copies of it printed and distributed throughout Ireland. Mathew never forgot his meeting with Duffy, and the two men remained friendly for years.[7]

In mid-September Mathew was in Limerick once again. Flanked by Bishop Ryan, he addressed the huge crowd that had gathered to greet him. In his remarks he sharply criticized doctors who prescribed alcoholic beverages for their patients. Although he conceded that small amounts of wine might hasten a person's recovery from an illness, he chastised physicians who directed their patients to consume beer, wine, or spirits on a regular basis. He counseled them to encourage their patients to drink water instead. In October, having heard more reports of doctors ordering teetotalers to drink, he decided to remove the medical exemption from the words of the pledge.[8]

In late November Mathew made yet another trip north to strengthen his organization in the region. After touring County Monaghan for a week, he arrived in Clones, one of the larger towns of the county. The people who gathered outside the church to greet him noticed two orange flags hanging from the bell tower. The gesture was clearly meant as a rebuff to Mathew, but he took it as a sign of welcome, remarking that he had never before seen Orange flags flying from a Catholic church. After hearing these remarks, the angry crowd settled down and allowed him to proceed with his work of administering the pledge.[9]

Through these Ulster tours, Mathew's movement was establishing itself as a force in each of Ireland's four provinces. Protestants may not have enrolled in the temperance societies in large numbers, but they did not show hostility to Mathew's crusade. Instead, at this time, Mathew's fiercest critic was his coreligionist, John MacHale, the "Lion" of the west.[10]

Bearding the Lion

By the spring of 1841, Mathew's difficulties with MacHale were becoming public knowledge. In April a column appeared in the London *Times* noting that MacHale had stopped Mathew from visiting Balla to administer the pledge. The correspondent, who disliked MacHale, believed that the conflict centered around Mathew's unwillingness to contribute funds to MacHale's parochial school system, which had been set up in opposition to the national schools. At the same time, the *Dublin Evening Mail* reprinted a letter from Mathew to a temperance supporter in Tuam in which Mathew criticized MacHale, writing, "I cannot conceive why your illustrious Archbishop, who is so anxious to promote the prosperity of this country and the great cause of morality, should suffer himself to be prejudiced against the Total Abstinence Society." In June the *Dublin Weekly Herald* published an editorial sharply critical of MacHale:

> We have been heretofore unwilling to give publicity to any thing reflecting on the conduct of this divine; but we feel we would not do our duty as journalists if we continued our refusal to lay before the public the conduct of any man, lay or clerical, who takes upon himself to check, in any degree, the progress of a movement which has done so much to banish crime and misery from the world, and especially our own country as that of teetotalism. . . . We have been informed that the bishop has carried his opposition so far as to order some of the clergy under his jurisdiction, not to administer the sacrament to any person whom they knew to have attended a teetotal meeting. . . . This, if it be true, which we hope it is not, deserves the censure of every friend to the cause of virtue.[11]

The following week a temperance society in the Tuam archdiocese made clear its opposition to MacHale. The Westport teetotalers, who were affiliated with Mathew, announced that they would begin withholding their financial support from all clergy who were unsympathetic to the temperance movement.[12] This represented a potentially serious challenge to MacHale, who was already strapped for funds. At the time Mathew was in England, witnessing the consecration of a new Catholic church, and was unable to respond to his society's resolution. In the meantime, Father Andrew O'Connell's Metropolitan Total Abstinence Society, which was completely independent of Mathew's organization, called a meeting to consider the Westport society's actions. O'Connell and his associates were outraged by the anticlericalism expressed by their Westport brethren: "We have read with the deepest pain and concern the [Westport Total Abstinence Society's] resolution. . . . We repudiate, in the strongest language of which we are capable, any such dictation to our beloved clergy; and that having the most unqualified reliance in their zeal, their piety, their love of country, and their long-tried affection for its people, we deem such dictation ungrateful, ungenerous and uncalled-for."[13]

When Mathew returned to Cork and learned of the Metropolitan Society's statement, he was annoyed. He considered himself the unquestioned leader of the temperance cause and would brook no interference from O'Connell or any other teetotal priest. Furthermore, since Mathew was thoroughly frustrated with MacHale by this time, he did not appreciate the implicit support accorded him in the Metropolitan Society's resolution. He answered O'Connell in an open letter in the *Freeman's Journal* in which he stated that he would have urged the Westport teetotalers to retract their statement had he known of it. Yet he concluded his letter with an expression of sympathy for the Westport teetotalers: "If the poor worm in its agony turns upon the proud foot that tramples upon it, why should you add the weight of your heel to crush the writhing victim, and be in at the death? I can scarcely credit the evidence of my senses, and believe that the Very Rev. A. O'Connell . . . would have arisen in his might and rushed with more than railway speed to Westport, in the Archdiocese of Tuam, to 'break the bruised reed.'"[14]

O'Connell might have been expected to resent this rebuke, but he seemed to take it in a good spirit. In answering Mathew, he defended his actions but apologized for any misapprehensions that he had caused. MacHale, in contrast, was angered. In his view, Mathew was challenging his authority in the archdiocese. In August, the Lion attacked, denouncing Mathew both from the pulpit of his cathedral in Tuam and from a small chapel in Kilmeena. After condemning Mathew, MacHale informed the teetotalers of the archdiocese that he was dispensing them from their pledges. MacHale had decided that lifelong pledges were too onerous, and he would henceforth administer the pledge for short terms. At the end of the period, the pledge could be renewed if the person desired.[15]

In response Mathew decided to write to Paul Cullen, his highest ranking friend in Rome. They had had a cordial meeting the previous year, when Cullen visited Ireland, and Cullen had also likely received favorable reports of Mathew's work from his uncle, Father James Maher, a staunch teetotaler from Carlow. A few months earlier, Cullen had obtained a favor for Mathew, arranging for his appointment as a commissary apostolic; this freed Mathew from any obligations to his Capuchin superior and placed him directly under the pope. (Mathew was already provincial of the Capuchins in Ireland, so only the minister general of the order outranked him. Still, he must have been afraid that the minister general would restrict his temperance work, or he would not have sought this dispensation from Cullen.)[16]

Under siege from the Lion, Mathew again sought Cullen's help. In a long, emotional letter, he described the difficulties he had been having with MacHale: "The Archbishop of Tuam is become an implacable enemy, though I have never willingly given him the slightest offence. In private and in public he has applied the most degrading epithets to me and the Teetotallers. He has dispensed with all in his Archdiocese [from] . . . the Total Abstinence Pledge. . . . Goaded by calumny and ill treatment, a few of the Teetotallers of Westport . . . came to a resolution not to contribute to the support of such clergymen as opposed them. As soon as I was informed of this I condemned the resolution and they have retracted it, and have apologized." He then summarized the remarks MacHale had made about him from the pulpit: "After a long tirade in Irish against the [temperance] society he said that I was a vagabond Friar, that I went about with a *woman*, that she sold medals for me, charging a shilling for bits of Birmingham pewter which cost only a few pence, and that we spent the money drinking brandy and water, laughing at the poor dupes whom we robbed. A thrill of horror ran through the whole congregation at the awful insinuation, that Father Mathew was living in sacrilegious guilt with this woman and that he was a brandy drinker." Mathew explained that the woman to whom MacHale was referring was a Mrs. MacGowan, "a respectable widow lady, [and] the mother of grown children." She had been traveling around County Mayo with two priests from Dublin who were active in the temperance movement. After assuring Cullen that he had not had any contact with the widow or the priests, Mathew implored Cullen to "devise some mode to induce his Grace to act with Christian Charity."[17]

One charge of MacHale's is rateworthy. His depiction of Mathew as a "vagabond Friar" suggests that MacHale resented him at least in part because he was a religious. Relations between the secular and regular clergy had been strained for at least a century. Many secular priests considered the friars lax because most of them lived outside of their convents, handled money, and did not wear their habits. At the same time, friars enjoyed substantial autonomy from their local bishops and were subject only to their provincials, who usually granted them considerable freedom.[18] By labeling Mathew a "vagabond friar," MacHale was accusing

Mathew of being another slack religious order priest who could do as he pleased without reference to any higher authority.

Cullen sent Mathew a generally reassuring letter in response. He had recently consulted with Pope Gregory XVI about Mathew's temperance crusade and was pleased to report that "he [the pope] immediately exclaimed: 'Digitus Dei est hic' [the finger of God is here], and he said he trusted that God would do something great for a people that with His grace had achieved so wonderful a victory over its ruling passion. The Cardinal Prefect of Propaganda [Cardinal Giacomo Fransoni] . . . fully coincided with the sentiments of the Pope . . . I mention these circumstances to you in order that the approbation of the first ecclesiastical authorities on earth may be a consolation to you in your troubles and an incitement to you to continue and prosecute with new ardour your useful labours." As far as MacHale was concerned, though, Cullen was not about to intervene, and he strongly urged Mathew to bear the archbishop's attacks in silence: "It is impossible to expect that any great good should be done without meeting with opposition and even persecution. . . . We should use the same arms of defence which they [Christ and His apostles] employed: patience, humility, resignation and above all the greatest charity. I would on no account enter into controversy with the ecclesiastical authorities even when they are not acting as they ought. The mischief which is done by dissensions between ecclesiastics can scarcely ever be remedied. I would bear every insult with patience and wait until heaven would show the justness of my cause." Cullen concluded his letter with a cautionary note that indicated that he, too, had some concerns about Mathew's attitudes: "[There] is a complaint against you . . . [that] you appear to entertain sentiments too liberal towards Protestants in matters of religion . . . It is well to be cautious. We should entertain most expansive sentiments of charity towards Protestants but at the same time we should let them know that there is but one true Church and that they are strayed sheep from the one fold. . . . Otherwise we might lull them into a false sense of security in their errors and by doing so we would really violate charity."[19]

Mathew followed Cullen's advice and refrained from further public criticism of MacHale. At the same time, he decided to accept invitations from teetotalers in Tuam to visit their towns. Mathew knew that

MacHale did not want him to set foot in his archdiocese but, armed with his new title of commissary apostolic, he felt he could travel wherever he wished without reference to the local ordinary. Despite regular trips to the area, he was not able to undo all the damage caused by MacHale. Teetotalism did not disappear from Tuam, but it remained weaker in this area than in most other regions of Ireland.[20]

Over the following months Mathew remained concerned enough about episcopal opposition that he wrote several more letters to Cullen and his assistant Father Tobias Kirby, asking for their help. What he was hoping for was some public gesture of support for temperance from the pope himself. In the fall of 1841 he sent Kirby a solid gold temperance medal to give to the pope. He also requested that the pope grant a plenary indulgence to all members of his society: "I am well aware of the infinite advantage it would be to Teetotalism to have my system approved by his Holiness, myself recommended to the Bishops and clergy, and a Plenary Indulgence with the usual conditions granted to the Teetotalers at the hour of death . . . I confidently hope that you will be able to procure these favours for me."[21]

When no indulgences seemed to be forthcoming, Mathew wrote again to Kirby and reiterated that any support from the pope would be helpful: "If the Most Holy Father would condescend to forward to me a letter containing his Apostolic benediction, and an encouragement to persevere in the sacred mission of Temperance, and an exhortation to the Bishops, Vicars Apostolic and pastors of Ireland, England and Scotland to invite me into their dioceses, districts and parishes, all opposition would cease, the foul demon of drunkenness would forever disappear, and the pure and spotless banner of Temperance would wave over the length and breadth of the land."[22]

Receiving plenary indulgences from the pope would have had its disadvantages for Mathew, one being that it would have been harder for him to claim that his society was nonsectarian. Still, it seems Mathew was concerned more with silencing MacHale and other critics within the Church than with reaching out to the people outside of it. In the end, the pope chose not to intervene: he would neither bestow the indulgences nor offer a public gesture of support. Ironically, Mathew's friend and patron, Daniel Murray, undermined him in this effort. When consulted by

Cardinal Fransoni in the fall of 1842, Murray warned that if indulgences were granted, the society "would then be considered Roman Catholic, which its leaders do not wish."[23]

Eluding the Liberator

In the beginning of 1841 Lord Melbourne's Whig government still clung to power, but all observers knew that its days were numbered. Daniel O'Connell was distraught, realizing that the Tories, led by his archenemy, Robert Peel, were likely to gain power.[24] Melbourne finally stepped down in June, and a general election was scheduled for July. O'Connell and his allies spent considerable time and money in their campaigns to retain their seats, but to no avail. The Tories won a landslide victory in England, which left them with a majority of more than eighty seats in the House of Commons. In Ireland they picked up 6 seats, giving them a total of 38 out of 105, while O'Connell's contingent fell from 28 to 20 or so.[25] Worse yet, O'Connell lost his own seat in Dublin and also lost a hotly contested race for a seat in County Carlow. He was, however, elected to a seat for a County Cork district and so remained an M.P.

Since Peel had a comfortable majority in Parliament, O'Connell had little incentive to participate in Westminster politics. Believing that no further reforms would be coming from Parliament, he decided to pursue his Repeal campaign with more zeal, but before he stepped up his crusade for Repeal, he had another, more immediate goal in mind. The Municipal Reform Act of 1840 had broken the Protestants' lock on Irish city governments, and O'Connell was determined to be the first Catholic to take advantage of the change in Dublin's governmental structure. Even with the reforms in place, Dublin's Protestant elite retained powers far in excess of their proportion of the population, however, and O'Connell knew that he had a difficult campaign ahead of him. Over the summer he campaigned strenuously—Oliver MacDonagh says "ruthlessly"[26]—to become the first Catholic lord mayor of Dublin and narrowly defeated the Tory candidate. He began his one-year term on November 1, 1841.

Busy with the official duties of the lord mayor's office, O'Connell at first had little time for political activism. Furthermore, he felt duty bound to maintain at least a semblance of nonpartisanship. The Repeal campaign would have to wait another year before he would be willing and able to devote his full energies to it. Until then, he spent much of his time promoting Mathew's movement, which was considerably less controversial.

O'Connell's support for temperance was nothing new, of course. He had been hailing the teetotal movement since 1839 and had taken the pledge in the fall of 1840, after which he frequently spoke at temperance meetings, declaring that his health had much improved since he had pledged; he claimed that he now "slept sounder than at any time in [his] life." By the beginning of 1841, he had emerged as a zealous teetotaler. At a speech in Cork in January, he voiced concern about lapsed teetotalers: "[I have] heard with regret that many who had taken [the pledge] in Cork ha[ve] returned to the vomit." He counseled his supporters to have no contact with these fallen away teetotalers. In May, chairing a total abstinence meeting in London, O'Connell praised the "great and glorious work" accomplished by his "esteemed friend," Father Mathew, and warned his listeners to reject even a moderationist approach to alcohol: "Temperate men have every chance of becoming intemperate; no man is secure who uses intoxicating drinks."[27]

As lord mayor, O'Connell intensified his promotion of temperance still more. When the *Dublin Weekly Herald,* the leading temperance newspaper in Ireland, needed money, O'Connell helped arrange a fundraiser. He attended local temperance society meetings dressed in his official robes. On Easter Monday, he traveled to Cork to march in Mathew's temperance parade—much to Mathew's consternation. O'Connell walked side by side with Mathew at the head of the procession and knelt for his blessing before the parade was over. This was the first time Mathew had been seen in public with the Liberator; until this point he had been able to elude O'Connell. Now with O'Connell the loyal teetotaler wanting to participate in his official capacity as lord mayor, Mathew could not possibly refuse him.[28]

O'Connell certainly saw the political capital he could gain by tying himself to Mathew, but his activities on behalf of temperance were not motivated solely by these considerations. He was genuinely impressed by Mathew and genuinely excited about the temperance movement's accomplishments. In his correspondence he made a number of references to teetotalism, all favorable. When writing to Paul Cullen in May 1842, he enthusiastically described Ireland's "modern miracle of temperance," noting that spirit revenues had fallen dramatically since Mathew had launched his campaign.[29]

In July 1842 O'Connell wrote Mathew to invite him to visit him and his family at Derrynane Abbey during his upcoming tour of County Kerry. O'Connell reminded Mathew that he had promised, presumably at their meeting on Easter Monday, to come to Derrynane. Mathew politely declined the offer. Although Mathew would not visit him, O'Connell made certain to see Mathew on his trips to Dublin promoting temperance. Indeed, one of O'Connell's last acts as lord mayor was to attend an address by Mathew in Dublin.[30]

O'Connell's efforts to link himself with Mathew and the temperance cause in general in 1841–42 must surely have irritated Mathew, but they still did not represent a threat to the temperance movement. As long as Repeal remained dormant, Mathew was not in any danger of being overwhelmed by O'Connell. In 1843, all this would change, and Mathew would find himself and the temperance movement imperiled by O'Connell.

The Repeal Year

After false starts in 1830, 1834, and 1840–1841, O'Connell finally began to devote all his time and talents to the Repeal movement in the fall of 1842. At the start of 1843 he promised his followers that this would be the "Repeal Year."[31] To ensure that his prophecy was fulfilled, he planned to hold a series of rallies promoting Repeal throughout Ireland. Nicknamed "monster meetings" by his critics at the London *Times,* these events attracted hundreds of thousands of people. The meetings were meant principally to stir up the faithful throughout Ireland, but they were also intended to serve as a warning to Peel. Throughout his long career, O'Connell had adamantly opposed violence in political campaigns. In this case, however, he realized that Parliament was no more sympathetic to Repeal than it had been in 1834, when it had rejected his Repeal motion by a margin of almost fifteen to one. Unwilling to organize a conventional parliamentary campaign or sanction violence, O'Connell chose an alternative route. His monster meetings were strictly nonviolent and yet menacing at the same time. The huge crowds and the inflammatory rhetoric used by many of the speakers were clearly meant to intimidate Peel.

In his efforts to promote Repeal, O'Connell was ably assisted by a cadre of talented young writers. In October 1842 the group, led by Thomas Osborne Davis, John Blake Dillon, and Charles Gavan Duffy, published the first issue of the *Nation*, which quickly became Ireland's most influential nationalist newspaper.[32] These men, later christened the "Young Irelanders," were skilled at journalism and poetry alike. Davis and Dillon had studied law at Trinity College in Dublin, where they had developed attitudes that would eventually conflict with O'Connell's Catholic nationalist vision,[33] and Duffy, a self-educated newspaperman, likewise had a more secular outlook than O'Connell. But in 1842 these tensions had not yet surfaced and Davis, Duffy, and Dillon were O'Connell's unwavering disciples. Every week, their newspaper reported on his travels and speeches in painstaking detail.

The meetings began in the spring of 1843. In April, 120,000 people gathered in Limerick to hear O'Connell describe the manifold virtues of Repeal. In May, O'Connell addressed three hundred thousand people in the historic town of Cashel and five hundred thousand in Cork. After learning of these vast demonstrations, officials at Dublin Castle became alarmed. Lord Lieutenant de Grey, a Tory hardliner, warned Peel that Ireland was on the brink of disaster. In early May, Peel decided to respond to O'Connell's provocations with a threat of his own. Speaking in the House of Commons, Peel solemnly assured his colleagues that "there is no influence, no power, no authority which the prerogatives of the Crown and the existing law give to the Government which shall not be exercised for the purpose of maintaining the Union. . . . I am prepared to make this declaration, that deprecating as I do all war, and especially civil war, there is no alternative which I do not think preferable to the dismemberment of the empire."[34]

Undeterred by Peel's stern speech, O'Connell appeared at another monster meeting less than a week later. This time, he spoke at Mullingar in County Westmeath, flanked by two prominent nationalist bishops, William Higgins of Ardagh and John Cantwell of Meath. At a banquet after the rally, Higgins declared that every member of the hierarchy supported Repeal, and he dared the British authorities to try to eradicate the Repeal movement in his diocese. Higgins was not exactly right when he claimed that the whole hierarchy supported Repeal; neither Murray nor Crolly was a Repealer, and shortly after Higgins's speech, Murray issued a statement reaffirming his neutrality on the issue. Higgins was not far from the truth, though. The great majority of the hierarchy supported Repeal and no bishop publicly opposed O'Connell's campaign.[35]

The same was true of the lower clergy. Hundreds of priests were active Repealers, and those who were less enthusiastic kept silent on the issue. Because of the Church's solid backing, O'Connell was able to raise a substantial amount of money. The bishops allowed O'Connell's supporters to collect the "Repeal Rent"—dues owed by members of the Repeal Association—in churches once a month. They also allowed Repeal agents to take up collections at all Catholic chapels for the support of O'Connell and his family. Known as the "O'Connell Tribute," these monies were collected on two fixed Sundays of the year. It is difficult to determine precisely how much money was raised through these funds, since accurate records were not kept for each year; however, from 1840 to 1845, O'Connell garnered at least £140,000 from the Repeal Rent and the Tribute. In 1843, the peak fundraising year, the Rent amounted to forty-eight thousand pounds and the Tribute exceeded twenty thousand pounds.[36] Without the clergy's support, O'Connell would never have been able to raise such large sums.

In June, O'Connell, growing increasingly confident that 1843 might indeed prove to be the Repeal Year, began to adopt a harsher, more threatening posture in his public appearances. Speaking at Mallow in County Cork, he delivered an unusually vehement anti-British harangue. The speech, later known as the "Mallow Defiance," seemed to encourage violent resistance to British rule:

> Gentlemen, you may soon have the alternative to live as slaves or die as freemen. In the midst of peace and tranquillity our Saxon traducers are covering the land with troops. . . . Are we to be called slaves? Have we not the ordinary courage of Englishmen? Are we to be trampled under foot? . . . They may trample on me, but it will be my dead body they will trample on and not the living man! Cromwell, the only Englishman who ever possessed Ireland,

sent 80,000 Irishmen to work as slaves, every one of whom perished beneath the uncongenial sun of the Indies. Peel and Wellington may be second Cromwells. They may get his blunted truncheon and enact . . . Cromwell's massacre of the women of Wexford. But I am wrong. By God, they never shall. . . . [T]here is no danger to the women of Ireland, for the men of Ireland would die to the last in their defence. We were a paltry remnant in Cromwell's time. We are nine millions now![37]

Meetings of this sort continued through this summer. In mid-August, O'Connell's followers organized the biggest rally of the year at Tara in County Meath. Both the date, August 15th, and the site were carefully chosen for their symbolic values. August 15 was a major Catholic feast day—the Assumption of the Blessed Virgin Mary—and Tara was the seat of the Irish high kings in the years before the Norman conquest. This time, 1 million men and women converged on the site to catch a glimpse of O'Connell.[38]

After Tara, still more meetings were organized at symbolic sites. As the summer drew to a close, O'Connell and his deputies decided to plan one final meeting for the year at Clontarf, a town just north of Dublin. Clontarf was another site rich with symbolism: there on Good Friday, 1014, Brian Boru, the Irish high king, had defeated the Vikings and put an end to their hopes of controlling Ireland. The Clontarf rally was to be even larger and more impressive than Tara and the other monster meetings.

Temperance and Repeal

After O'Connell committed himself to the Repeal campaign, he had less time to spare for other causes, such as teetotalism. By 1843 he had withdrawn from the temperance movement, claiming that he had to consume alcohol for medicinal reasons.[39] Still, his interest in the cause did not flag. In January 1843 he spoke in Dublin at a meeting honoring Mathew (who was not present). While continuing to praise Mathew's work in the most extravagant terms—describing it as a "mighty moral miracle"—he took issue with the rhetoric used by some temperance advocates: "[I]n forming a contrast with their [the Irish people's] present state and that from which they had been rescued, there was some appearance that they had been previously in a state of degradation, and that in praising what has been done there was too heavy a censure passed on the former condition of the country.... It would appear as if prior to the temperance movement the Irish people were a depraved people—emphatically a drunken population.... I utterly deny that the people of Ireland were at any time inferior to their neighbours or to the people of any foreign country."[40] He furnished data indicating that other European peoples—particularly the Scots—were much heavier drinkers than the Irish had ever been.[41]

Although he did not mention Mathew by name, O'Connell was implicitly criticizing him. Mathew had time and time again referred to drunkenness as Ireland's national sin and had said that intemperance had made the Irish people the laughingstocks of the world. To O'Connell this sort of language was far too critical of the Irish and may have sounded too much like the condescending language some English observers used to describe the Irish.

By the summer months, O'Connell was still praising Mathew, but his rhetoric had shifted once again. Mathew's movement was now laudable because it had laid the groundwork for Repeal—or perhaps even for armed conflict. At a Repeal meeting at Roscommon in August, O'Connell remarked,

> Oh how I love teetotalism! I have made it a rule that anyone who disregards its solemn obligation, and breaks his pledge, shall not be admitted to the Repeal ranks. Napoleon boasted of his bodyguards; but I can boast of more than an Imperial Guard—a Christian guard of virtuous teetotallers. The mighty moral miracle of five millions of men pledged against intoxicating liquors has come from the hand of God, and I hail it as the precursor of the liberty of Ireland.... If I had to go to battle I should have the strong and steady teetotallers with me. The teetotal bands should play before them, and animate them in the time of peril ... I tell you there is not an army in the world that I would not encounter with my teetotalers. Yes teetotalism is the first sure ground on which rests our hope of sweeping away Saxon domination, and giving Ireland to the Irish.[42]

There was a considerable amount of truth to O'Connell's assertions. Certainly, had it not been for Mathew's crusade, O'Connell would never have been able to hold peaceful monster meetings. Ten years earlier, such meetings would probably have degenerated into drunken brawls. In the

1830s, local fairs, which drew much smaller crowds than the monster meetings, were often disrupted by fighting. James Grant, an English journalist, recounted what typically occurred at the Donnybrook Fair outside of Dublin in the 1820s and 1830s: "One hardly ever meets with a Paddy of the last generation who did not himself, at some period or other of his life, receive a broken head at Donnybrook Fair, or break the head, for the mere love of the thing, of some one or other of his dear friends. Breaking heads and breaking bones were then, indeed, considered an essential part of the . . . Fair."[43]

Local temperance affiliates helped support the Repeal campaign as well. Temperance musical bands often entertained the crowds at the monster meetings. Temperance reading rooms, which were supposed to be free from political and religious controversy, were used for Repeal meetings in some towns, and the *Nation* and other Repeal newspapers were received in many temperance halls and reading rooms. These links between teetotalers and Repealers were reported on by the British press. As a result, some British officials, including Peel, became more suspicious of Mathew and the temperance movement.[44] Mathew was aware that these displays of political partisanship by teetotalers were alienating key elements of English and Irish society, but he believed there was little he could do to restrain his rank and file during this time of political excitement.

Mathew also seems to have been worried about touring for temperance. As O'Connell intensified his drive for Repeal, Mathew curtailed his travels in Ireland and set his sights on England.[45] It could have been coincidental that Mathew chose to go abroad during the height of the Repeal agitation, but he had been invited to England three years earlier and waited until this time to make his trip.

Mathew in England

In late June 1843 Mathew set off on an extended English tour accompanied by his English-born secretary, James McKenna. Mathew had enjoyed a successful weeklong visit to Scotland the previous summer and was hopeful that the English would be as receptive as their northern neighbors had been.[46] After landing in Liverpool, he spent almost a month visiting the major cities in the north and midland regions—Manchester, Birmingham, Leeds, York—and a number of small towns as well. In Liverpool he met William Rathbone, a wealthy Unitarian merchant, who would become his intimate friend and benefactor in the years following. Although he met other influential Protestants on several occasions, most of the people he encountered were Irish Catholics. Brian Harrison claims that Mathew's principal concern was to minister to his exiled Irish brethren and help them assimilate. By enrolling them into the total abstinence organization, Mathew hoped that the Irish would become respectable and responsible members of English society.[47]

It does appear that the Irish were Mathew's first priority, if not his sole concern. The 1841 census counted three hundred thousand Irish in England, with the great majority of them massed in the growing industrial cities of the north and in London. These were the cities he visited. At almost every stop on his tour, he spoke at least once at the local Catholic church, which was frequently named St. Patrick's. When administering the pledge, he often spoke in Irish as well as English, since many of the new immigrants were not yet fluent in English.[48]

The Catholic clergy were generally receptive to Mathew. Priests were on hand to welcome him to every town he visited. One of his more noteworthy clerical friends was Father George Spencer, a well-heeled convert who was then teaching at Oscott College, the principal Catholic seminary. Although Spencer was favorably disposed to Mathew's work and a teetotaler himself, he was concerned chiefly with converting the English people to Catholicism and devoted most of his energies to that quixotic project.

Mathew had some supporters among the bishops as well. At this time, the Catholic Church in England was not governed by a regular hierarchy. Since England was considered mission territory, the Church was administered by eight bishops known as vicars apostolic, each of whom presided over a district rather than a diocese. Nicholas Wiseman, a longtime supporter, welcomed him to Birmingham, and John Briggs, vicar apostolic of the Yorkshire district, welcomed him to Manchester and traveled with him to several towns.[49] At least one bishop, however, was careful to keep his distance from Mathew: Thomas Griffiths, vicar apostolic of the London district. An old Catholic of the most timid sort, Griffiths appears to have had no theological objections to total abstinence but was determined to avoid any and all controversy.⁵⁰ Consequently, he did not oppose Mathew in any overt way; he simply ignored him during his London tour.

With the clergy's assistance, Mathew's tour of the northern cities progressed fairly well. At each stop, he celebrated Mass and took part in banquets and processions in his honor. In York, accompanied by Briggs, he told a large crowd that since arriving in England, he had received several anonymous letters accusing him of "substituting teetotalism for the Gospel." His response was to point out that he had already distributed at his own expense more than one thousand copies of the Bible and was then arranging for an inexpensive edition of the Scriptures to be published so that a Bible would be available "to every teetotal head of a family in Ireland."

Two days later Mathew delivered a wide-ranging talk at a breakfast meeting in Leeds:

> When I see around me Christians of all sects, I cannot but exclaim, 'How lovely are thy tabernacles, O Lord! and how pleasing it is that brothers should dwell in unity' [Ps. 86:1, 133:1]. I trust that there will be frequently meetings similar to this present delightful one. Some to whom I was lately speaking told me that they were total abstainers in principle, but that they did not wish to take the pledge; and yet a pledge is merely the simple expression of a determination to be total abstainers. . . . It is not a vow but a simple resolution. . . . It is thought by some in England that the teetotallers of Ireland have taken a part there in the great political movement. 300,000 persons assemble and disperse without any occurrence to mar peace and order. . . . If I am to be blamed upon that ground, I must bear it.⁵¹

From Leeds Mathew traveled to the surrounding towns and then spent several days in Liverpool and Manchester. All together, he enrolled at least forty-five thousand in Liverpool, fifty-five thousand in Manchester, and another forty thousand in Leeds, York, and the smaller towns.⁵² Not all of these pledge takers were new converts to the total abstinence cause. Some had already been teetotalers but wanted to take the pledge specifically from Mathew.

At the end of July Mathew reached London, which he had previously described as a "sink of drunkenness" with thirty thousand Roman Catholic drunkards.⁵³ He decided to spend five full weeks there, tending to the Irish population. Upon his arrival, he was greeted by a handful of notables, and both Earl Stanhope, a Tory and a Protestant, and the earl of Arundel and Surrey, a Whig and a Catholic, took the pledge at his hands.[54] Stanhope had been one of the earliest proponents of teetotalism, having renounced alcohol in 1831, and had been instrumental in the establishment of several temperance societies. Although staunchly anti-Catholic, he admired Mathew and appeared on the platform with him at a number of his public meetings in London. Another influential supporter was Jane Welsh Carlyle. In an effusive letter to her husband, Thomas Carlyle, Jane described how Mathew had let her sit next to him on stage during one of his meetings in London. On parting he had given her a silver medal, even though she did not take the pledge. She declared Mathew "to be the very best man of modern times" (and then added diplomatically, "*you* excepted").[55]

Mathew spent most of his time, however, not visiting with dignitaries but trying to minister to the eighty thousand Irish who populated the slums of London.[56] Almost all of his appearances were arranged in neighborhoods with high concentrations of Irish, such as St. Giles, Wapping, and East End.[57] Here again, he was often obliged to give the pledge in Irish. Virtually all of his public appearances in London were disappointments. Although sizable crowds—sometimes as large as fifty thousand—regularly gathered to hear him, few took the pledge. Most onlookers were simply curious to see the famed Irish friar in the flesh. Some days five hundred would enroll, and on better days one thousand to two thousand would join. According to the *Illustrated London News,* many of those who did take the pledge in London had "black eyes and bruised faces, [and] appeared to have recently been making great sacrifices to Bacchus."[58] Considering that London's population was roughly 2 million, this was an embarrassingly small and motley harvest for Mathew.

As Mathew continued his labors in London, his troubles began to mount. After his initial meetings, hecklers, many of whom were drunk, came to taunt him. When he appeared at Greenwich, publicans milled about the crowd, selling beer and proclaiming that they were "members of the malt and hop society." Instead of wearing medals around their necks, as the teetotalers did, they wore pewter mugs. Such minor incidents were to be expected, since drink vendors often attempted to disrupt teetotal meetings in London. On August 28, however, the opposition turned violent. At Bermondsey, Mathew's meeting was broken up by several dozen men and boys who forced their way to the platform. Most of the group dispersed when they encountered a police cordon in front of the platform, but a few of the more brazen protesters made a second attempt to reach the platform and were almost able to sever the ropes supporting the stage. Colm Kerrigan claims that if the ropes securing the platform had been cut, a number of people, including Mathew, could have been killed. Some of the hecklers hurled rocks at Mathew and threw beer in the faces of the policemen guarding him.[59]

About a week later, Mathew left London for Norwich, a stronghold of dissenting Protestantism. Here, too, he encountered vehement opposition. The night before Mathew's arrival, a minister warned his congregants not to kneel at "the feet of a Roman Catholic priest, and tak[e] the pledge, together with a Papistical blessing, at his hands." At the same time, handbills were posted throughout the city describing Mathew as a "priest of an idolatrous Church" and a "worshipper of the wafer God." When he arrived the next day, he received only a polite, low-key welcome from the townspeople. Nevertheless, that evening, the local Anglican bishop, Edward Stanley, presided over a sizable meeting in his honor. Alluding to the posters, Stanley described them as "trash so gross, so scurrilous and abusive." Referring to Mathew as "a Christian brother," Stanley offered him a warm welcome.[60]

As the incidents in Norwich suggest, much of the opposition to Mathew was religiously based. Some Protestant clergy in London had also used anti-Catholic rhetoric to discredit Mathew. One London minister strongly urged his listeners to shun Mathew's "Popish movement," saying it was "calculated to shake the basis of the Protestant faith" in England. An Anglican cleric in Greenwich was similarly alarmist, warning that Mathew's campaign was part of an Irish plot to destroy the Church of England.[61]

That many Protestant clergy viewed Mathew with suspicion is not surprising, considering the prevalence of anti-Catholic sentiment in England at this time.[62] Indeed, it is surprising that Mathew was not subjected to considerably more Catholic baiting. Still, what was said about Mathew and Catholicism undoubtedly influenced English opinion.

Consequently, when Mathew appeared before largely Protestant audiences, as he did in London and Norwich, many of his listeners were predisposed to reject him and his message. At the same time, Mathew's tour may have helped to allay the anti-Catholic inclinations of many English Protestants. Brian Harrison claims that Bishop Stanley's public handshake with Mathew in Norwich made a profound impression on many Protestants.[63]

Although anti-Catholicism was a factor in the opposition shown to Mathew, it was not the only source of his problems. Harsh economic realities played their part. Most people who were connected with the liquor industry resented Mathew, fearing that his campaign might bankrupt them. This had been the case in Ireland, and it was certainly to be expected in England. What made the English situation more troublesome for Mathew was the large percentage of people, especially Londoners, who were involved in some aspect of the liquor trade. Because the Beer Act of 1830 had reduced the fee for a license to sell beer, beer houses had multiplied in England in the 1830s.[64] Many shopkeepers and tradesmen would sell beer and perhaps food as a way to supplement their incomes. In addition to beer houses, gaudily decorated establishments known as "gin palaces" were springing up throughout London at this time.[65] Thus many more people had a stake in the liquor industry in England than in Ireland. When one combines these two factors, economic fears and nativism, the hostile reaction of many Londoners is understandable. To many of the Protestant working people of London, Mathew was a popish monk attempting to deprive honest men and women of their livelihoods.

The Pledge Revisited

Just as Mathew was preparing to leave England, Frederick Lucas, editor of the Catholic journal the *Tablet,* began to raise objections to Mathew's work. The *Tablet* had provided thorough and sympathetic coverage of Mathew's tour in July and August, but it changed its tune in early September. Claiming that the English temperance movement was dominated by evangelicals, many of whom believed that alcohol was intrinsically evil, Lucas said he could not understand why Mathew was willing to give the pledge to people who subscribed to such a heresy. He then took aim at the pledge itself: "As the intention of the pledge is not a *promise* or a *vow*, but a simple *resolution,* it occurs to us that instead of the word 'promise,' . . . it would be well to use the word which exactly conveys Father Mathew's meaning—'I *resolve,*' etc. The pledge might then . . . have appended to it a clause like the following: 'And I declare that in making this *resolution,* I do not believe intoxicating liquors to be in themselves unlawful or forbidden by the law of God.'"[66]

Lucas continued to raise questions about the pledge. He claimed to have surveyed the clergy of Ireland on their understanding of the pledge and received fourteen different interpretations. Some priests considered it a solemn vow, some a promise, and still others a mere resolution. Mathew himself seemed just as ambivalent on the subject as he was in 1840, when it was first raised. Although in July at Leeds he had explicitly stated that it was a simple resolution, in October he declared that it was a vow if the person pledging considered it such.[67] These conflicting statements troubled Lucas, who had taken the pledge from Mathew and been one of his strongest supporters in England.

Mathew surely had his reasons for giving hazy explanations of the pledge. If word were to get out that the pledge were a mere resolution, many of his followers might be tempted to break their pledges. It would be better for them to think that the simple resolution they had made was a solemn vow. Mathew was certainly not going to disabuse any teetotaler of this notion.

Despite the opposition that Mathew met from many quarters, on balance his English trip was successful. Counting the sixty thousand people he enrolled in London, Mathew pledged two hundred thousand people during his ten-week stay. Many who took the pledge stayed faithful to it for the rest of their lives. Thirty years later, when Archbishop Henry Manning was organizing the League of the Cross, a Catholic teetotal society, he found that many of the people who formed the nucleus of the league had taken the pledge from Mathew and kept it. In 1876, Manning boasted, "Since the foundation of the League four years ago, 58,000 pledges have been taken, and 13,000 in this last year alone. I think, therefore, we may say that our hands have not been slack in doing Father Mathew's work."[68]

When Mathew returned to Ireland in mid-September, a crowd of twenty thousand waited at the dock in Kingstown to welcome him home. After spending a couple days in Dublin administering the pledge, he headed for Cork, where he remained for the next several weeks, recuperating from his trip and attending to business. On the outskirts of Cork, another welcome awaited him: a wealthy teetotaler, William O'Connor, decided to build a monument to commemorate Mathew's trip to England. In November, a round stone tower was erected to celebrate Mathew's "enthusiastic reception [by] the citizens of London, without distinction of religion or politics." Dubbing it the "Tower of Temperance," O'Connor filled its rooms with images of Mathew and Queen Victoria, along with Irish and English flags. He encircled the tower with acres of shrubs and flowers and declared that the whole property was to be open to the public as a park.[69]

CLONTARF AND THE DECLINE OF REPEAL

While Mathew maintained a low profile in Cork in the fall of 1843, O'Connell was on center stage and Repeal was in full swing. Energized by Tara and the other monster meetings, Repealers were astir about the Clontarf meeting, set for October 8, which they expected to draw at least 1 million people. Just as all the preparations were in place, however, Peel took action. He had remained silent all summer, not responding to O'Connell's "Mallow Defiance" or any of the other provocative speeches given at the rallies, but upon learning that a "Repeal Cavalry" of mounted, uniformed men would appear at Clontarf, Peel decided he had justification for intervening.[70] Declaring the Cavalry a quasimilitary force, even though none of its members were armed, he banned the Clontarf meeting less than twenty-four hours before it was scheduled to occur.

Peel had called O'Connell's bluff at last. O'Connell, ever the dutiful constitutionalist, canceled the meeting. Nevertheless he and eight of his colleagues were arrested the following week for seditious conspiracy. Brought before a carefully screened, all-Protestant jury, O'Connell and his codefendants did not have much of a chance. At the trial, the prosecutors described the uniforms that some Repealers wore to the rallies in an effort to show that the Repeal movement had a militaristic dimension. The defense countered by noting that some people at Mathew's teetotal rallies wore uniforms as well. Predictably, the jury sided with the prosecutors, and O'Connell and seven other defendants were fined and sentenced to jail terms of up to one year. (One of those arrested, Father Peter Tyrrell, had died during the trial.) Perhaps fearing violence, the British took pains to ensure that the group's stay in prison was not unpleasant. On May 30, 1844, O'Connell and his colleagues, christened the "Repeal Martyrs" by the nationalist press, arrived at the Richmond Penitentiary in Dublin in the lord mayor's coach. During the course of their confinement, each prisoner was given his own apartment, was treated to excellent meals, and was allowed to receive as many visitors as he wanted.[71]

While the "Martyrs" bided their time in prison, Mathew continued to spend most of his time in Cork. His interest in temperance had certainly not flagged, but his English tour had cost him five hundred pounds and left him strapped. Still, he managed to do some traveling. In June he toured around County Sligo, in July he visited Clonmel in County Tipperary, and in August he went to Dublin to preach a charity sermon.[72] While in Dublin, he stopped by the jail to pay his respects to O'Connell, Duffy, and the others. Writing to John Sheil, one of his anglophile friends, Mathew explained, "Mr. O'Connell has honored me with his friendship for more than twenty years. . . . Three of those [imprisoned], Mssrs. Gray, Ray and Duffy are faithful teetotallers. Not to visit such individuals in prison would be culpable in the extreme and an act of political partisanship."[73]

With O'Connell in jail, the Repeal leadership was taken over by Smith O'Brien, a wealthy Protestant landlord and recent convert to the cause. One of O'Brien's first initiatives was to announce that he was taking the "Repeal pledge." In other words, he would not drink alcohol again until Repeal was achieved.[74] When questioned by Daniel O'Connell Jr., Mathew said he welcomed all new adherents to teetotalism. In private, he was more critical. To a fellow clergyman, Mathew wrote,

> It is true that in reply to Mr O'Connell's inquiry whether I had any objection to Mr Smith O'Brien's pledge I evidently said "Not the least, sir." That was all that passed on the subject. I rejoiced when Mr Smith O'Brien pledged himself to abstain from all intoxicating drinks until the Repeal of the Union, and I would be completely happy if every Repealer in Ireland who was not a

teetotaller, would follow his example. The evil that has been caused by the association of drinking Repealers is unutterable. At the great O'Connell banquet in this city, there were over three hundred persons drunk. . . . The Repeal wardens throughout the country hold their meetings in public houses and many publicans are wardens and hundreds of our own faithful teetotallers have yielded to the temptation. I do not anticipate much success for Mr. Smith O'Brien's pledge against intoxicating drink . . . I would not oppose it, even were it given only for a month. Besides my opposition would effect no good, and would raise a clamor against me amongst interested individuals [claiming to be] patriots. . . . It is for you and me and any true teetotaller to have no connection with this new agitation. I have never and never will administer the Total Abstinence Pledge for a limited term. The very name of a teetotaller proclaims the renunciation to be teetotally, that is forever.[75]

In early September, O'Connell and his seven comrades received welcome news from an unlikely quarter. The judges of the House of Lords reversed their convictions, citing irregularities in the jury selection. O'Connell promptly declared that his early release was a miracle worked through the intercession of the Virgin Mary. To celebrate, O'Connell's followers planned a triumphal procession from the prison gates through the city. The people flooded the streets to see their hero and hear his plans for a renewal of the Repeal crusade. Two days later, he appeared at the Repealers' meeting place, Conciliation Hall, and delivered a meandering address that made no reference to Repeal. In October he sent out a long letter from his home in Kerry endorsing a federalist scheme that would have increased Irish representation in Parliament and given the Irish more control over local matters. The plan angered most Repealers and yet was still too sweeping for most English Whigs to countenance.[76]

O'Connell's biographers have speculated about his change of course. Some argue that O'Connell—by this time almost seventy—had become a bit feeble mentally. Others say he was distracted by his infatuation with Rose McDowell, a twenty-three-year-old Belfast woman who had visited him in jail.[77] Whatever the explanation, in the fall of 1844, O'Connell was not as sharp or strong as he had once been. As a result, the Repeal movement, which had been slipping since Clontarf, continued to lose strength through 1844.

Repeal was far from finished in Irish politics, but it would never regain the dominant position it had held in the summer of 1843. Mathew could breathe a little easier. Teetotalism was no longer in danger of becoming an auxiliary to O'Connell's political campaigns. Although O'Brien's Repeal pledge was worrisome to Mathew, it never became popular, and Repeal leaders began to focus their energies on other matters. Mathew and the temperance movement had weathered the storm. The Repeal Year had come and gone without inflicting any lasting damage on Mathew.[78]

Mathew's Accomplishments

Mathew began his seventh year in the temperance crusade in the spring of 1844. Supporters estimated that he had enrolled 5 million people into his movement. In December Mathew informed James Grant that his rolls had increased further: "You have not over-rated the number when you state that five millions and a half have taken the pledge. This includes females and children. . . . In [Cork] we have more than 60,000 teetotallers, which is more than half the population."[79]

Mathew and his coworkers could point to other statistics as well to demonstrate the success of the movement. First, the number of gallons of spirits consumed in Ireland fell 48 percent from 12.3 million in 1838 to 6.45 million in 1844. Since the population increased during these years, the decline in per capita consumption of spirits was even greater. Of course, these figures refer only to legally distilled spirits; they do not include poteen production. Considering that the police found many more poteen stills in 1843 than they had in 1840, it is likely that poteen production was rising.[80] Even so, this increase would not have offset the steep decline in legally distilled whiskey.

Likewise, from 1838 to 1844, the number of distilleries decreased 29 percent from 87 to 62; the number of spirit dealers declined 30 percent from 455 to 317; and the number of whiskey retailers dropped 38 percent from 20,399 to 12,646. Maurice O'Connell, the editor of Daniel O'Connell's papers, notes that one of the Liberator's friends, Denis Cormac, was "a member of a Kilkenny brewing family ruined by Father Mathew's temperance movement." Occasionally Mathew received letters from former distillers and publicans who hoped that he would help them get started in new professions. From Castlebar, County Mayo, Patrick Toole wrote to Mathew, identifying himself as one who was engaged "in the cursed trade, the public business," but "owing to the change in the times ... is reduced to a state of destitution." Another victim of the temperance crusade was Mathew's younger brother, Thomas, a distiller in Cashel. Writing to an acquaintance, Major John Russell, after his brother's death, Mathew remarked sadly, "Though my poor brother never uttered a complaint, I have the sorrowful conviction that his death at the early age of 47 was occasioned by the failure of his trade. For until then, he was prosperous in business, and he became desponding when he found his prospects blighted. I wish some wealthy London Company would purchase the concern for a factory."[81]

Some publicans attempted to adjust to the new climate by selling nonalcoholic beverages. When the English novelist William Thackeray visited Ireland in 1842, he noted that the tavern keepers of Killarney were "now condemned to sell 'tay' in the place of whisky." Many others who were involved in the liquor industry could not adapt and decided to leave Ireland. Kerby Miller, an expert on Irish emigration, estimates that as many as twenty thousand tavern keepers and other persons associated with the liquor industry left Ireland for the United States from 1840 to 1844.[82]

As the temperance movement progressed, crime rates in Ireland declined. Visiting a police barracks in County Tipperary, Mrs. Asenath Nicholson was told by the officers that "Father Mathew has so changed everything, that our profession is entirely needless in some parts of the country." Colm Kerrigan notes that convictions for serious crimes decreased 33 percent in Ireland from 12,049 in 1839 to 8,042 in 1844. In contrast, convictions in England and Wales increased slightly in the same period. Kerrigan cautions that criminal statistics are not an entirely reliable indicator of illegal activity, since arrest and conviction rates can be affected by the size and efficiency of the police force and the attitudes of judges and juries. Furthermore, he points out that the crime rate was declining already before Mathew launched his temperance crusade.[83] The establishment of an organized police force in 1836 may have contributed to the decreasing crime rates. Thus there is a certain ambiguity surrounding these data, but it is nonetheless clear that crime declined somewhat between 1839 and 1844 and Mathew's campaign was a factor in this change.

James Haughton obtained data from the warden of Dublin's Richmond Penitentiary that also indicated that crime rates declined in this period. Whereas 3,457 men were committed for drunk and disorderly conduct in 1841, only 2,507 were arrested in 1844. Surprisingly, more women than men were arrested for public drunkenness, and their committal rate had decreased only slightly over the same period. From 1841 to 1844, the number of arrests of women dropped from 4,786 to 4,520. Overall, women comprised 40 percent of the prison population in Dublin. Many of the women arrested were prostitutes; rescue workers in these years estimated that there were 1,700 prostitutes working in Dublin and 350 in Cork. These were women whom Mathew found it almost impossible to reach.[84]

Maria Edgeworth did not resort to statistics when talking about Mathew and temperance. Writing to Richard Allen, a Quaker teetotaler, Edgeworth hailed the temperance movement as a "wonderful crusade" and remarked, "I consider Father Mathew as the greatest benefactor to his country, the most true friend to Irishmen and to Ireland."[85]

A number of foreign visitors shared Edgeworth's enthusiasm. Several commented on the dramatic changes they had witnessed in the behavior and attitudes of the Irish people. Thackeray offered the following observations:

> [A] delightful old gentleman . . . said that all the fun had gone out of Ireland since Father Mathew had banished the whisky from it. Indeed, any stranger amongst the people can perceive that they are now anything but gay. I have seen a great number of crowds and meetings of people in all parts of Ireland, and found them all gloomy. There is nothing like the merry-making one reads of in the Irish novels. Lever and Maxwell must be taken as chroniclers of the old times. . . . On the day we arrived at Cork, . . . a stout, handsome, honest looking man of some two-and forty years, was passing by, and received a number of bows from the crowd around. It was Theobald Mathew with whose face a thousand little print shop windows had already rendered me familiar.[86]

J. G. Kohl, a German who toured Ireland in the fall of 1842, was similarly impressed by Mathew's work: "I do not remember to have passed through any Irish town, in which I did not see a spick and span new school-house, and a distillery, either shut up or going evidently to decay."[87] In Wexford, Kohl found only one of seven breweries operating, and in New Ross and Enniscorthy, he learned that the principal distilleries had shut down.

James Grant, who visited in 1844, was even more lavish in his praise for Mathew. Describing him as "incomparably the greatest man of the day," Grant claimed that drunkenness had all but disappeared from Ireland. Those who had taken the pledge had kept it "wondrously well. A few, and only a few, comparatively out of the masses who have taken it, have violated [it]." With crime on the decline, the educational system improving, and temperance principles "all but universal," Grant was sanguine about Ireland's future prospects.[88]

In August 1844, with the threat from Repeal waning, Mathew was faced with another challenge that had the potential to cripple his burgeoning movement. Visiting Chapelizod, a Dublin suburb, to administer the pledge, Mathew was met by a bailiff who first knelt for his blessing and then informed him that he was under arrest for having failed to pay his debts to medal manufacturers in Birmingham.[89] Out of respect for Mathew's feelings, the Irish press did not carry the news of his arrest. Still, he would have to find a way to extricate himself from this financial crisis. He needed seven thousand pounds to satisfy his various creditors and several hundred more pounds just to cover his travel expenses over the short term. Without these funds, he would be forced to further curtail his travels on behalf of temperance.

{ CHAPTER FIVE }

Temperance in Crisis, 1844–1845

> *I did not anticipate [my debts], I was hurried forward by zeal in the sacred cause and before I was aware of it, I was inextricably embarrassed. I claimed no sacrifice too great that promised to promote the object to which I had devoted all my energies. . . . I was unaided and alone, and never sought or accepted pecuniary assistance.*
>
> Father Mathew, writing to Joseph Sturge (1844)

In the summer of 1844 Mathew became increasingly preoccupied with his financial problems. Before his arrest, he had spent money freely on a host of projects associated with temperance and had not worried much about his finances. After his encounter with the bailiff, though, he recognized that he would need to raise a considerable sum if he was planning to pay his creditors and continue traveling on behalf of temperance. And with reports of pledge breaking becoming more widespread, Mathew felt that it was imperative that he encourage his followers to abide by their pledges.

Mathew's Fiscal Crisis

Mathew's financial troubles did not come upon him all of a sudden. He had been losing money since he joined the teetotal movement in 1838. He gave to each new member a copper medal, for which he was charged three-and-a-half pence by the English manufacturer. In 1839, when the movement was still in its early stages, the *Dublin Weekly Herald* reported that he was spending five pounds per week on medals.[1] As the movement expanded dramatically in late 1839, the cost of providing cards and medals to all new members ballooned accordingly. In addition, there were considerable expenses associated with the establishment and maintainence of musical bands and reading rooms. Band members needed instruments and uniforms, and reading rooms needed furniture and a generous supply of books and newspapers as well as temperance tracts. He also donated monies to many of the churches and schools that he visited on his tours and gave liberally to most of the indigent teetotalers who approached him.

In 1840 James McKenna recognized that Mathew had fallen deeply into debt, owing five thousand pounds to various creditors.[2] He persuaded Mathew to sell the medals for a shilling apiece. If each new member paid a shilling, Mathew would realize enough of a profit to free himself from debt. Unfortunately, selling medals did not generate nearly as much money as McKenna envisioned. Representatives of a few local temperance societies forwarded money to the headquarters of the Cork Total Abstinence Society, but Mathew was not reimbursed for the bulk of the medals he distributed.[3] In districts in which the local teetotal officials protested that the people were too poor to pay for the medals, Mathew did not press them for payment. Instead, he continued to distribute medals to all who asked, regardless of their ability to pay. The loose organization of the movement also hampered the fundraising effort. Since Mathew at no point employed more than three clerks, he never had an adequate staff to oversee a movement with millions of adherents.[4] Consequently, he and his aides were unable to keep track of how many medals they had distributed and how much money they had received from their numerous affiliates. Writing to Richard Allen shortly after his arrest, Mathew claimed that "hundreds of thousands of medals were sent by order to different parts of Ireland for which I never received any return."[5]

Mathew's decision to charge for temperance medals was seized on by his critics as an indication of his mercenary motives. From England and Scotland, teetotalers wrote Mathew to inform him that foes of the temperance movement were reciting limericks mocking him for his greed.[6] Mathew's Irish critics made similar insinuations against him. A columnist for the *Dublin Evening Mail* remarked sarcastically, "Whenever Uncle Toby gets his money, there is more where it came from; and, accordingly, he has set up a laboratory of his own—[he] coins his medals and meddles with the coin; in short, he makes a very pretty thing of it."[7] Bishops John MacHale and William Higgins were also under the impression that Mathew was accumulating large sums of money through the sale of medals, which heightened their suspicion of him and his movement.

Although the sale of medals was proving a failure, Mathew remained confident that he would be able to right his financial position. For years he had been expecting to inherit a considerable sum of money from Lady Elizabeth Mathew, his wealthy Protestant cousin. Lady Elizabeth had never married and had no surviving brothers or sisters. She had always been especially fond of her younger cousin and promised him on several occasions that she would remember him in her will. However, upon his cousin's death in December 1841, Mathew was shocked to learn that he had been appointed executor of her estate but had not received any portion of her legacy. She had willed the bulk of her estate to a French relative, Vicomte Rohan de Chabot. It seems she was afraid to give any money or land to Mathew because she thought the Capuchin order would take possession of it. Whatever her reasons, Lady Elizabeth's decision meant that Mathew would be unable to solve his financial difficulties on his own. From this point on, he was more careful about the money he spent. Whereas in 1840 he regularly contributed twenty pounds or more to churches and charities in the towns he visited, after his cousin's death he was much more cautious about giving away money. Still, his "pecuniary embarrassments," as he called them, increased incrementally from 1841 to 1844, reaching seven thousand pounds at the time of his arrest.[8]

Finally, in October 1844, two months after his arrest, Mathew agreed to have his financial plight publicized. An English Unitarian friend, the Reverend Thomas Hincks, revealed the news in his denomination's newspaper, *The Inquirer*. Friends and well-wishers in both England and Ireland responded swiftly to the announcement. Writing to James Haughton, Daniel O'Connell argued that prompt action had to be taken on Mathew's behalf: "Father Mathew must be relieved from all his difficulties—difficulties brought on in the performance of that astonishing moral miracle of which he has been, under Providence, the instrument. It would be the basest ingratitude in the world not to make him perfectly independent in pecuniary circumstances. It must not be. Let us set about at once affording the remedy. . . . *In short, the thing must be done.*"[9]

To coordinate the fundraising effort, the Mathew Relief Committee was established in Cork under the aegis of the mayor, William Fagan, and an alderman, Thomas Lyons. In Dublin another committee had already been established to aid Mathew in 1843. This group, the Mathew Testimonial Committee, was led by Peter Purcell, a wealthy Protestant businessman, and included Haughton, the Duke of Leinster, and other dignitaries. Purcell and his colleagues hoped to raise money to honor Mathew in some way—through the erection of a statue of him or by creating a library or botanical garden in his name. The committee had not yet decided how it would honor Mathew, but it claimed to have raised a sizable sum for him. Haughton, the committee's treasurer, saw himself as the logical choice to oversee the relief effort for Mathew, and he wrote to Mathew, volunteering his services and suggesting that Mathew specify exactly how much money he owed his creditors and for what.[10] In Haughton's view, the more the people knew, the more inclined they would be to contribute.

By early November, a Mathew Relief Committee had been established in Dublin with many of the same people who had served on the Mathew Testimonial Committee: the Duke of Leinster (chairman), Haughton (secretary), Peter Purcell, Daniel O'Connell, Maurice O'Connell, R. R. Guinness, R. D. Webb, and others. At their initial meeting, the committee members declared their intention of raising twenty thousand pounds for Mathew. Maurice O'Connell was of the view that every Irish person should give up one day's wages and contribute it to the fund.[11]

Mathew was not happy about the establishment of a Dublin-based relief committee and not at all pleased by Haughton's proposal that he furnish a complete account of his expenditures and debts. He thought Haughton was not only meddling in his private affairs but might be trying to gain control over him and the temperance movement. As Mathew's earlier disagreement with Father Andrew O'Connell demonstrated, he had no tolerance for challenges—whether real or imagined—to his authority. He curtly rejected Haughton's proposal and stressed again and again in his correspondence that he wanted all contributions sent to Fagan and Lyons in Cork rather than to Haughton's Committee. Writing to Father John Spratt in Dublin, Mathew assured him, "Nothing could be more repugnant to my feelings and to my conviction than the appointment of a Treasurer and a Committee in Dublin. After a desperate effort, I have yielded to the importunity of a friend . . . the Rev. Mr. Hincks . . . who made an appeal to the public; an appeal that has elicited such true sympathy. It is not for me, under these circumstances, to place myself under the controls of a Committee and to place at its disposal the gifts of a generous public."[12]

Mathew then wrote to Purcell, requesting that all monies raised by the Testimonial Committee be forthwith sent to him. After some hesitation, Purcell and Haughton turned over all the committee's funds to Fagan and Lyons. To Mathew's great dismay, Purcell's group had collected only £2,168, because most of the subscribers had never fulfilled their pledges. The *Freeman's Journal* reported that "not 1/20th of the subscribers ever paid." The problem, according to W. W. Simpson, an English Protestant supporter of Mathew, was that temperance bands were taking part in Repeal demonstrations. Simpson concluded that although Mathew did not sanction these activities, this was the "cause of the great Protestant party withholding their subscriptions from the testimonial." Still more disappointing was the revelation that the Testimonial Committee had spent almost half of the money it had received so it only had £1,150 on hand to forward to Cork.[13]

When apprised that more than nine hundred pounds had been spent on clerks' salaries, postage, stationery, and other items, Mathew told Spratt that "the account of the expences of the Testimonial Committee is awful." John Maguire, one of the leaders of the Cork committee, shared Mathew's anger about the Testimonial Committee's extravagance. At a public meeting of the Cork committee, Maguire rebuked Purcell and the other leaders for their irresponsibility. Purcell's feelings were hurt. He had invested considerable time and money in an effort to assist Mathew and did not appreciate Maguire's criticisms. Mathew apologized profusely to Purcell, assuring him that "nothing in my whole life ever gave me so much pain as this speech of Mr. Maguire's. Do not, dear Mr. Purcell, think more about it."[14]

In spite of the tensions among the temperance leaders, the effort to relieve Mathew progressed more or less steadily through the winter of 1844 and the spring of 1845. Undaunted by Mathew's rebuff, Haughton and the other members of his committee continued to meet regularly in Dublin. Daniel O'Connell attended several of the meetings and at one noted that fifty thousand pounds could be raised if one million Irishmen each contributed a shilling. Although the committee never raised anything remotely near that amount, Haughton periodically forwarded sums of two hundred pounds or more to Mathew.[15]

Fundraising efforts were much more successful in England. In December 1844 Lord John Russell, a leader of the Liberal Party, appeared at London's Exeter Hall—a bastion of evangelical Protestantism—to plead Mathew's cause. Through Russell's appeal and Hincks's efforts, considerable sums were raised in England on Mathew's behalf. Writing to Father John Fitzgerald in Castletown Delvin in May 1845, Mathew noted that his "circumstances became known to friends in England, and with their aid, and some partial help from Ireland, a sum over £7000 has been raised, and my debts are liquidated."[16]

As his words indicate, Mathew was not nearly as satisfied with the Irish response as he was with the English response. In a letter to Haughton, he expressed his disappointment with his compatriots: "I'm justified in saying that the teetotalers of Ireland have not upheld me—have not contributed for my relief half of what I expended for their happiness." There were several reasons for Mathew's difficulties in raising funds in Ireland. First, most Irish people were desperately poor in these years. Joel Mokyr, an economic historian, contends that the Irish were poorer than almost any other European people in the first half of the nineteenth century and poverty "was almost synonymous with life in Ireland."[17] Besides, some rural Irish did not use money for their transactions. They gave a certain share of their produce to the landlord instead of paying in cash and bartered for any essentials they required.[18] Thus, many Irish people may have been interested in helping Mathew but simply did not have the resources to do so.

Furthermore, most of the Irish who had disposable income had already committed money to the support of the Church or to O'Connell. Emmet Larkin estimates that the Catholic Church required about six hundred thousand pounds annually for the support of its clergy and the upkeep and improvement of its churches, schools, and convents. And since 1840, O'Connell had been drawing large sums from the Repeal Rent and the Tribute. Although his revenues had fallen off somewhat after 1843, he still collected approximately sixty thousand pounds in

1844–45 from the Repeal Rent alone; there are no figures available for the O'Connell Tribute in 1844–45, but it probably exceeded ten thousand pounds. With these two expenses bearing down on them, Irish Catholics could not have had much money to spare for other charitable causes.[19]

O'Connell had been greatly aided in his fundraising efforts by the Catholic bishops, who actively promoted the Repeal Rent and the Tribute. These monies were generally collected on church grounds after Mass each Sunday. If the bishops had supported a Mathew tribute and authorized a collection to be taken up for him in churches throughout Ireland, Mathew would have been able to raise considerably more money. A handful of bishops spoke out on Mathew's behalf and sent contributions to the relief committees, but the bishops as a body made no effort to assist him.[20]

With these obstacles before him, it is no wonder that Mathew had trouble raising money in Ireland. In spite of these problems, the Mathew Relief Committee in Cork reported in 1845 that eighty-three hundred pounds had been sent to Mathew. This was not a large sum compared to the monies pouring into O'Connell's coffers and it was not enough to secure Mathew's future. Still, the money settled Mathew's immediate crisis and enabled him to maintain his touring schedule.

Broken Promises

Even though he worried about his debts, Mathew was determined not to stop touring for temperance. Indeed, with reports of pledge breaking becoming more common, he redoubled his efforts to persuade the wavering to remain faithful to their pledges. In December 1844 he demonstrated that he could still draw large crowds. Visiting Thurles at the request of Archbishop Michael Slattery, he spent three days preaching in the cathedral and giving the pledge to boys in the Christian Brothers school and girls in the Ursuline school as well as adults. After spending Christmas in Cork with one of his brothers, he set off for another tour of Limerick. Father Augustine claims that over the course of three days Mathew enrolled fifteen thousand people, but it is not clear whether these were new members or lapsed teetotalers returning to the fold.[21]

O'Connell, too, continued to promote temperance. At a temperance soirée held in his honor in Killarney in January, he praised Mathew in the most extravagant terms:

> If the Very Rev. Mr. Mathew had not proceeded me—the really greatest man that Ireland has ever produced—had not been my precursor, I would not venture to consult millions of men listening to the story of their wrongs, and determined to have their country righted, but that they were checked by the moral miracle of the teetotal movement. The year 1843 was the triumph of Father Mathew, not of me. The monster meetings were his work, not mine; their perfect safety was produced by his system. . . . Hundreds of thousands, nay millions, assembled without the slightest force or violence, and such was their forbearance towards each other that they were unstained even by a single accident. . . . In Ireland alone the name of Mathew is a spell word, a magic, a talismanic word of Irish liberty.

He then took up the issue of pledge breaking. First he denied that appreciable numbers of Irish were breaking their pledges. Using the sectarian rhetoric of which he was a master, O'Connell declared that the pledge "will be kept just as Catholicism was kept in spite of three hundred years of oppression." For those few, however, who had not adhered to their pledges, he had no sympathy: "I would not keep a pledge-breaker in my house, or in my employment. They are traitors who deserve shunning."[22]

In March the question of pledge breaking again arose, when it was announced that more people were arrested for drunkenness on this St. Patrick's Day than had been in the previous year. The editors of the *Freeman's Journal* were quick to claim that the problem lay with prostitutes rather than pledge breakers. Still, with the impression spreading that temperance was in decline, Mathew and the other teetotal leaders began to warn the Irish people about the awful things that often befell pledge breakers. In April Haughton wrote a letter to the *Freeman's Journal*, reporting the drowning of a pledge breaker. He concluded dolefully, "It is melancholy to know that many who do so, soon come to a bad end." In May Mathew sent Haughton an upbeat letter, recounting his recent trip to Adamstown in County Wexford: "More new members were gained to our Sacred Society, than ever lapsed from it, during the last seven years." Nevertheless Mathew was concerned about pledge breaking and, like Haughton, was perfectly willing to employ scare tactics to keep members from breaking their pledges. At the end of June he appeared at Swords, a Dublin suburb, with both Spratt and Haughton. At the meeting, which netted twenty-five thousand new members, Mathew offered a cautionary tale of a man in Ennis, County Clare, who had broken his pledge, become desperate, and murdered his wife.[23]

Mathew received some assistance in his fight against pledge breaking from the Irish Protestant novelist William Carleton. In *Art Maguire: or the Broken Pledge,* which Carleton dedicated to Mathew, the protagonist's life steadily deteriorates after he breaks his pledge. Art loses his once promising job, starts abusing his wife and young son, and finally ends up a beggar. In case readers had somehow missed his point, Carleton concluded the novel with a stern warning: "Do not [repeat] the errors of his life as you find them laid down in this simple narrative of *The Broken Pledge.*"[24]

Ireland Old and Young

While Mathew was using all his powers to fight pledge breaking, Ireland's nationalist leaders were spending much of their time fighting with each other. Since the fall of 1844, fissures between O'Connell and the Young Ireland leaders had been steadily widening. Part of the problem stemmed from Sir Robert Peel's decision to offer a series of concessions to Irish Catholics. In quick succession he had established a Charitable Bequests Board to oversee grants to religious institutions; proposed trebling the government allocation to Maynooth College; and called for the establishment of nonsectarian colleges in Belfast, Cork, and Galway. These proposals left O'Connell in an awkward position. While willing to accept more money for the seminary, O'Connell lined up with the MacHaleite bishops in opposing the Charitable Bequests Board and the so-called Queen's Colleges. The latter issue proved so volatile that it divided not only the hierarchy but the Repeal Association.

In the view of the Young Irelanders, Peel's education scheme was commendable: the colleges would help uplift the Irish people and alleviate many of their problems. These were Mathew's sentiments as well, but he was careful not to make any public statements on the matter.[25] O'Connell, however, accepted MacHale's argument that the proposed system would endanger the faith and morals of Catholic youth.[26] He took to denouncing Peel in the strongest possible terms for trying to foist "Godless colleges"[27] on the Irish people, but he was unable to stop Parliament from approving the measure. The issue of the Queen's Colleges brought to light the cleavage between the more secular and militant Young Irelanders and O'Connell and his loyalists.

Frederick Douglass Comes to Cork

Mathew welcomed Frederick Douglass to Cork in October 1845. A twenty-seven-year-old former slave, Douglass was one of America's leading abolitionists and the movement's preeminent black voice. Having just published his autobiography and fearing that proslavery forces might seek his arrest, Douglass had decided to take an extended tour of England, Ireland, and Scotland.[28] He had spent September in Dublin attending O'Connell's Repeal meetings and delivering lectures on slavery and temperance.[29] He knew that both O'Connell and Mathew were committed abolitionists. Their names had topped a lengthy antislavery petition that had been sent to Irish Americans in 1841.[30] The letter had condemned slavery in unequivocal terms: "SLAVERY IS A SIN AGAINST GOD AND MAN. *All who are not for it must be against it.* NONE CAN BE NEUTRAL. . . . Irishmen and Irishwomen! treat the colored people as your equals, as brethren. By all your memories of Ireland, continue to love Liberty—hate slavery—CLING BY THE ABOLITIONISTS—and in America, *you will do honor to the name of Ireland.*"[31]

In Cork, Douglass participated in temperance meetings on four occasions. On October 21 he appeared as Mathew's guest at a gathering of members of the Cork Temperance Institute.[32] Before a mostly female crowd of 250 well-wishers, Douglass gave a speech titled "Intemperance and Slavery," in which he noted how much the free black population in America had benefited from temperance: "I set my voice against intemperance. I lectured against it, and talked against it, in the street, in the wayside, at the fire-side; wherever I went during the last seven years, my voice has been against intemperance . . . I am pleased to be able to say, that the change in their situation, with regard to intemperance, has been great." In concluding, Douglass alluded to the widespread belief that Ireland's temperance movement was on the wane: "We may answer . . . as a man once answered it [the question] in America. He said—'Twas going down—going gloriously down—going *down east, down west, down north, down to every point of compass*—going into every family—spreading peace and comfort and gladness over the entire community.' It may be said to be *so* going down in Ireland."33

The following morning, Douglass breakfasted at Mathew's home and took the pledge from him. He had been a teetotaler for eight years but wanted to renew his pledge before Mathew.34 After parting, Douglass wrote an effusive letter to William Lloyd Garrison, his abolitionist colleague, recounting his meeting with Mathew: "On the 21st inst. [instant, or this month], Father Mathew, the living saviour of Ireland from the curse of intemperance, gave a splendid soirée, as a token of his sympathy and regard for friend Buffum and myself. . . . So entirely charmed by the goodness of this truly good man was I, that I besought him to administer the pledge to me. He complied with promptness, and gave me a beautiful silver pledge. I now reckon myself with delight the fifth of the last five of Father Mathew's 5,487,495 temperance children."35

Not all of Douglass's letters home were so upbeat. For while he enjoyed his weeks in Ireland, he was shocked by the poverty he witnessed. Describing to Garrison the condition of a farm family's home that he visited, he noted that the dwelling was made of mud and was windowless with "a piece of pine board laid on top of a box—a picture representing the crucifixion of Christ, pasted on the most conspicuous place on the wall—a few broken dishes stuck up in a corner. . . . I see much here to remind me of my former condition, and I confess I should be ashamed to lift up my voice against American slavery, but that I know the cause of humanity is one the world over." He then told Garrison what he thought was the cause of all the Irish wretchedness: "The immediate . . . cause of the extreme poverty in Ireland is intemperance. . . . Drunkenness is still rife in Ireland. The temperance cause has done much—is doing much—but there is much more to do, and as yet, comparatively few to do it. A great part of the Roman Catholic clergy do nothing about it, while the Protestants may be said to hate the cause."36

The Onset of the Famine

Ireland's economy in 1845 centered largely around agriculture: about two-thirds of its 9 million people were engaged in farming. Ireland did not have much industry at this time, and two of its leading enterprises, brewing and distilling, had been weakened by the temperance campaign. In Mokyr's view, Mathew's campaign contributed to the "deindustrialization" that was occurring in Ireland in the late 1830s and early 1840s.[37] Consequently, a higher proportion of Irish people depended on farming for their livelihood in 1845 than in 1835.

Most tenant farmers, cottiers, and laborers in turn depended on the potato for their survival. Since potatoes provide a high yield and most farmers leased small tracts of land, they had little choice about what crop to plant. For generations the potato had been the centerpiece of the Irish diet. A typical working man ate about fourteen pounds of potatoes each day, along with small quantities of onions and green vegetables.[38] This virtually meatless diet provided farmers and their families all the nutrients they needed. Scarcely anyone suffered from scurvy or any other diet-related disease.[39]

Still, the Irish people were taking a risk in relying so heavily on the potato. Since potatoes could not be stored for long periods, farmers needed a sizable crop each and every season. If the crop failed, farmers would be in danger of starvation. Farmers had experienced partial losses of their potatoes several times in the first three decades of the nineteenth century.[40] Since only isolated districts were affected each time, government officials did not normally take much notice. In September 1845, though, Peel and his aides were informed that the season's potato failure was of a greater magnitude than the losses of the previous years.

Peel responded swiftly to the crisis. First, he established a scientific commission to investigate the cause of the blight. Two leading English scientists, Lyon Playfair and John Lindley, were dispatched to Dublin to join an Irish scientist, Robert Kane, in an inspection of the diseased potatoes. Although unable to discover the fungus that was destroying the potatoes, they were at least able to alert Peel that half the season's harvest was going to be lost.[41]

With this dire prediction in mind, Peel decided to provide some immediate relief. He imported twenty thousand tons of American maize and oatmeal into Ireland, hoping they would substitute for the potato in farmers' diets.[42] He also established a variety of relief work projects throughout the country. James S. Donnelly Jr. estimates that 140,000 men were put to work building roads, bridges, and piers; the income from these jobs enabled them to buy maize and other necessary foods.[43]

Peel could have taken more dramatic steps, but his laissez-faire outlook restrained him. He could have stopped all food exports from Ireland; instead, large quantities of wheat, barley, oats, corn, and livestock continued to leave Irish ports. He could have banned distilling and brewing in Ireland to save grain, as O'Connell had urged him to do.[44] Finally, he could have given food away to indigent families. But since each of these measures would have violated free trade principles, Peel refused to consider them. He was convinced that Great Britain's economy needed to be freer to cope with the famine. To achieve this aim, he decided to try to dismantle the Corn Laws. Enacted in 1815 by the Tories, the Corn Laws imposed high tariffs on all grain imported into Great Britain. Farmers in England staunchly defended the laws, but city dwellers had long resented them because the duties inflated the price of bread.

In late October 1845 Peel put the question of Corn Law repeal before his cabinet and found that most of his ministers were ardent protectionists. After trying several more times without success to convince his cabinet to support him on this question, Peel decided to resign in early December. But the Liberal leader, Lord John Russell, was unable to form a government and Peel was returned to office.

Peel hadn't achieved repeal of the Corn Laws, but he had nonetheless deftly handled the worst crisis in his five-year administration. The famine had destroyed at least 40 percent of Ireland's potatoes and yet no one had died as a result. Perhaps emboldened by his success, Peel would press again in 1846 for repeal of the Corn Laws, which he was confident would provide further relief for Ireland's poor.

Father Mathew wearing the temperance medal, c. 1850. Library of Congress.

Temperance soirée in Cork, 1840. *Illustrated London News,* February 1840. Brown University Library.

Opposite: Police circular investigating Mathew and the temperance movement, 1840. National Archives, Dublin.

CIRCULAR.

CONSTABULARY OFFICE, DUBLIN CASTLE,
12th March, 1840.

[STRICTLY CONFIDENTIAL.]

WITH a view to receive as much information as possible on the subject of the present movement of masses of the people in certain parts of the Country, in favor of Temperance, as encouraged by the Rev. Mr. MATHEW, I request you will send me, at your earliest convenience, detailed and unreserved answers to the following Queries—on the understanding that whatever use may be made of the information itself, the sources from whence it proceeds shall not be made public.

1. State the period of the Rev. Mr. MATHEW's visit to your District. *Have not yet visited.*
2. The probable proportion of Protestants to Roman Catholics in your District. *1 Protestant to 120 Catholics.*
3. The total number of Persons who have taken the Temperance pledge, and what proportion of this number are Protestants. *Over 600 Catholics and only 1 nominal Protestant.*
4. Whether any, and what number of Women, or of Men above those of the Working Class have taken the pledge. *About 12 Women about 30 Men.*
5. Whether the Society is supposed to have any particular Religious or Political object or bearing, and what that is. *It has — all Catholic.*
6. Whether any who have taken the pledge have since violated it, and in what numbers. *2 Women only.*
7. Whether those in general who have taken the pledge were formerly of sober or intemperate habits, and what is the feeling of those who have refused the pledge towards those who have taken it. *The greater number intemperate, a good [few]*
8. Is it true or false, that numbers of the People take the pledge in a state of intoxication, or at least get drunk after determining to take it? *It is true, that several has got Drunk.*
9. Does the taking of the pledge appear to be associated with superstitious feelings, in many instances;—such as the expectation of immediate manifestations of the Divine judgment, in the event of violating it, &c.? *It does. Yes.*
10. What influence has the pledge had on the general conduct of the People, especially at Fairs, Races, and on similar occasions? *It has made them sober. And they seldom fight.*
11. How many Public Houses have been closed since the introduction of the Temperance pledge, or have the applications for Publicans' Licenses been sensibly diminished? *Only 2 has shut up.*
12. State the effect which the Temperance Society has produced upon crime, by enumerating the crimes committed during the six months preceding, and the corresponding period immediately after Mr. MATHEW's visit, confining your attention exclusively to crimes that have their origin in drunkenness, as homicides and other acts of violence. *I cannot say, as he has not yet visited, but every thing*
13. Are those who take the pledge bound by any rules beyond the pledge itself—are they united as a Society in which there are any thing like office bearers, who exercise a control over the members, &c., or have they any regular places or times of meeting, or do they wear any badge except the medal, and when is that worn? *They are. Yes. They have. I saw no badge, but the medal is worn at their meetings.*
14. State the number of Protestant and Roman Catholic members of the Force in your District, and the number of each persuasion who have taken the pledge. *4 Protestants. 10 Catholics. None have taken the pledge*
15. *Any and what increase of Depositors in the Savings Banks.* You will see the importance of weighing well the foregoing Queries, and of carefully concealing from *every* individual the object you have in collecting the information *Know of any, no bank being here.* that will enable you to answer them satisfactorily. I am aware of the difficulty of specifying, in several of the cases, the exact numbers, but still you may be able to approximate to the truth.

I need scarcely add, that I shall be glad to receive from you such further observations as the subject referred to may suggest.

D. M'GREGOR,

Inspector-General.

Daniel O'Connell, Lord Mayor of Dublin. Painting by C. Grey and J. Peterkin, 1842. Courtesy of the National Library of Ireland, Prints and Drawings.

Daniel O'Connell taking the pledge from Father Mathew, c. 1840. Courtesy of the National Library of Ireland, Prints and Drawings.

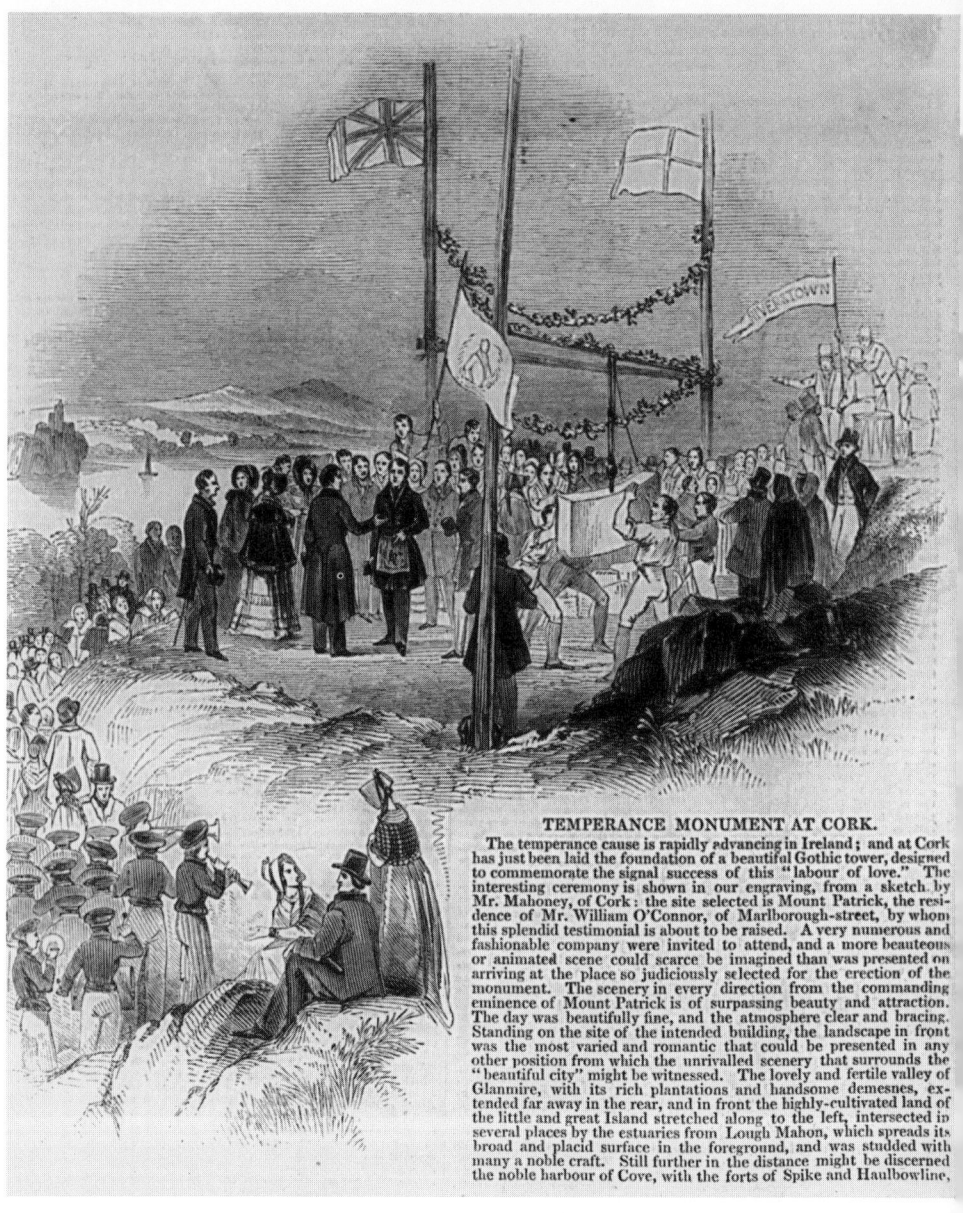

Temperance monument in Cork. From *Illustrated London News,* November 18, 1843. Brown University Library.

Frederick Douglass. From *Illustrated London News,* August 15, 1846. Brown University Library.

Father Mathew. Photograph by Matthew Brady, 1849. Library of Congress.

Sir Charles Gavan Duffy, Young Ireland leader and friend of Mathew, c. 1880. Courtesy of the National Library of Ireland, National Photographic Archive, Lawrence Collection, Royal 21539.

"Temperance: A Centennial Allegory," an engraving paying tribute to the Catholic Total Abstinence Union and Father Mathew (depicted on the left), 1876. Library of Congress.

Father Mathew statue, Fairmount Park, Philadelphia, erected 1876. Photograph by Christopher Barth, 2000.

Father James A. Cullen, S.J., founder of the Pioneer Total Abstinence Association, c. 1900. Courtesy of Maureen Manning, Pioneer Association, Dublin.

{ CHAPTER SIX }

The Famine Years, 1846–1849

> *God alone can effectively rescue from famine and death a whole population destitute of food and money . . . The Lord has sent another messenger of His wrath amongst us. Pestilence is increasing in our country and the living are scarcely able to bury the dead. We are overwhelmed by the magnitude of the calamity that has afflicted us. . . . Pray for us . . . that the Lord may speedily stay His chastening hand.*
>
> Father Mathew, writing to the Reverend Dr. Martin Spalding, May 1, 1847

From 1846 until Mathew's departure for the United States three years later, the teetotal movement was beset by crises. Financial difficulties would continue to plague Mathew, and his health would start to deteriorate in April 1848, forcing him to cut back on his work on behalf of temperance. In addition to these personal problems, Mathew had to struggle with external difficulties. Several members of the hierarchy remained hostile to him and undermined him at critical junctures. Most damaging, however, was the onset of the Famine, which had first hit parts of Ireland in the autumn of 1845 and would recur with devastating force from 1846 through 1849. The Famine would deal the temperance movement a blow from which it would never fully recover.

Corn Law Repeal

Peel once again took up the issue of the Corn Laws in the spring of 1846. Aware that many members of his own party were adamantly opposed to the repeal of these laws, Peel reached out to the opposition party for support. By May he had drawn together a fragile coalition of Whigs, Tories, Radicals, and Irish Repealers willing to support his plan. Over the strenuous opposition of Lord George Bentinck, Benjamin Disraeli, and a majority of the Tory rank and file, Peel's free trade proposal passed the Parliament. The victory proved costly to Peel, however, as dozens of infuriated protectionist Tories, led by Disraeli, joined with Whigs to unseat him a month later. Although Daniel O'Connell had supported Peel on the question of the Corn Laws, he was only too happy to join forces with Disraeli against his old archrival.[1]

Peel's replacement was Lord John Russell, the Whig leader. A friend of O'Connell, Russell had long promoted reforms for Ireland and had several new measures in mind when he took office. At the same time, Russell was an even more dogmatic proponent of laissez-faire principles than Peel. As such, he was skeptical about Peel's public works programs and grain purchases. On the issue of Famine relief, Russell would allow himself to be guided by Charles Trevelyan, the permanent head of the Treasury. Able and hardworking, Trevelyan was utterly committed to both evangelical Protestantism and unfettered capitalism.[2] It was Trevelyan's view that if the potato crop were to fail again, the government should not intervene in any substantial way. Purchases of Indian corn should be reduced and the public works should be scaled back. Instead, private enterprise should generally be relied on to solve the problems.

Nationalist Schism

With the Whigs back in power, O'Connell abandoned his Repeal agitation. Since his campaign had been stalled for the past two years, O'Connell must not have thought he was giving up much by jettisoning it in favor of cooperation with the Russell administration. Russell, for his part, was proving amenable to appointing Irishmen—some of whom were nationalists, some of whom were Catholics—to key legal and political offices. In the view of Young Ireland militants, however, O'Connell was selling out the nationalist cause.

In early July, O'Connell presided over a tense meeting of the Repeal Association in Dublin. The rank and file sided with him overwhelmingly when he declared that the association would continue to press for Repeal but only by "peaceable, legal and constitutional means, to the utter exclusion of any other." This caveat was clearly directed at the Young Irelanders, who were not wedded to nonviolence. Assuming that the issue was settled, O'Connell returned to London to attend to his parliamentary duties.[3]

Two weeks later, the Repeal Association met again with O'Connell's son John in the chair. When Thomas Francis Meagher, a twenty-three-year-old Young Ireland firebrand, tried to deliver a speech defending revolutionary nationalism, he was twice silenced by O'Connell for advocating violence.[4] In response, Smith O'Brien, Charles Gavan Duffy, Meagher, and several other Young Ireland leaders walked out of the meeting. The split that had been looming for more than a year had finally come. Six months later, the Young Irelanders formed their own organization, the Irish Confederation, to promote a more radical nationalist alternative to the Repeal Association.[5]

Mathew Seeks English Money

Mathew was certainly aware of the political struggles going on around him in 1846, but as always he tried to remain above the fray and instead devoted his energies to raising money for himself. In January 1846 he decided to hire an agent, Major John Russell, to raise money for him in England. Since the Famine had struck his homeland, Mathew did not feel he could seek funds for his cause in Ireland. He provided Russell with a list of names of wealthy business owners and nobles to contact in London. One man he did not want Major Russell to contact was O'Connell, who was spending much of his time in London. Mathew was concerned lest his well-heeled English benefactors might think that his movement had ties to O'Connell and the Repeal Association:

> You have it in your power to disabuse [the English nobility] . . . of the false idea, that Mr. O'Connell had the most distant connection with the Total Abstinence Society. He never pledged himself to the observance of our rules, and he never observed them. To gain the support of the teetotallers he boasted of being a member and even walked in one [of] our Processions wearing a medal. It required my utmost efforts to exclude his agitation from our halls, and it was in a spirit of opposition [that] he established Repeal Reading Rooms. It was he who caused the failure of the Mathew Testimonial Subscription. . . . To avoid any connexion with him, I was obliged to give up the Procession of last Easter Monday, twelve months. The Repeal agitation damaged our cause very much for the principal collectors and contributors to the Rent were Distillers, Brewers, Publicans, [etc.] and we were sacrificed. The Repeal press is hostile or at least indifferent to the progress of temperance as you are aware.[6]

Anxiety about money did not prevent Mathew from traveling widely. Father Augustine notes that in January alone Mathew visited Limerick, Ennis, Galway, Kilkenny, and a number of smaller towns; in March he toured County Kerry and visited Lorrha in County Tipperary.[7] Although pledge breaking and alcohol consumption were on the rise, Mathew could still turn out large crowds.[8] According to the *Tipperary Vindicator*, at Lorrha, "The large open space . . . was literally thronged. The spacious parish Chapel, in which the pledge was administered, was also densely crowded." In April a temperance parade was again held in Cork on Easter Monday, and between fifty thousand and sixty thousand people reportedly took part.[9]

In May Mathew spoke to a group in Cork in characteristically confident tones: "I rose this morning before six o'clock, walked through the principal streets of the city, and I am proud to say that I did not see a single drunken person. Neither did I during the day nor in the evening. This is a fact of which we may feel proud when we remember that . . . Sunday was, not many years since, a day devoted to riot and dissipation, to all kinds of profanation of the Lord's Day."[10]

The summer brought discouraging news from Major Russell. In April a committee had been formed to raise an annuity for Mathew. The organizers—Lord Landsdowne, Lord Russell, S. C. Hall, and W. W. Simpson—had hoped to collect enough money to furnish Mathew with at least five hundred pounds per year.[11] Although several hundred pounds—perhaps one thousand—were collected over a three-month period, Lord Landsdowne concluded that the committee was not getting anywhere near its goal. After consulting with Major John Russell, he suggested to Lord John Russell that the British government provide Mathew with a pension. Various notables received pensions honoring them for their contributions to British society, including Prince Albert, who was awarded thirty thousand pounds annually, and Alfred Tennyson, whose poems had gained him three hundred pounds per year. Lord Russell agreed to the proposal and promptly set to work arranging a one hundred pound pension for Mathew. When Queen Victoria learned of Russell's plan, she immediately wrote to him expressing her dissatisfaction: "[A pension for] Father Mathew [is] a doubtful proceeding. It is true that he has done much good by preaching temperance, but by the aid of superstition, which can hardly be patronised by the Crown."[12]

The queen's opposition to the pension may have disconcerted Lord Russell, but the real obstacle proved to be Mathew himself. He sent the prime minister a polite letter saying that he did not feel it would be appropriate for him to accept aid of this sort. To Major John Russell, Mathew was more forthright: "The pension I do not take into consideration, as I could have obtained a much larger one before now, but I declined it from an apprehension of weakening my influence with the people. I would prefer remaining quietly in Cork, to the degradation of a paltry pension, totally inadequate to meet my unavoidable expenditure."[13]

Major Russell then remonstrated with Mathew to reconsider the prime minister's offer. He believed that the government pension could be combined with monies raised for the Annuity Fund to give Mathew an adequate annual income. Mathew angrily dismissed the suggestion: "You labour under a delusion for the sum proposed by Lord John Russell was not £500 or £300, but £100 a year. This would be indeed a ridiculous, a contemptible termination of my Mission. When in despair of pecuniary funds to enable me to continue my labours, I said I would accept aid from the Government, I had not the most distant idea that you would have solicited a pension for me, without having previously consulted me . . . I would sooner take a staff in my hands and walk through the country than degrade the Temperance Society by the acceptance of such a petty pittance. . . . As to the idea of procuring subscriptions to increase the annuity to £800 a year, do not for an instant harbor it, not £1 would be given to a pensioner."[14]

The Famine Returns

In the late summer of 1846 Lord Russell was informed that a potato blight was once again striking, and this time all over Ireland, destroying virtually the entire crop. Apprised of the scope of the failure, Russell decided to follow Trevelyan's plan: the government would intervene as little as possible. Some Indian corn would be purchased, but not as much as had been bought by Peel. Public works would be allowed to continue, provided that the Irish landlords, whom Russell considered lazy and prodigal, shouldered most of the expenses.[15]

O' Connell immediately started writing to his friend to inform him of the gravity of the situation; in August he sent Russell a note couched in deferential language but underscoring

> the frightful state of Famine, by which the people of that County [Cork] are, not merely menaced, but actually engulfed. . . . I respectfully submit that the forms of the law . . . must yield to the pressure of a death-dealing famine. And I submit whether her Majesty's Government may not feel, at such an awful crisis, it right whether Parliament might not . . . confer upon the Government extraordinary powers of directing, *without any delay*, the execution of works of public utility and of supplying the immediate means of paying the wages of the labourers employed in such works. Nothing but the fearful state of my county could justify me in this urgency. Whilst I feel convinced that due attention will be paid to the merits (if any they have) of my suggestions.[16]

At about the same time Mathew sent his first letter to Trevelyan, describing the severity of the potato failure:

> Divine Providence, in its inscrutable ways, has again poured out upon us the vial of its wrath. A blast more destructive than the simoon of the desert has passed over the land, the hopes of the poor potato cultivators are totally blighted, and the food of a whole nation has perished. On the 27th of last month I passed from Cork to Dublin, and this doomed plant bloomed in all the luxuriance of an abundant harvest. Returning on the 3rd instant, I beheld, with sorrow, one wide waste of putrefying vegetation. In many places the wretched people were seated on the fences of their decaying gardens, wringing their hands, and wailing bitterly the destruction that had left them foodless. It is not to harrow your feelings, dear Mr. Trevelyan, I tell this tale of woe, but to excite your sympathy on behalf of our miserable peasantry.[17]

In August Mathew set up a soup kitchen in Cork and began corresponding with philanthropists in England and the United States, telling them what was needed. A number of individuals and organizations sent money to Mathew to distribute as he saw fit. Although willing to accept money, Mathew preferred donations of food because market prices for grain in Cork had become so inflated that bread and other staples had become extremely expensive. Even Indian corn, always the cheapest food available, had jumped in price.[18] To Archbishop J. B. Purcell of Cincinnati, Mathew wrote, "One thousand pounds sent in food would do more good than three thousand in money."[19]

In late August he wrote again to Trevelyan, urging him to have Indian corn shipped to Ireland: "The country is in an awful position, and no one can tell what the result will be. For the sake of our common humanity, I anxiously hope that Her Majesty's Government will adopt the wise precaution of providing as large a supply as possible of Indian corn, to protect the wretched people against famine and pestilence." In September he wrote a long letter to Trevelyan in which he gave a frank evaluation of the condition of the Irish people:

> I have been during the last four weeks, in many parts of the Kingdom, and I found everywhere the population in a state of sullen desperation. The recent, I may call it, abandonment of the Repeal agitation by Mr. O'Connell has produced this state of mind, much more than the potato blight. The people were elated, with false hopes, of, I dare not say what, and now are utterly confounded on finding themselves disappointed. The men . . . who were accustomed to take a lead in the Repeal movement, acting as Wardens, etc, now seek to continue their occupation by exciting to tumult the poor stricken people. Hence the riots that have lately occurred. The measures of the government to provide remunerative employment are above all praise, . . . but no rate of wages will save the people from extreme distress, unless the price of provisions, will be kept down. . . . Our people are as harmless . . . as flocks of sheep, unless when inflamed and maddened by intoxicating drink. . . . Were it not for the temperate habits of the greater portion of the people of Ireland, our unhappy country would be before now one scene of tumult and bloodshed. Thank God temperance is now based on such a firm foundation, nothing can weaken its stability! Intemperance, with the Divine assistance, will never again be the national sin of the Irish people.[20]

Despite these letters, Trevelyan did not become alarmed about conditions in Ireland. Like Mathew, he saw the hand of God at work in the Famine, but rather than viewing the Famine as an expression of God's judgment, Trevelyan saw it as a gift of sorts from God. Writing to the Irish nobleman Lord Monteagle in October, he declared, "I hope I am not guilty of irreverence in thinking that, this being altogether beyond the power of man, the cure has been applied by an all wise Providence in a manner as unexpected and unthought of as it is likely to be effectual. God grant that we may rightly perform our part and not turn into a curse what was intended for a blessing."[21] He saw the Famine as a means of modernizing Ireland's economy and freeing farmers from their dependence on potatoes and irresponsible Irish landlords.[22]

Mathew, too, felt that the Irish people had to turn to sources other than potatoes for their livelihoods. He began corresponding with James McAdam of the Belfast Flax Cultivation Society to see if flax could be grown in large quantities in southern Ireland. Bluntly he declared to McAdam, "The potatoe must be abandoned and flax would prove a much more profitable crop." At the same time, he recognized that if flax were to be extensively cultivated, mills would have to be built throughout southern Ireland and the people would have to be taught how to raise the crop. Perhaps because of the expense involved, Mathew's scheme was never tested. A few farms, his brother's among them, tried growing flax, but it was never attempted on a large scale.[23]

As winter approached, the condition of much of the peasantry became desperate.[24] Mathew, increasingly alarmed, started writing to Trevelyan and other government officials with greater frequency. In November he informed Trevelyan of the problems associated with the public works projects: "When these . . . works are commenced, public houses are immediately found, the magistrates with culpable facility, granting licenses. The overseers and pay clerks had their offices in these pestiferous erections, some of these officers have a pecuniary interest in these establishments. It often happens that the entire body of labourers, after receiving payment, instead of buying provisions for their famishing families, consume the greater part in the purchase of intoxication drink." Both Cormac Ó'Gráda and Cecil Woodham-Smith confirm Mathew's charge. They note that taverns were often established adjacent to public works projects and the workers' minimal wages were often disbursed in pubs.[25]

By December 1846, thousands were starting to die of starvation, and many more, weakened by malnourishment, were contracting typhus, dysentery, and scurvy.[26] Shortly before Christmas, Mathew again wrote to Trevelyan to inform him of the grim conditions prevailing in Cork: "*Men, women and children are gradually wasting away. They fill their stomachs with cabbage leaves, turnip tops and the like to appease the cravings of hunger.* At this moment, there are more than five thousand half-starved wretched beings, from the country, begging in the streets of Cork. *When utterly exhausted, they crawl to the workhouse to die.*" O'Connell, too, tried to impress on the government the desperate plight of the Irish people. Although his health was failing and his feud with the Young Irelanders weighed heavily on him, O'Connell tried to mobilize the Repeal Association to press for famine relief. At a meeting of the association in Dublin in December, he criticized the Russell administration for its unwillingness to intervene and called on the Irish of all classes to come together and lobby for more assistance from London.[27]

Father John Spratt: Mathew's "Worthy Coadjutor" or Rival?

The Famine certainly sapped the strength of the temperance movement in 1846–47. The historian Mary Daly argues that its impact must be viewed as "roughly akin to major wars or other natural disasters."[28] With the Famine raging, many Irish lost interest in teetotalism and focused instead on simply staying alive. The Famine, however, was not the only difficulty Mathew faced in 1846–47. Internal squabbles were again weakening the movement. In the fall of 1846 he quarreled with another key temperance leader and erstwhile friend, Father John Spratt, a Dublin-based Carmelite friar.[29] Many temperance activists believed that Spratt would take over the leadership of the movement from Mathew at some point; in newspapers he was often described as Mathew's "worthy coadjutor."[30]

Spratt had angered Mathew by holding a temperance rally at Finglas, a suburb north of Dublin, on the same day that Mathew was in Dublin promoting temperance. Spratt explained that his meeting had already been advertised before he had been notified of Mathew's appearance, so he felt obliged to hold it. Mathew did not agree and began to suspect that Spratt was interested in challenging him for control of the movement. Writing to his friend Patrick Duff, Mathew revealed his deep disappointment with Spratt: "I never would have believed that the V. Rev. Dr. Spratt could have acted with so much discourtesy towards me. It is now manifest that he has other objects, besides the promotion of teetotalism. A rival meeting at Finglas could only gratify our most violent opponents."[31]

In September Spratt traveled to Dundalk in County Louth without first getting the approval of the local bishop or the parish priest. Mathew, who made it a practice to visit only towns where the parish priest was a teetotal sympathizer, was disturbed that his "coadjutor" would behave in such a fashion. He decided to write a public letter to the pastor in Dundalk disavowing Spratt's actions. He explained his rationale to Duff: "I considered his visit to Dundalk . . . a violation of ecclesiastical discipline and dangerous to the faith of the people by raising altar against altar. . . . He has taught the Catholic people . . . that they can do without their pastors. [He] was well aware of the strictures with which I adhered to the rule of not holding a temperance meeting in any parish, unless expressly invited by the Parish Priest. He also knew that it was this motive of propriety that prevented me from going to Dundalk, Belfast, Londonderry, Loughall, Armagh, etc."[32]

James Haughton, no doubt still bristling from his own tangle with Mathew, rebuked him for his treatment of Spratt: "I have read with surprise and sorrow, and indeed with other feelings which I shall not characterize, a letter in a Dundalk newspaper, signed with your name . . . in which you say 'I have no connexion with the proceedings of Dr. Spratt, and the gentlemen with whom he acts'. . . . You repudiate a connexion with the only clergyman, may I not say in all Ireland, who has given his heart to the cause you support. . . . You should rejoice and thank God for having such a coadjutor as Father Spratt. It would be well indeed that we had such a man in every parish in Ireland."[33]

Haughton was certainly correct in describing Spratt as Mathew's most loyal clerical supporter. In 1844, Spratt had contacted the Dublin newspapers telling them that Mathew wanted all monies sent directly to Cork rather than to Haughton's relief committee. At the same time, Mathew had his differences with Spratt and probably had entertained doubts about him before this point, for Spratt was a committed Repealer who regularly appeared at meetings with Daniel O'Connell and his son Maurice. At one of Spratt's temperance rallies in 1844, Martin Brennan, a Repealer, fused temperance and Irish nationalism in classic O'Connellite fashion: "[Irishmen] must . . . put on the armour of sobriety, and then will heaven back their efforts, and Erin will stand redeemed, emancipated and disenthralled by the irresistible influence of teetotalism." Brennan's fiery rhetoric so alienated Peter Purcell that he wrote to Mathew complaining about it. While surely disturbed by the report, Mathew was not about to upbraid Spratt at this point. Replying to Purcell, he explained his inaction by saying that his position was "one of great difficulty."[34]

Although Mathew was troubled by Spratt's open advocacy of Repeal, he was probably more worried that Spratt threatened his leadership of the movement. Since taking the pledge in 1838, Mathew had consistently worked by himself and never made any attempt to draw other priests into the movement to assist him. This was not an oversight: Mathew believed that he was to be the sole instrument of the temperance reformation. In 1842 he admitted as much to his friend Tobias Kirby: "Do not, my dear Mr. Kirby, consider me guilty of vanity, when I [declare that] all . . . [Irish teetotalers] have taken the Pledge from me. In fact the people do not look upon themselves as Teetotallers unless they have received my blessing."[35] Statements such as these suggest that Mathew may have been vain—or perhaps even beset to some degree by a messianic complex. On the other hand, as Kerrigan notes, he may very well have believed that it was God's plan that he should singlehandedly direct the movement.[36] Whatever the explanation, he was not interested in a coadjutor, especially not one with Repeal sympathies. Spratt's missteps in 1846 gave Mathew justification for separating himself from his "worthy coadjutor."

The Liberator's Last Days

During the winter of 1846 O'Connell's health had deteriorated to such a degree that he wasn't sure whether he would be able to return to England. At the end of January 1847 he decided to go to London to make one last speech warning the Russell administration about the magnitude of the Famine. The reports from O'Connell, Mathew, and other Irish leaders must have made some impression on Russell, because in January he decided to replace the public works projects and inadequate Indian corn purchases with direct relief. The harsh weather had made it hard for the men to get to the work sites and the limited supply of Indian corn had left food prices out of reach for many Irish. He followed the example of Mathew and the Quakers and ordered soup kitchens to be established in all distressed areas of Ireland.[37] Although there were seemingly endless delays in getting them set up, by the summer of 1847 the soup kitchens were providing free food for 3 million Irish people.[38] Agreeing to establish soup kitchens was a dramatic step for such a laissez-faire advocate as Russell. When Irish representatives first came to inform him about the Famine in the late summer of 1846, Russell would listen to their accounts and then read aloud to them chapters from Adam Smith's *Wealth of Nations*.[39]

Although O'Connell was hopeful that the soup kitchens would give relief to many of the starving Irish, he felt that much more needed to be done. On February 8, he mustered almost all of his remaining strength and spoke before the House of Commons. With trembling hands and a quivering voice, he warned his colleagues that the Irish people were "starving in shoals, in hundreds—aye, in thousands and millions. . . . Ireland is in your hands. . . . She is in your power. . . . If you do not save her she can't save herself. And I solemnly call on you to recollect that I predict with the sincerest conviction that one quarter of her population will perish unless you come to her relief."[40]

After giving his speech, O'Connell wanted to return to Ireland, but his doctors prevailed on him to travel to the warmer climes of southern Europe. O'Connell heeded their advice and set off in March on a pilgrimage to Rome in hopes of meeting the newly elected Pius IX. Accompanied by his son Daniel, a servant, and a chaplain, Father John Miley, O'Connell decided to go in stages to Rome. At the end of March they arrived in Paris, where O'Connell was called on and fêted by the archbishop of Paris and other church leaders. By the beginning of May they had reached Marseilles, and from there they set sail for Genoa. By this time, though, he was physically broken and mentally tormented by scruples; he could go no farther. When it became apparent to him that he was not going to make it to the Papal States, he asked that his heart be sent on to Rome and the rest of his body be shipped back to Ireland. His wishes were followed; his heart was encased in a silver urn and sent on to the pope.[41]

Mathew before Parliament

In the winter and spring of 1847 Mathew spent almost all of his time in Cork, trying to assist the Famine victims. In his free time he continued writing to people in England and America whom he thought could be of help. He sent a grim letter to Mrs. S. C. Hall, a wealthy Irish Protestant friend who resided in England: "This has been a sorrowful Christmas to all here who have bodies to suffer or hearts to sympathize. . . . The evils under which we suffer are grievously aggravated by the high price of the bread stuffs. No wages a poor operative can earn are sufficient to purchase an adequate supply of food for his generally large family. They hardly suffice to afford food of the cheapest kind to himself, leaving his wretched wife, children and aged parents to fill their stomachs with the offals of the vegetable gardens. O Great Father of all what spectacles do we not daily behold in all parts of this wretched Kingdom."[42]

He wrote again to Trevelyan, thanking him for establishing soup kitchens but reminding him that the people of Cork were still in desperate straits: "You have done, all that could be done, to alleviate the calamity with which it has pleased the Lord to visit the Irish Nation. You'll pardon me for saying that I am more sanguine in my hopes of a . . . cheap supply of food than you appear to be. America . . . is coming to help us not with contributions but in breadstuffs. The soup kitchens are affording very great relief, and have lightened in an unexpected degree the pressure upon the corn and flax markets. We are in a deplorable state in Cork, from the influx into the city of more than ten thousand foodless, houseless people, young and old, from the several counties around us. I am in a horror whilst I walk the streets and return to my besieged dwelling in sadness and hopelessness." At the end of his letter Mathew offered some advice regarding the soup kitchens: "It should be incumbent on Soup Committees to introduce flesh meat, fish and milk into their soup otherwise it will not be fit food. The multitudinous deaths in the workhouses, especially amongst children is to be attributed to the want of animal food."[43]

At the end of March, Mathew notified Trevelyan that "corn-laden vessels" were en route to Ireland. In his letter he also applauded the administration's decision to allow rum to be imported cheaply into Ireland. He had been a voluntarist ever since he had joined the temperance movement, and the Famine hadn't changed his perspective. He reasoned that Russell's Distillery Act would "save an incalculable quantity of homegrown corn from destruction. This simple act will accomplish more good, than hundreds of laws, prohibiting distillation for grain could ever effect. The more numerous and stringent such enactments, the more would private distillation and smuggling increase."[44]

The American aid that Mathew had long been anticipating arrived in April. A group of Protestant philanthropists and reformers, including William Lloyd Garrison, had raised a substantial sum of money and outfitted the USS *Jamestown* with provisions.[45] Setting sail from Boston, the *Jamestown* arrived in Cork carrying eight thousand barrels of wheat, corn, ham, beans, bread, and peas.[46] This was just what Mathew wanted; he could now flood the market with cheap wheat, which would force down the prices of other foodstuffs as well. The ship's captain, Robert Forbes, asked for a tour of the city so that he could see for himself what state the people were in. Mathew obliged and proceeded to lead him around Cork's poorest neighborhoods: "I went with Father Mathew, only a few steps out of one of the principal streets of Cork, into a lane; the valley of the *shadow of death* was it? alas, no, it was the valley of death and pestilence itself! I saw enough in five minutes, to horrify me—hovels crowded with the sick and dying, without floors, without furniture . . . some called for water to Father Mathew, and others for a dying blessing." When they stopped by one house, they discovered seventeen people lying on the floor, afflicted with famine fever. Although Mathew had them rushed to a hospital, none survived.[47]

In June Mathew was asked to testify before a parliamentary committee chaired by Lord Monteagle that was investigating the Famine. The committee members, especially Monteagle, were interested in emigration and thought perhaps that as a way of dealing with the crisis, the government should assist or even promote emigration, for example, by paying for people's passages. The Irish people had already begun leaving in droves, boarding often unseaworthy and overcrowded vessels bound for America, Canada, England, and Australia, in the summer of 1846. The hardier ones continued to leave by the thousands in the winter, when transatlantic journeys were especially hazardous. In 1846, 106,000 had emigrated; in 1847 the number rose to 215,000; and by the time the Famine was over, the total number would exceed 1 million.[48]

Mathew eagerly accepted the invitation to address the committee.[49] For months he had been trying to tell anyone who would listen about the plight of the people of southwestern Ireland. At the hearings he furnished some statistics on Cork: twenty thousand destitute people from the surrounding villages were then in Cork, seeking relief. Seven soup kitchens were operational, and his was feeding between three thousand and four thousand people each day. Six thousand people had already been interred in his free cemetery, and each day sixty to seventy more paupers were brought there.[50]

When asked about emigration, Mathew acknowledged that many of the Irish poor were anxious to leave and that he had received a number of upbeat letters—some with money enclosed—from Irishmen and Irishwomen in America. Still, like many of his fellow priests, Mathew was of two minds on the subject. He hated to see so many people leave their homeland forever. Instead he hoped that new jobs could be found for them, growing flax or fishing, to free them from their dependence on the potato. Although he was ambivalent about emigration, he was convinced that the government should not get involved in it by paying for people's voyages to other countries. As far as he was concerned, the less part the government played in the process, the better.[51]

Mathew's "Well-Earned Tribute"

As the Famine continued to ravage Ireland, Mathew became increasingly pessimistic about his own financial prospects. In the spring of 1847 he reconsidered the previous year's pension scheme and asked Lord Russell if a larger grant could be arranged. In June, Russell offered him a pension of three hundred pounds. This was still considerably less than Mathew had hoped for, but, desperate for money, he accepted it. This proved to be a fateful decision. The London *Times* deemed the pension a "well-earned tribute" for a "pious and good man," but most Irish weren't nearly as approving.[52] Mathew was accepting money from the British in the midst of the Famine, when anti-English sentiments were at an unprecedented high. For years Mathew had striven to present himself as a man without any political affiliations, but in the eyes of many Irish people, he was showing himself to be a British ally.[53]

Mathew's decision must have been especially irksome to many of his fellow priests, who for years had been strenuously resisting government proposals to put the parish clergy on the English payroll. According to Father Donal Kerr, state payment of the clergy had first been broached in 1782, and in 1799 and 1825 it was proposed by government officials in return for Catholic Emancipation.⁵⁴ By the 1830s, most clergy were adamantly opposed to state payment, fearing it would lessen their standing with the Irish people. When Alexis de Tocqueville visited Ireland in 1835, he found that the clergy wanted no part of the government's largess. In 1837 Bishop William Higgins informed Pope Gregory XVI that he and all his brother bishops would "beg [their] bread throughout any diocese rather than ever receive a pension." Despite widespread opposition from both Catholics and English Protestants, who had no interest in subsidizing popery, Lord Russell informed the members of the House of Commons of his support for it in July 1846. Kerr claims that state payment of the clergy was the cornerstone of Russell's program for Ireland.⁵⁵ By accepting a pension, Mathew may have encouraged Russell to press on with his state payment scheme, which he would bring up again in 1848.

It appears that Mathew immediately recognized the fallout from his decision. In his view, Major Russell was to blame. Russell had been instructed to raise subscriptions for an annuity; nothing had been said about a pension. It seems that Russell also sought more money for his services than Mathew had anticipated. In June Mathew sent him a curt note, informing him that his services were no longer needed: "I deeply regret my total inability to comply with your request. All my resources are exhausted. There is not £1 in my house, and as you are well aware, any fund upon which to draw for a fresh supply. Since your return from London I have, at great inconvenience given you a larger sum than you, at first, said was due. . . . I consider this letter final."⁵⁶

A Miter for Mathew?

In the midst of all these troubles, Mathew and the temperance movement received a sudden boost in May 1847. The parish priests of the Cork diocese held a meeting to elect a successor to the late bishop, John Murphy, and they put Mathew at the top of their list of candidates.⁵⁷ Three days later, twenty-three priests who were ineligible to participate in the election sent Mathew a letter endorsing the parish priests' decision. This was just the expression of confidence that Mathew and the temperance movement needed. Congratulatory letters poured in to Cork. Father James Quinlivan wrote from Cambridge, England, to tell him of the "joy I experienced at seeing your name stand at the head of the 'trio,' or dignissimus of those sent to Rome." Father Augustine described the election as the "crowning honour of Father Mathew's life, and the most signal testimony that could be paid to his worth."⁵⁸

After the parish priests' election, the bishops of the province convened to offer recommendations to Rome on the relative merits of the three candidates. At this meeting they took an unusual step: the archbishop of Cashel, Michael Slattery, and a majority of the other bishops sent Rome a letter asking that Father William Delany, the second choice on the *terna*, be appointed bishop in lieu of Mathew. In a letter to Cullen, Slattery contended that if Mathew were appointed, the independence of the hierarchy might be jeopardized. As a nationalist, Slattery would have felt that the pension tied Mathew too closely to the British government.⁵⁹ Bishop Higgins also wrote to Cullen on the Cork appointment, even though his diocese was not in the Cashel province. Higgins expressed the same criticisms of Mathew, except he was not nearly as circumspect as Slattery: "How will we persuade the poor people that a pension can be bad when Dr-Fr Mathew, with the Cork crozier in one hand, receives his government bribe with the other! He will be in all the secrets of the ministry—will be a check and a spy in our deliberations . . . [S]hould he be appointed I must look upon the event in conjunction with all my episcopal friends as a national disgrace and a national calamity." Recognizing that some bishops were hostile to him, Mathew sent one of his Capuchin confreres, Father Denis McLeod, to Rome to plead his case before Cullen. He armed McLeod with the following urgent plea: "[The appointment] is a case of life or death for me and for the Temperance cause in Ireland. After being honoured with the unsolicited suffrages of my very Rev'd and Rev'd brethren, the pastors of this Diocese, it would degrade me in the eyes of the whole world if I were set aside. This is my sole motive for sending the Rev'd Denis F. McLeod to Rome. . . . He is perfectly well acquainted with everything respecting my public and private conduct. . . . The information you will receive from the Rev'd Mr. McLeod will enable you to vindicate me and the Temperance movement."⁶⁰

Cullen must have had a difficult decision to make. He knew Mathew well and liked him, but Mathew's willingness to accept a British pension would certainly have rankled his nationalist sensibilities. In the end,

Cullen sided with Slattery and the other Cashel bishops. Father Delany was appointed bishop of Cork in July and consecrated in August.[61]

Being denied the bishopric after having been nominated by the parish clergy certainly was a grave disappointment for Mathew, and since the parish priests' election had been well publicized in the newspapers, his embarrassment was all the greater.[62] When questioned about the affair, he generally claimed that it was all for the best that he was not appointed bishop. Writing to Sister Basil Lonergan, an Ursuline nun, he affected nonchalance: "Do not take to heart the announcement from Rome, it has not come upon me by surprise . . . I feel lighthearted and happy to be sacrificed for the sacred cause of temperance. The Archbishop [Slattery] expressly declared in his letter to Rome that it was this motive that influenced the Prelates."[63]

When writing to Cullen, Mathew was considerably more candid. He sent a long letter that severely criticized Slattery and was implicitly critical of Cullen for following Slattery's recommendation:

> His Grace says I am not as good a Theologian as Dr. Delany. I have no hesitation in asserting that I am, and have also made Canon Law my particular study. My knowledge and observance of ecclesiastical discipline are well known. The clergy can bear testimony of my labours as a missionary, though his Grace states my inexperience in this respect as one of his objections. He accuses me of imprudence in the management of temporal affairs. I am not, it is true, a lover of money. I have shut up my gold and silver in the bowels of the poor. . . . His Grace also states that my nomination would not be pleasing to the great body of the clergy. The contrary is the fact. In speaking of me his Grace has not enumerated my labours for three and thirty years for the glory of the great God, the exaltation of the Holy Church and the salvation of souls. His Grace . . . principally objected to my appointment on the grounds that it would be an approval by the Holy See of the Temperance movement in Ireland. But the setting of me aside by the Holy See is a public disapproval of my exertions in this sacred cause . . . I am crushed. I am actually annihilated by this decision. . . . I am degraded forever, having been dignissimus on the list and set aside.

He concluded his letter with a plea that Cullen obtain some "mark of approbation" from the pope to show that he had no misgivings about the temperance campaign.[64]

With a few of his friends Mathew was even blunter about the treatment he had received from his former friend Slattery. Writing to Maurice Lenihan, a journalist and teetotaler, he bitterly recounted the actions taken by Slattery and the other bishops:

> You are aware of the manner in which I have been treated by your bishop Dr. Kennedy who came to Cork breathing vengeance against me, and by the Archbishop and the new bishop of Cloyne Dr. Walshe [*sic*]. The Archbishop also signed against me, and in favor of the Rev. Mr. Delany, the names of Doctor Foran and Doctor French who were absent and knew not who were the candidates. The Archbishop acted with great treachery, pretending the warmest friendship, dining at my table and then stabbing me in the dark. The principal motive assigned by the Archbishop . . . for putting me aside, was the unwillingness of the Prelates, to pronounce in favor of the Temperance movement by voting for my elevation to the episcopacy. . . . It is I trust, all for the better yet I cannot prevent myself from feeling acutely [sic] the malevolence of the Prelates.[65]

The Famine Eases?

In the summer of 1847 Irish farmers finally had some good news to report: the potatoes harvested were free of the blight. The crop was still disturbingly small, though, because many farmers had eaten their seed potatoes over the winter and had nothing left to plant.[66] After this news, Trevelyan did not concern himself with the continuing potato shortage. He took the disease-free harvest as a clear sign that the Famine had ended.[67]

Having reached that conclusion, Trevelyan and Lord Russell decided there was no need to continue operating the soup kitchens. In September the government ordered them to be closed. Henceforth, anyone needing food was to go to the local workhouses, which in most cases were overcrowded and disease-ridden. The workhouse guardians were directed to provide "outdoor relief" to the sick, the elderly, the widowed, and even the able-bodied poor. A harsh amendment was added to this Poor Law Act, however, by William Gregory, a Protestant landlord from Galway. The "Gregory clause" specified that anyone who occupied more than a quarter acre of land was ineligible for public assistance. To qualify for relief, small leaseholders would have to abandon their lands. Many farmers and their families would soon find themselves facing terrible dilemmas.⁶⁸

Although the Famine was far from over, Mathew was encouraged enough to resume his temperance work in August. At the invitation of the bishop of Derry, Edward Maginn, Mathew set off on a tour of Derry and the surrounding towns.⁶⁹ In the fall, Mathew visited Dublin, several Ulster towns, and then Waterford and had some success at each stop. He was still not traveling as extensively as he had in the early 1840s; he continued to spend some of his time on Famine relief work and he may have been obliged to reject some invitations because of his financial difficulties. Nevertheless, in the beginning of 1848, the temperance movement finally seemed to be righting itself after three years of turmoil.

In the spring Mathew began to plan a trip to the United States. He had first been invited to America in 1841 by the Young Men's Total Abstinence Society, and in April 1843 he had received a formal invitation from Francis Patrick Kenrick, the Irish-born bishop of Philadelphia, to visit his diocese and stay at his residence.⁷⁰ Kenrick had been vigorously promoting teetotalism throughout Pennsylvania since 1840. Mathew had accepted and had hoped to come in 1844, but the sectarian violence that erupted in the city that spring had convinced him to postpone his visit. The conflict, known as the "Bible Riots," had been sparked by Kenrick's request that Catholic children in the public schools be allowed to use the Douai-Rheims translation of the Bible rather than the King James Version. Rumors then spread among nativists that Kenrick and his intemperate Irish followers were trying to ban the Bible from the public schools.⁷¹ Riots had broken out in May and again in July leaving twenty dead and more than one hundred wounded.⁷² To an ardent ecumenist like Mathew, this violence among Christians was shocking. In a letter to the Reverend John Marsh, a Congregationalist minister and secretary of the American Temperance Union, Mathew expressed his sorrow and disbelief: "I have been long and anxiously looking forward to the happiness I expected to enjoy during my sojourn in the States. Recent calamitous occurrences in Philadelphia have blighted all my hopes. Why cannot the citizens of America, like the people of the Old World, contend in political strife without conflagration and bloodshed?. . . . Since I heard the fearful details from Philadelphia I can speak or write or think of nothing but churches in flames and streets flowing with blood."[73] Mathew assured Marsh, however, that he was still intent on visiting America as soon as peace was restored.

By 1845 nativism had entered into a period of dormancy in America, but with Ireland in the midst of the famine, Mathew was unwilling to travel abroad.[74] By the spring of 1848 he felt that Ireland's crisis was lifting, so he again prepared to visit America.[75] If only he could obtain funding from some wealthy supporter, he could set off on his long deferred journey. To accomplish this aim, he sent his friend, John Sheil, a teetotal physician from Donegal, to England to raise money for him. In March, Mathew told Sheil, "My entire dependence is upon your personal application to moneyed individuals. For want of means I have been obliged to postpone my voyage to the States until Autumn."[76] Sheil, like Major Russell before him, had little success; he asked two leading Catholic nobles, the earl of Shrewsbury and the earl of Arundel, for support, but both declined.

When news of Mathew's plans became public, the editors of the *Freeman's Journal* reported the story and denounced Mathew. For years, the newspaper had been strongly supportive of him and faithfully covered all of his tours. At this point, though, they decided that he was simply too close to the British government:

> We understand that the Rev. Theobald Mathew, the great Apostle of Temperance, visits America this month. We trust that the Irish in America will receive him as he deserves, *in his capacity as Temperance Apostle,* and that the reverend gentleman will not be tempted, through his unwise devotion to the British Government, to travel out of his proper province and use his high name to influence the political sentiments of the Irish whom he visits. We respect and reverence the man and his mission in Ireland and it is one of our causes of deepest regret that he should have sullied his high name by associating himself with the cause of his country's oppression. That he has done so in Ireland and England is alas too true. May an all-wise Providence guard him from committing a similar error in the free land which he is now about to visit. His visit to America ought to be solely as the Ambassador of Temperance and in nowise as the secret ambassador of the British Ministry.[77]

Mathew was unable to respond immediately to these charges, for he was "prostrate on the bed of sickness, weak in mind and body from the effects of [his] malady, *paralysis.*" Early in April he had suffered a stroke that initially left him paralyzed on the left side. After several weeks of rest, he began to recover. Though his left leg continued to trouble him, the paralysis left him, and by the summertime, he had taken up his temperance duties once again. When the American missionary Asenath Nicholson came to Cork that summer, she was pleased to see that the city was "rallying a little" from the Famine but was quite disturbed by her meeting with Mathew. He seemed to have aged considerably in the four years since their last meeting: "A palsy shook his body," and his expression now seemed shaded with a "pencil of sorrow."[78]

Despite his weakened condition, Mathew was not about to cut back on his schedule. One of his top priorities was to answer the editorial in the *Freeman's Journal*. Rather than reply to the charges directly, he wrote a letter to an American friend, Colonel J. H. Sherburne, which was later printed in various newspapers. After acknowledging that his feelings had been wounded deeply, he asserted that the only grounds for their criticism was his acceptance of the pension, which he was using to pay the premiums on a life insurance policy that he had taken out the previous year. The policy, worth six thousand pounds, would pay off all his creditors in full.[79]

The editors of the *Freeman's Journal* issued a statement explaining what had prompted their previous editorial. Admitting that Mathew was Ireland's "greatest social benefactor," the editors nonetheless felt obligated to warn Irish Americans about his political views. They saw Mathew as a pawn of the English administration and were afraid that he would promote these views in America. What they claimed to be upset about was not the pension but a letter that Mathew had written in the spring in which he praised Lord Clarendon, the lord lieutenant.[80]

Mathew let the matter drop and turned his energies to raising money for his American tour. If he could just raise a few hundred pounds, he would finally be able to reach America's shores and bring the temperance message to the hundreds of thousands of Irish who had emigrated there in the previous decade.

The Battle of the Widow McCormick's Cabbage Patch

In July 1848 Mathew's attention was abruptly drawn back to his homeland's woes. Uprisings had recently occurred in Paris, Berlin, and Vienna. In France, King Louis Philippe had been forced to abdicate; in Austria,

Prince Klemens von Metternich, the conservative foreign minister, had fled for his life. English authorities were concerned that the revolutionary fever might spread to Ireland. They had cause to worry; the ease with which France's king had been toppled certainly made an impression on Irish nationalists. John Mitchel, a radical member of the Irish Confederation, was so taken with the events in France that he began publishing a newspaper, the *United Irishman*, which openly advocated a "holy war" to free Ireland.[81]

In March Mitchel was arrested and in May was convicted of sedition by a packed jury and sent to Tasmania to serve a fourteen-year sentence. The authorities then turned their attention to Smith O'Brien's Irish Confederation and Charles Gavan Duffy's *Nation*, both of which had become increasingly strident of late. In early July the government made a preemptive strike, arresting Duffy and several of his associates. A couple weeks later, the *Nation* was shut down and Confederation clubs were banned. O'Brien, in part responding to English provocation, launched an uprising of sorts in County Tipperary on July 29. At Ballingarry he and perhaps five hundred men who were armed mostly with pikes skirmished with several policemen who had barricaded themselves inside the Widow McCormick's house. Two men were killed and several wounded. When police reinforcements arrived, the farcical affair came to an abrupt end. O'Brien's men scattered, and he and the other leaders were soon captured. When Mitchel heard about the events, he sneered at O'Brien's "poor extemporized abortion of a rising."[82]

Writing to Richard Dowden, the former mayor of Cork who was in London at the time, Mathew recounted the events: "The bubble has burst. . . . It was a strange delusion to imagine that the most powerful Government in the world could be overthrown . . . I was not mistaken, and I always asserted that the great body of the People, were not implicated. The teetotaller every where remained faithful. You can easily imagine what the position of Cork would be, were it not for this dragchain. If the people of Ireland, were as in former days, slaves to drunken habits, our greenest fields would have been deluged in blood."[83]

Over the following months Mathew watched closely as O'Brien and Duffy and the other defendants were brought to trial. He was especially concerned about Duffy, his friend and fellow teetotaler. In November,

Duffy, who dreaded the prospect of being convicted, contacted Mathew and asked him if he would be willing to appear at his trial as a character witness.[84] Although poles apart politically from Duffy, Mathew was quite willing to help: "Neither time, or distance of place, are of any importance to me, when I have the even remote prospect of being of the slightest service to you."[85] In December he went to Dublin and testified on Duffy's behalf. He said nothing about Duffy's politics, of course, but confined himself to discussing Duffy's long and active involvement in the temperance movement. Mathew's testimony, along with that of William Carleton and Michael Blake, Duffy's bishop, may very well have helped.[86] He was finally acquitted in April 1849 and took up editing the *Nation* again in September.[87]

In the spring of 1849 Mathew turned all of his remaining energies back to temperance. He was still intent on visiting America and had written to his friend Colonel Sherburne, asking for more help: "I have received, it is true, from Temperance friends in the States, and also from benevolent individuals in England, occasional remittances of money; but the last Famine devoured everything I could scrape together. I could not address assemblages of Teetotallers, with sunken eyes and hollow cheeks, on the benefits of total abstinence without supplying them with bread." With no funds forthcoming from America, Mathew decided to resume touring while waiting to see if Sheil would have any success in England. In January he visited Dublin, Limerick, and then Ennis, where, although too weak to deliver a sermon, he administered the pledge to four thousand people.[88]

By March he had learned that William Rathbone, an English Unitarian friend, was to provide him with five hundred pounds for his American trip. As he prepared for his voyage, he was comforted by the "happy conviction . . . of the prosperous position of Teetotalism in Ireland." Lord John Manners, a friend of Disraeli's who toured Ireland at this time, shared Mathew's view. During a voyage to the Skelligs, he "found Teetotalism triumphant; only one of our crew would touch a drop of the cratur, wherewith we had provided ourselves, and he seemed to lead but a sorry life, being constantly girded at by his pledged companions."[89]

Many of Mathew's followers had remained faithful through the Famine, but the movement had nevertheless lost ground. In 1848 the Irish consumed about 7.1 million gallons of legal whiskey, 10 percent more than they had consumed in 1844. The per capita increase was actually greater than that, because Ireland's population had dropped about 20 percent in these four years because of emigration and Famine-related deaths. Of course, the returns on legal whiskey do not tell the whole story; some Irish still preferred poteen to Parliament whiskey and others were beer drinkers. Beer production hovered around six hundred thousand barrels a year from 1844 to 1848, and it is impossible to know how much poteen was produced during this time.[90] It is certainly conceivable that poteen consumption was declining. Since taxes on spirits had been lowered in 1846 and again in 1847, some Irish may have been induced to switch from poteen to legal whiskey. Even were this the case, it is highly unlikely that the decline in poteen consumption would have equaled the increased intake of legal spirits. The evidence strongly suggests that the Irish people drank more in 1848–49 than they had in the early 1840s.

{ CHAPTER SEVEN }

Mathew's American Tour and Final Years, 1849–1856

I am truly sorry to learn that Father Mathew has acted a cowardly part on the question of Slavery since he arrived in America. . . . I am sorry he has fallen; I am sorry he has bowed down before the slave power. I am sorry he contemplates a visit to the Slave States. . . . But I will yet hope better things of Father Mathew.

James Haughton in *The North Star,* November 2, 1849

MATHEW AT LONG LAST prepared to set sail for America in May 1849. He had already warned his friend Colonel J. H. Sherburne not to expect much from him during his tour: "The portrait that you have of me, is I regret, too flattering for my present age. From illness and excessive toil, my friends in the States, will find in me, but a mere wreck of what I was, and I must throw myself on their kindness and forbearance, whilst I shall be amongst them. I fear that I will not be able to exert myself, as I have hitherto; nor can it be expected that I will address public meetings. . . . [The Americans] must be satisfied with the result of my past labours." Before departing from Cork, he assured a large crowd of well-wishers that not much work remained to be accomplished in Ireland, for "the greater part of the Irish people have taken the total abstinence pledge." Consequently, he was going to America—where his efforts were much needed—for twelve months. The prospect of visiting a nation where Irish people were faring well thrilled him: "I go also to afford myself the pleasure and consolation of beholding my exiled countrymen, not, as here, lingering thro' a life of protracted starvation and constant misery, but in the midst of prosperity, enjoying the remuneration of their industry, and all the comforts that plenty and domestic comfort confer." From Cork, Mathew traveled to Dublin and then to Liverpool, where he embarked for America, in the company of his secretaries, David O'Meara and Cornelius Mahony.[1]

Mathew hoped to accomplish a variety of goals during his American sojourn. As he told his supporters in Cork, he was intent on bringing more people into the temperance movement and encouraging those who had taken the pledge in Ireland to remain faithful to it. He was probably more concerned with solving his own problems, though. He believed that he would be able to restore his health by spending time in the mild climate of the southern states. Certainly winter in the South would be easier on him than a cold, damp Irish winter. And he was still most anxious about money. He hoped to raise substantial sums of money on his tour. Americans of all religions had been generous during the Famine, and Mathew knew that many Irish emigrants had prospered in America. He trusted that Americans would also be magnanimous to him. Indeed, he was so optimistic about Americans' largess that he believed he would be able to raise enough money to pay off his own debts *and* complete Holy Trinity Church in Cork, which he had started in 1832 and left half-finished.

Assisting him with his financial projects was Patrick Donahoe, the editor of the *Boston Pilot*, the leading Irish American newspaper. Months before Mathew left Ireland, Donahoe began promoting the "Mathew Liberating Fund." He urged every teetotaler in America to give one dollar to allow Mathew to "resign the miserable British pension."[2]

Temperance in America

The United States was a temperance stronghold in the middle of the nineteenth century. The movement had originated in America and spread to Ireland and England in 1829; by the 1830s and 1840s, temperance had gained a wide following throughout America. Teetotal societies had been established north and south of the Mason-Dixon line and attracted both the middle class and the working class. Whereas the American Temperance Union catered to the more affluent teetotalers, the freewheeling Washingtonians promoted temperance among the workers.[3] Women, too, were beginning to take an active role in temperance work in the 1840s. Susan B. Anthony, Elizabeth Cady Stanton, and Amelia Bloomer were committed not only to women's suffrage but to teetotalism and Prohibition.[4]

Together these groups had begun exerting pressure on local and state officials to enact restrictive legislation. In the 1830s and 1840s most temperance activists were lobbying for "high license" or "no license" regulations that would subject tavern owners to expensive fees. In 1851, Neal Dow, the mayor of Portland, went a step further and helped secure the passage of a law prohibiting the manufacture and sale of alcoholic beverages in Maine. The new statute thrilled many teetotalers, including Lyman Beecher, who exclaimed, "This thing is of God. . . . [the] Maine Law was a square and grand blow right between the horns of the Devil."[5] Henceforth, most American temperance advocates worked to obtain legislation similar to the Maine Law in other states. By 1855, twelve states and territories had followed Maine's example, and two had passed restrictive legislation that fell short of full Prohibition.[6]

Although Irish American Catholics took no part in its Prohibitionist dimension,they were involved in the teetotal movement. In Philadelphia Bishop Francis Kenrick had strongly encouraged the men in his diocese to pledge. In June 1840 he had issued a pastoral letter calling for the establishment of "a society similar to that, which has been established by the zeal of a humble priest in Ireland, with the pledge of total abstinence from all intoxicating liquors." By August Kenrick noted approvingly in his diary that five thousand men had taken the pledge in Philadelphia.[7]

Although Philadelphia was the focal point for Catholic teetotalers, societies were also established in New York City; Washington, D.C.; Rochester, New York; Boston; and even Dubuque, Iowa. Cincinnati, too, must have had its share of Catholic teetotalers, because when Charles Dickens visited there in 1842 he witnessed a massive temperance rally and noted the large number of Irish participating. In his journal he wrote, "I was particularly pleased to see the Irishmen, who formed a distinct society among themselves, and mustered very strong with their green scarves; carrying their national Harp and their Portrait of Father Mathew, high above the people's heads. They were as jolly and good-humored as ever; and . . . were the most independent fellows there, I thought."[8]

Not all American Catholics shared the Irish enthusiasm for temperance. Writing from Sandusky, Ohio, in 1842, Father Joseph Machebeuf informed his ordinary, Archbishop Purcell, of the difficulties he was encountering in his effort to promote temperance among his parishioners: "On St. Patrick's Day which was celebrated here with great solemnity such as high mass, procession and public dinner, after as good an exhortation as was possible to me I took first the temperance pledge and was followed by twenty-five Irishmen. . . . The number of members is now raised to 162. . . . At Easter I had the pleasure of seeing coming to their duty number[s] of those who, the year before were strong pillars of taverns and groceries. Now the grocerykeepers are complaining very loud of the hardness of the times. . . . Among the Irish Catholics I do not now know one single man who might be called a drunkard. It is not so with the germans, [a] few of them are often giving very bad example and only one of them took the temp. pledge."[9] As Father Machebeuf learned, for most Germans total abstinence had little appeal. Perhaps because they drank beer rather than whiskey, the Germans had not experienced the sort of alcohol problems that had plagued the Irish and could not see the need for teetotalism. Furthermore, brewing and drinking beer were integral parts of their culture; few were interested in foregoing their lager for any cause.[10]

German opposition notwithstanding, the Catholic temperance movement expanded steadily in the 1840s. At their Fourth Provincial meeting in Baltimore in 1840, the American bishops took up the question and offered some encouragement to temperance activists: "Our attention has been repeatedly given to the subject of intemperance; this vice has spread wide desolation through many lands. . . . We . . . commend the resolution of those persons who, to guard the more effectually against temptation, and to endeavor by their example and influence, the eradication of vice, and having no need of their use, abstain altogether from ardent spirits." The bishops did not encourage total abstinence, however: "We neither feel ourselves warranted to require, nor called upon to recommend . . . total abstinence from a beverage which the Sacred Scriptures do not prohibit, and of which the most holy persons have occasionally partaken."[11]

For the next couple of years, the bishops remained ambivalent about the temperance movement and about Mathew's campaign in particular. At their Fifth Provincial meeting in 1843, the bishops issued another guarded statement on temperance. This time they commended teetotalism as well as abstinence from distilled spirits: "The enormous evils of intemperance, which no tongue can portray, have given occasion to a remedy apparently extreme. Millions in Ireland, and many thousands in this country have publicly pledged themselves to abstain from the use of all intoxicating liquors. We cannot but approve." They then offered their judgment on the nature of the pledge, an issue which had plagued Mathew since 1840. They declared that the pledge should be seen not as a solemn vow but rather "as a resolution, which . . . imposes no new obligation, so that the person who should fail in its observance, sins only by excess." They concluded their statement by urging teetotalers to stay away from non-Catholic groups: "We warn you against uniting in societies not based on religious principles, nor directed by the ecclesiastical authority, or otherwise organized in such a way as may suppose mere human influences and means."[12] Although the American Temperance Union and the Washingtonians were no doubt uppermost in the bishops' minds, the objection could be applied to Mathew's society as well. And some bishops had begun to question Mathew's methods. By September 1843 Kenrick, Mathew's erstwhile admirer, had begun to have doubts about him. In a letter to his brother Peter, who was bishop of St. Louis, Kenrick expressed his fear that Mathew "seems to detract from religion and to rest too much on the pledge alone, not without injury to the grace and truth of God. I am sorry therefore that I gave consent to the petitions of those who wished him invited to America." Two months later he wrote to Father Paul Cullen, declaring that "if not checked and regulated, it [Mathew's movement] would degenerate into fanaticism." Michael O'Connor, the Irish-born bishop of Pittsburgh, was also skeptical about Mathew's methods. Writing to Cullen in 1842, he remarked, "Our success [with teetotalism] has hitherto been great. We have established it on a more religious basis than it is in Ireland. The pledge is administered before the altar. We profess to regard it as a religious act, and though we cannot refuse to give it to Protestants who come publicly for it in the crowd, we have declined all official connection with Protestant societies." Thus, in America, just as in Ireland, the bishops were considerably more critical of Mathew and his movement than were the laity.[13]

Mathew's Tour

Inasmuch as temperance appealed to disparate and mutually exclusive groups in America—slaveholders as well as abolitionists, nativists as well as Irishmen, workers as well as patricians—Mathew was bound to encounter difficulties on his tour. Troubles started for him as soon as he stepped off the ship in New York harbor on July 2nd. There waiting to greet him were the city's Whig mayor, Caleb Woodhull, and its formidable Irish-born bishop, John Hughes.[14] At first, the mayor and various Protestant temperance activists controlled Mathew's schedule. They had him staying at a fashionable residence, Irving House, and attending temperance meetings in Protestant churches. Feeling that the Protestants were exploiting Mathew, Hughes prevailed on him to move to the bishop's residence. For the duration of his stay in New York, he was shepherded about the various Catholic churches, schools, and charities.[15]

Despite the squabbling among his supporters in New York, Mathew enjoyed his first weeks in America. Writing to Richard Dowden in Cork, he gave a glowing account: "Nothing could exceed the kindness and attention I have invariably received, since my arrival in this great and happy country. My health, I find, thank God, continues to improve. In fact, everything here continues to cheer me on." What did trouble him, though, were further reports in the Irish press about his acceptance of the British pension: "With regard to observations that have appeared concerning the pension granted me by the British Government, I hope you will be kind enough to defend me and my motives, and explain by your remarks in the [Cork] *Constitution* and other papers, my position. You are aware that I was solicitous for an increase of the pension and that it was not granted and that the present sum is barely sufficient to pay the premium of insurance on my life not taking into account that I have to pay the interest of the debts due to my creditors. Altho' I am grateful for the aid granted by the British Government still if my friends here who do not wish me to be a pensioner would extricate me from my difficulties, I would relinquish the stipend."[16]

AVOIDING ABOLITIONISTS

Mathew left New York for Boston, where serious problems were awaiting him. Upon his arrival, he was greeted by the governor of Massachusetts, the mayor of Boston, and several Protestant ministers, including Lyman Beecher. The bishop of Boston, John Fitzpatrick, was just as concerned as Bishop Hughes had been that public officials and Protestant activists were taking advantage of him. Fitzpatrick remarked in his diary, "It is much to be regretted that Father Matthew[sic] comes to this country from Ireland somewhat in the character of the Nation's guest. His actions must consequently be controlled in a great measure by the public authorities who tender to him the civilities of the cities which he visits, and by those ultra-reformers & pseudo-philanthropists who are public men and leaders more by their own ostentation & impudence than by any virtue or merit. . . . The platform was also covered by sectarian fanaticks, calvinistic preachers and deacons. . . . The appearance of fellowship between a Catholic priest and such men can hardly be without evil results."[17]

The day after this initial public appearance, however, Mathew had a cordial visit with Fitzpatrick. For the rest of his stay, Mathew spent much of his time at the bishop's side, visiting Catholic churches. On July 26th he accompanied Fitzpatrick to Worcester to attend the first commencement exercises of the College of the Holy Cross.[18] After returning to Boston, Mathew started giving the pledge at Faneuil Hall and at the cathedral and other Catholic churches.

Mathew's troubles in Boston came to a head after he was paid a visit by William Lloyd Garrison, the fiery abolitionist leader. Garrison, an ardent teetotaler, admired Mathew both for his temperance crusade and for his opposition to slavery.[19] Although concerned first and foremost with abolition, Garrison had been interested enough in teetotalism to travel to London with Frederick Douglass to attend the World Temperance Convention in 1846.[20] Sponsored by abolitionists, the meeting brought together the leading antislavery teetotalers from England, Ireland, and America. Mathew had considered going but had withdrawn at the last moment. He told a Quaker friend, R. D. Webb, that he wanted to go to the convention to express publicly his "abhorrence of that detestable system, American slavery."[21]

Presuming that he and Mathew had much in common, Garrison presented him with a letter inviting him to take part in a rally in Worcester the following week commemorating the abolition of slavery in the British West Indies.[22] Garrison remembered that Mathew had joined Daniel O'Connell in signing the Anti-Slavery Address to Irish Americans in 1841 and had warmly received Frederick Douglass in Cork in 1845. Garrison was also well aware that most Irish in America were quite hostile to abolitionism. The Anti-Slavery Address had not influenced them in the least.

Initially some Irish Americans had argued that it was a forgery but when that theory proved untenable, they did their best to ignore it.[23]

For Garrison, Mathew's visit offered a critical opportunity to raise the consciousness of the ever increasing Irish population in New England. If Mathew appeared publicly with Garrison and renewed his commitment to abolitionism, this might persuade some Irish Americans to join the cause. At the very least, such an appearance would silence Garrison's critics at the *Boston Pilot* and other Irish American newspapers.[24]

When Garrison presented Mathew with the invitation, Mathew rejected it out of hand, saying, "I have as much as I can do to save men from the slavery of intemperance, without attempting the overthrow of any other kind of slavery!"[25] He knew that slavery was an explosive issue in America and was determined to avoid it.[26] Furthermore, since he planned to spend much of his time in the South recuperating from his stroke, he was afraid to align himself publicly with Garrison and his radical associates.

Garrison, bitterly disappointed and angered by Mathew's response, decided to devote most of his remarks at the Worcester rally to his unhappy meeting with Mathew. Speaking before a crowd of four thousand people, Garrison offered a detailed account of Mathew's vague, noncommittal statements, to which his listeners responded, "Shame! Shame!" After the rally, Garrison decided that he still had more to say on the matter and began publishing open letters to Mathew in his newspaper, *The Liberator*. Over a six-week period in September and October 1849, Garrison published five letters documenting Mathew's cowardly and contradictory behavior. The final letter was scathing:

> In Ireland, you professed to be an uncompromising abolitionist; you found time to bear a strong testimony against American slavery, as a disgrace to the country, and a sin against God; . . . Now that you are on American soil . . . you have signified your determination to give the slave no token of your sympathy, and his oppressor no cause of uneasiness! As for the abolitionists, in no shape or manner are you willing to be identified with them! You volunteer the expression of a doubt whether there is any specific injunction in the Scriptures against slavery! You recollect that the signing of the [anti-slavery] address . . . brought a good deal of odium upon you, and you are not disposed to encounter any more of it on that score, especially as you are every where feasted and flattered by a pro-slavery people. . . . [Y]ou have added to the

anguish, horror and despair of the poor miserable slaves, made their yokes heavier, and fastened their chains more securely!"[27]

Mathew was certainly stung by Garrison's rebukes. Writing to John Maguire in Cork, he remarked, "I have been badly treated by Mr. Garrison . . . who strove to entrap me." Still, Mathew kept at his business and made no attempt to answer Garrison's charges; he no doubt hoped the issue would fade away. From August til October he traveled around Massachusetts, Rhode Island, Connecticut, and Maine, stopping at virtually every sizable town as well as several Indian settlements.[28] While Mathew remained silent, most of his supporters in the North, including some abolitionists, rallied to his defense.[29] Antislavery Whigs such as William Seward of New York took his side against Garrison, arguing that the latter was acting in a shrill and tiresome manner. Catholic leaders were likewise relieved to see Mathew break with Garrison and were happy to have an excuse to lash out at Garrison. Patrick Donahoe responded in the *Boston Pilot* in terms just as withering as those that Garrison had used: "We protest, we would rather be the slave of the bloodiest planter than of the demon passion that, palpably, horsewhips the heart of William Lloyd Garrison. . . . We did not think human malignity could be so staunch, so steady to its purpose—as it seems on the weekly columns of the *Liberator*."[30]

Unfortunately for Mathew, southern temperance advocates also took notice of the controversy engendered by Garrison. Their objections were precisely the opposite of those voiced by Garrison: they were disturbed to learn about Mathew's abolitionist past. In September, Judge Joseph Lumpkin, the president of Georgia's temperance society, wrote to Mathew asking whether it were true that he had signed an antislavery address in 1841 and whether he presently considered himself an abolitionist. In reply, Mathew sent Lumpkin a letter in which he clearly distanced himself from Garrison and the New England abolitionists without alluding to his own views on slavery: "In referring Your Honour to the conversation I had with Mr. Garrison . . . I vainly thought my solemn declaration of being firmly resolved not to interfere in the slightest degree with the institutions of this mighty republic, would have been amply sufficient to calm the anxieties of even the most sensitive American. I now, dear and honoured judge, renew this declaration, and I most respectfully urge that no man, who enjoys himself freedom in this emphatically free country can require more from one."[31] Finding this reply too evasive, Lumpkin withdrew his invitation to visit Georgia.[32]

In spite of the slavery controversy and the sectarian tug-of-war that Mathew was frequently enmeshed in, the tour was still proving to be a success. In New York and Boston, he had administered the pledge to twenty thousand and thirty-five thousand people, respectively, most of whom were Irish.[33] In early November he left Boston for Philadelphia,[34] but pains in his side and leg forced him to stop in New York for medical attention. Surely his nonstop touring had wearied him, and perhaps the conflict with Garrison had taken a toll as well. After resting for a couple of days, Mathew started again for Philadelphia and arrived there on November 20.[35]

Though Bishop Kenrick was still leery about Mathew and in fact had never renewed his invitation to him, he nevertheless was quite impressed when he finally met him face to face. Writing to his brother, Kenrick lauded Mathew as a "very excellent man [who] . . . ought to be welcomed by all bishops." He was struck by Mathew's popularity among people of all creeds and classes and was astounded to see hundreds of sick and blind people crowding around him in hopes of obtaining a cure.[36] Evidently he had not heard of this dimension of Mathew's movement.

After three weeks in Philadelphia, Mathew left for Baltimore. During a short stay, he met with the archbishop, Samuel Eccleston, and gave the pledge to nearly one thousand people, including the mayor. The editor of Baltimore's Catholic newspaper noted that Mathew looked "a little worn by his labors, as well as suffering from a slight paralytic affection. . . . We sincerely hope that his visit to the more genial climate of the southern states will recruit his strength."[37]

CONTROVERSY AT THE CAPITOL

Mathew elected to make a brief stopover in Washington, D.C., before heading deeper south. Upon his arrival, he paid a visit to Georgetown College, whose president, Father James Ryder, S.J., was a thoroughgoing teetotaler.[38] Mathew was warmly received by the faculty and students alike, and the students were given the following day off so they could go downtown and watch Mathew tour the Capitol.[39]

Mathew planned to pay only a brief social call at the Capitol, but to his dismay he found himself engulfed in another controversy over slavery. In an effort to honor him, several representatives offered a resolution admitting him to a seat on the floor. Although the proposal was approved unanimously, a similar measure in the Senate met with considerable opposition. Among Mathew's critics were two of the Senate's most militant apologists for slavery: John Calhoun and Jefferson Davis. The future president of the Confederacy denounced Mathew in no uncertain terms. He prefaced his remarks by avowing that he bore no ill will toward the Irish race or the Catholic Church and was only concerned with the friar's politics.[40] Describing him as an "ally of O'Connell," Davis said Mathew had attempted to "incite the Irishmen . . . to unite as a body with the Abolitionists in their nefarious designs against the peace, property and constitutional rights of the South." Several senators, including Whig leaders Henry Clay and William Seward, promptly rose to Mathew's defense. Clay pointed to Mathew's exchange with Garrison as evidence that a "change had taken place in the opinions of Father Mathew, and that he now stood before the country unbiassed [sic] in his sentiments." Stephen Douglas, an Illinois Democrat and future presidential candidate, reminded his colleagues that temperance, not slavery, was the issue at hand: "It is doing injustice to the character of this distinguished philanthropist to attempt to connect his name with the subject of slavery. . . . He comes here on a great mission, which commands the admiration and sympathy of all men who have a heart to feel and a mind to comprehend the philanthropic efforts of a great and noble soul . . . [W]e ought not to attempt to [draw him into] our party struggles." In the end, the Senate rejected the protests of Davis and the other slavery advocates and, by a 33–18 vote welcomed Mathew to assume a seat on the floor.[41] The Marquis de Lafayette was the only other visitor to have been so honored.

The next day Mathew dined at the White House at the invitation of President Zachary Taylor. A southern Whig who owned slaves but opposed the extension of slavery, Taylor was probably not disturbed by Mathew's abolitionist past. Although not a teetotaler himself, Taylor well knew that many leading members of his party, including William Seward, Henry Clay, and Abraham Lincoln, were sympathetic to temperance.[42] Furthermore, Taylor may have hoped to use Mathew's visit to appeal to the burgeoning Irish immigrant community.[43] Whatever his motivations, Taylor received Mathew warmly and toasted him—with water, of course—at the banquet.

From Washington Mathew traveled farther south, stopping first at Richmond, Virginia. Here his audiences were composed largely of evangelical Protestants who sympathized with his cause but tended not to take the pledge at his hands. From Virginia he passed through Charleston and Columbia, South Carolina; Wilmington, North Carolina; and Savannah, Georgia before arriving in Mobile, Alabama, in March 1850. At Mobile, he was the guest of Michael Portier, the city's French-born bishop. To his brother Charles, he sent an optimistic letter saying that the mild climate of Mobile was helping to restore his health. After Mathew departed for New Orleans, Portier sent Bishop Antoine Blanc of New Orleans a glowing report on him: "I will forever thank God for the good this truly pious, humble and charitable religious has done in my diocese by his holy and benevolent labours, by his fervent exhortations and his apostolic example. New Orleans, will offer to his zeal an immense field, a field worthy of his heavenly mission."[44]

Mathew took up residence with Bishop Blanc and set to work. New Orleans was the South's largest city, and its Irish population had been growing steadily for decades. With about 20,000 Irish among its 115,000 residents, New Orleans would prove to be Mathew's most successful stop in the South. During his two-month stay, roughly fourteen thousand people took the pledge from him. In financial terms, though, his days in New Orleans were a disappointment. He told his brother that he had raised only sixty dollars during his stay there. His previous stops had been just as disheartening. From Boston he had written to his friend John Maguire, informing him that he was "too sanguine as to the result of the subscriptions in the United States. . . . The Irish in America are not rich and the Native Americans do not sympathise in our affairs." Patrick Donahoe had not had much success, either. He had hoped to raise thirty thousand dollars for his Mathew Liberating Fund but was able to collect only about a thousand dollars.[45]

After leaving New Orleans, Mathew rode up the Mississippi River to Natchez and Vicksburg. In Natchez he preached at the cathedral and enrolled four hundred people. The bishop, John Chanche, S.S., also offered a favorable account to Blanc: "Father Mathew left us this morning early for Vicksburg. His stay here has been of great good. Many more persons have taken the pledge than I expected. To be sure many women and children. But a good many men too, to whom it will be of great service. I am rather pleased with him and his visit."[46]

Mathew's next stop was Little Rock, Arkansas. Little Rock at this time was still a small town, so Mathew was not occupied with pledging hundreds of new members. Instead he followed the advice of the city's Irish-born bishop, Andrew Byrne, and spent several weeks resting in an effort to regain his strength before continuing northward on his tour. He tried bathing in the waters at Hot Springs, but it did not help much, and he resumed his travels in a wearied state.[47]

He headed north to St. Louis, where he was the guest of the Irish-born archbishop, Peter Kenrick. For a month he was back on his old schedule, speaking, preaching, and giving the pledge all over the city. Appearing at a High Mass with the Jesuit missionary Peter de Smet, Mathew preached an hour-long sermon that one reporter described as "forcible, elegant and deeply persuasive." All told, ten thousand people enrolled in St. Louis.[48]

All this exertion tired him out. With winter coming, he decided to return to New Orleans to rest in its warmer clime. By Christmas he was back in New Orleans, giving the pledge to new members and chastising those who had broken their pledges since his last visit. Shortly after St. Patrick's Day in 1851, he set off for Nashville, but along the way he suffered a second, nearly fatal stroke. At this point he knew he must return to Ireland. He had hoped to reach a few more cities in the Midwest and Southwest before his departure—the Sons of Temperance[49] had invited him to Chicago, Bishop John Odin had asked him to come to Galveston, Texas, and Father Edward Sorin had invited him to visit Notre Dame, his fledgling school in northern Indiana. To Sorin he sent a short note lamenting that a "renewed attack of Paralysis . . . has much enfeebled me."[50]

Upon reaching Kentucky, Mathew stopped to visit Henry Clay at Ashland, his famed six-hundred-acre plantation outside Lexington. Clay had been one of only a few slaveholding senators to defend Mathew during the debate of 1849.[51] Now Mathew hoped that the aging senator could help him raise more funds. Clay agreed and published an "Appeal to the

American Public," in which he noted that Mathew had fallen between twenty-five and thirty thousand dollars in debt as a result of his work during the potato famine. Hailing him as "one of the greatest benefactors . . . that our country has ever entertained," Clay implored his fellow citizens to come to Mathew's aid.[52]

Although clearly ailing, Mathew made several more stops on his way to New York City. By the end of June, he was in Cincinnati, preaching in the cathedral. He boasted that he had come across thousands of people in America who had taken the pledge from him in Ireland as children and kept it. During his weeks in Cincinnati, he was able to add twelve thousand more people to the temperance rolls, even though he was "laboring under partial paralysis."[53]

In July he reached Pittsburgh and took up residence with one of his former critics, Bishop Michael O'Connor.[54] From there he traveled to upstate New York, stopping in Albany, Buffalo, and Utica. By the end of September he finally reached New York City and began to make plans for his departure. At St. Patrick's Cathedral, he delivered an impassioned farewell sermon that was uncharacteristically severe in tone. Having for months praised America for the economic opportunities it offered, he now warned his listeners about the dangers of money: "With what a trembling hand . . . ought we to receive the boon of prosperity. When our path is strewed with flowers, how prone are we to forget ourselves till the hand of death severs the golden chain that linked us to the earth! Then we mourn the misspent hours lost in seeking for imaginary happiness; and find out the errors of our ways, when perhaps it is too late." He concluded by exhorting those present to keep eternity always before their eyes: "Time flies, our span of existence here is but a moment compared with eternity. What difference does it make to us if our path is strewed with choicest flowers, when the day is fast approaching, and may be tomorrow, when we shall lose them all. . . . When we are afflicted, therefore, let us consider that it is less than we deserve, and that we must be afflicted either here or hereafter—that the strokes of the rod of our heavenly Father in this world are to save us from the wrath to come. Kiss the smarting rod. It is right that our tears of sorrow should wipe away the stains of our prosperity."[55]

After giving a few more farewell addresses, Mathew finally set sail for his homeland on November 8. In reporting on his departure, the *New York Herald* noted all that Mathew had accomplished during his stay: "He has visited, since his arrival in America, twenty-five States of the Union, has administered the temperance pledge in over three hundred of our principal towns and cities, has added more than half a million of our population to the long muster roll of his disciples; and in accomplishing this praiseworthy object, has travelled thirty-seven thousand miles."[56] The *Herald*'s editors were right. Mathew had literally crisscrossed the nation promoting temperance. Considering his age and ill health, his extensive touring was an extraordinary feat. During his tour, five hundred thousand—perhaps even six hundred thousand—people took the total abstinence pledge at his hands.[57] Of course, many would break their pledges in the years following.[58] Even so, Mathew's tour was largely a success. He drew thousands of Irish Americans into a movement that had largely been a Protestant preserve, and he charmed the American bishops, many of whom had had misgivings about him. In the latter decades of the nineteenth century, many influential Irish American bishops, priests, and laymen would be temperance advocates. Certainly Mathew's labors laid the groundwork for the later Irish involvement in the movement.

The trip did nothing to solve Mathew's personal problems, however. He left America physically broken, without any money to show for his labor. None of the fundraising campaigns had succeeded. Even Henry Clay's appeal had fizzled, netting only a few hundred dollars, a far cry from Clay's goal of twenty-five thousand. Clay told his friend Henry Grinnell that anti-Catholic sentiment had hindered their campaign: "I regret extremely that [the Appeal has] not been more successful, and I lament the influence of . . . religious prejudice. . . . There is not, I believe, the slightest foundation for the assumption that contributions to him are to enure to the benefit of the Catholic Church. . . . All religions are interested in the cause of temperance; and I had hoped that all would have cordially united in testifying [to] the great merits of [Father Mathew]."[59] Although it is likely true that some temperance advocates would not support Mathew because of his religion, many would have funded him if they were sure that the money would go to support temperance. But Mathew was determined to raise money for his church in Cork as well as his temperance society. Thus the "assumption that contributions to him are to enure to the benefit of the Catholic Church" was not so far-fetched.[60]

Mathew's Last Years

In December 1851—two-and-a-half years after his departure—an exhausted Mathew returned to Ireland and went directly to his brother Charles's home outside Cork to recuperate. As time passed and his condition did not improve, he resigned his positions as provincial of the Capuchins—which he had held since 1822—and superior of two local convents.[61] By March 1852 he had concluded that he was too ill and impoverished to do any more temperance touring. To an American friend he declared that he had "given up the idea of appealing to Louis Napoleon," and instead had "formed the resolution of calling on the citizens of Cork to aid me in my difficulties." He ended the letter by dolefully acknowledging that he had "relinquished the idea of again resuming the temperance mission. My health is so impaired that it would [be] worse than folly to think of it unless the Almighty worked for me a miraculous cure—which I do not hope for."[62]

Convinced that Ireland's damp climate was detrimental to his health, Mathew decided to seek a favor from Paul Cullen, who had been appointed archbishop of Dublin in May after the death of Daniel Murray. He asked Cullen to intercede on his behalf so that pope Pius IX would appoint him vicar apostolic of Jamaica, St. Lucia, or any other available Caribbean island.[63] Aware that Cullen was an intimate of the pope, Mathew believed that a recommendation from the archbishop would secure his appointment.

Cullen, however, was not anxious to help. At this point, he was probably less sympathetic to Mathew than he had been in 1847, when Mathew had sought his help in obtaining the bishopric of Cork. In 1850 Cullen had convened the first national synod in Ireland since the twelfth century. The Synod of Thurles—held near Slattery's home because he was in poor health—dealt with several issues, but temperance was not one of them. The bishops were concerned mainly with reaching a definitive judgment on the Queen's Universities. This subject pitted Cullen, Slattery, and MacHale against Murray and his allies in a bruising battle. Cullen and his supporters wanted the nonsectarian colleges condemned and ultimately prevailed over the Murray faction by a fifteen to thirteen vote.[64]

The struggle at the synod must have alienated Cullen further from the anglophile elements in the clergy. He was not about to recommend Mathew—a British pensioner—for a bishopric of any kind. In his reply, he tried to put Mathew off politely by telling him that he thought an episcopal appointment would be too demanding for a man in his frail condition. Mathew responded to Cullen's letter immediately, hoping to change his mind before Cullen sent off a negative letter to Rome. Mathew assured Cullen that his ailments had not left him incapacitated and then added plaintively, "The race is not to the swift, nor the battle to the strong [Eccl. 9:11], and should your Grace sanction my wishes in this respect, I confidently hope with the Divine Blessing, and through the intercession of the Immaculate Mother of our Lord Jesus Christ, to make St. Lucia a worthy daughter of the Islands of Saints." Cullen remained unconvinced, and Mathew never obtained an appointment to a Caribbean see.[65]

Mathew made one final public appearance in the fall of 1853. At the request of the Christian Brothers, he traveled to Limerick and administered the pledge to ten thousand people.[66] After this trip, he made no further efforts to lead the movement but continued to receive people at his brother's home. A steady stream of pilgrims came to him to take or retake the pledge at his hands, while others came seeking either financial assistance or relief from their infirmities. Although his health had broken down completely, many visitors implored him to place his trembling hands on their foreheads and give them his blessing.[67]

Saddened by the decline of his movement, Mathew came to the conclusion that his voluntarist approach was not sufficient. When the United Kingdom Alliance, an openly Prohibitionist society, was founded in 1853 by English enthusiasts of the Maine Law, Mathew sent a warm letter of support to its secretary: "My labours, with the Divine aid, were attended with partial success. The efforts of individuals, however zealous, are not equal to the mighty task. The United Kingdom Alliance strikes at the very root of the evil. I trust in God the associated efforts of the many good and benevolent men will effectually crush a monster gorged with human gore."[68] In 1854 he made an even more explicit declaration to a temperance advocate in Belfast: "The principle of prohibition seems to be the only safe remedy for the evils of intemperance. This opinion has been strengthened by the hard labor of more than twenty years in the temperance cause."[69]

In August 1854, Mathew was able to leave Ireland for the warmer climate of the Madeira islands, a trip made possible by donations from Archbishop Slattery and several priests of the province.[70] A year later he returned feeling somewhat stronger and, upon arriving in Dublin, was able to administer the pledge to the thousands who crowded around him. From Dublin he returned to his brother's home, hoping to renew his work. In February 1856, though, he suffered another stroke. From this point on, he was unable to celebrate mass or engage in any strenuous activity. Mathew died on December 8, 1856, at the age of sixty-six.

All of Cork seemed to mourn Mathew's passing. Bishop Delany and seventy priests offered a requiem mass for him in his own church, Holy Trinity, which stood unfinished, lacking a steeple. City officials, Protestant ministers, temperance leaders, and tens of thousands of ordinary Irish marched alongside the Catholic clergy in a solemn procession through the streets of the city.[71] He was interred in St. Joseph's Cemetery, the nonsectarian burial ground that he had established twenty-six years earlier. Here clothed in the Franciscan habit—a garment he had never worn in life—Mathew was laid to rest.

{ CHAPTER EIGHT }

Mathew's Legacy: Temperance after 1880

The task is much easier than it was for Father Mathew. Total abstinence is no longer a novelty; it has made its record and proved its efficiency, and the church has set Her seal upon it. . . . There remains, now, no excuse for indifference or inactivity.

John Ireland in *The Catholic World*, October 1890

AT MATHEW'S DEATH, the temperance movement was in a weak and disorganized state in most areas of Ireland. In America, too, the effects of Mathew's trip had proved temporary. In both countries, the teetotal movement entered a period of virtual dormancy that lasted a generation. By the 1880s, though, temperance was on the rise again. In Ireland, Father James Cullen, S.J.,[1] the founder of the Pioneers, linked total abstinence to Catholic devotions and Irish nationalism in language often reminiscent of Daniel O'Connell. In America, Archbishop John Ireland was probably the leading Irish teetotal proponent. For him and most Irish Americans in the temperance movement, teetotalism was a means to assimilation, a way for Irish immigrants to gain acceptance from the nation's Protestant majority. Ireland eagerly joined hands with Protestants to promote temperance—just as Mathew had—and spoke often and earnestly of his attachment to America. As an ecumenist and assimilationist, John Ireland had much in common with Mathew, while Cullen, the Catholic nationalist, shared much of O'Connell's vision.

TEMPERANCE IN IRELAND AFTER MATHEW

Evidence of the state of the Irish temperance movement in the 1850s was furnished by Sir John Forbes, an English physician who visited Ireland in 1852 and took extensive notes. Although Forbes did not traverse the whole island—he never reached Dublin or the southeastern counties—he offered a thorough account of the movement's strength in Munster, Connaught, and Ulster. In some of the towns in Munster, temperance societies had all but disappeared. At Skibbereen, County Cork—the site of Ireland's first teetotal organization—Forbes reported that the "system of Father Matthew [sic] had fallen sadly into decay. From a muster of many hundreds at one time, the professed teetotallers had sunk down . . . to two or three." Yet at Killarney and Limerick the societies were much more vibrant. Three temperance halls, each well stocked with newspapers and books, were functioning in Killarney, and Limerick had four active temperance halls; the one he visited was well appointed and claimed three hundred members.[2]

The societies in Connaught tended to be weaker than those in Munster. In both Westport and Castlebar the temperance movement had virtually collapsed. Forbes concluded that Archbishop John MacHale's hostility to Mathew had stifled the cause in these towns, because when he reached Galway, which was outside of MacHale's jurisdiction, he found that the local society had two hundred members and an active bank.[3]

In Ulster, Forbes found the movement vigorous in some towns and moribund in others. He noted that Protestant clergy had become enthusiasts for the cause in several towns. In the 1830s and early 1840s, John Edgar and some of his fellow clergy had objected to the teetotal movement on scriptural or pragmatic grounds. After the Famine ended, many ministers changed their minds, but Edgar remained hostile to teetotalism. Forbes noted that in Armagh, Newry, Larne, and Limivaddy, Protestant teetotal societies were enjoying some success. Catholics had established their own societies in several Ulster towns, but they were generally small.[4]

Forbes's notes do not indicate that temperance remained strong in one region of Ireland but had failed in another. The movement had of course declined everywhere since its zenith in the early 1840s, but there were still towns throughout Ireland where teetotalism remained a vital force. Generally, a person or group had taken up the cause after the Famine and helped breathe new life into it. In Ulster, Protestant clergy had become involved; in Ballina, the Sisters of Mercy had begun administering the pledge; and in Killarney, the Catholic clergy were strongly supportive.[5]

Although Forbes was generally pessimistic about the state of the temperance movement, he was nevertheless convinced that the effects of Mathew's campaign were still evident. He had witnessed almost no drunkenness during his travels and concluded his report on a confident note: "My memorandums clearly establish the fact, that the great banded army of Pledged Abstainers from intoxicating drinks, has been long broken in pieces, and the numbering of the host has come down from millions to thousands.... They show, however, at the same time, that though the organisation is gone, the influence of the movement for good, has survived its formal existence. It has left Ireland, comparatively speaking, a temperate nation; and the seeds scattered by it throughout the land in its days of triumph, are now, after lying dormant for a season, springing up everywhere with a broader root and a firmer stem."[6]

Forbes was too sanguine about the temperance movement's prospects—at least in the short run. After Mathew's death, a project was launched by John Maguire to erect a statue of him in Cork. In 1864 the statue was finally complete, and on October 10, Mathew's birthday, one hundred thousand people gathered to see it unveiled and listen as Maguire saluted Mathew as "the greatest reformer of the age."[7] This show of strength in Cork notwithstanding, little was being done in the 1860s to continue Mathew's work. When offering parish missions, Vincentian, Redemptorist, and Passionist priests normally devoted at least one of their sermons to temperance and often administered the pledge, but the only people who were campaigning day in and day out for temperance were Father John Spratt and James Haughton. Spratt pressed on with it until his death in 1871, exhorting the ten thousand members of his society to remain faithful to their pledges. Haughton supported his work in Dublin and lobbied for Sunday closing bills and other restrictive legislation.[8]

As far as the bishops were concerned, only three seemed exercised about the drink question. Patrick Leahy, archbishop of Cashel, Thomas Furlong, bishop of Ferns, and John MacEvilly, bishop of Galway, strongly believed that all taverns should be closed on Sundays.[9] Each prelate prohibited Catholics in his diocese from buying or selling alcoholic beverages on Sundays. Indeed, MacEvilly was so upset by the practice that he declared it a reserved sin.[10] In 1867 Paul Cullen, by this time a cardinal, and several other bishops took up the issue and endorsed a Sunday closing law for Ireland. After a protracted battle, Parliament approved a compromise bill in 1878 that closed pubs on Sundays but exempted those in Dublin, Cork, Belfast, Galway, and Limerick.[11]

Advocating Sunday closing was as far as the bishops were prepared to go to promote temperance. No bishop offered any support to the total abstinence movement in the twenty years following Mathew's death. In 1875 the bishops gathered at the Synod of Maynooth to consider the problems facing the Church. The bishops' pastoral letter described drunkenness as an "abominable vice" and acknowledged that it was still widespread among the Irish people, but it did not recommend total abstinence as a remedy.[12]

FATHER CULLEN'S PIONEERS

In the 1880s the pendulum finally started to swing back and the total abstinence movement began to revive. In 1884 the St. Patrick League of the Cross was established in Cork. Although this organization, an offshoot of the society Archbishop Manning had established twelve years earlier for Catholic teetotalers in England,[13] enjoyed some success, teetotalism's resurgence in Ireland was more closely tied to the work of Father James Cullen, S.J., who had become a teetotaler in October 1874. Praying after Mass one Sunday, Cullen promised to "imitate, however feebly, the great example of Father Mathew,"[14] and in 1876 he began establishing teetotal societies in his native Wexford. A few months later, the new bishop of Ferns, Michael Warren, took the teetotal pledge and established a diocesan total abstinence society with Cullen as its secretary. Under Cullen's energetic leadership, Warren's society boasted twenty-five thousand members by 1879.[15]

In 1881 Cullen, who had been a diocesan priest for seventeen years, joined the Jesuits. As part of his formation, he had to spend two years at a novitiate on the Continent before returning to Ireland. Upon his return, his superiors ordered him to conduct retreats and missions throughout Ireland. Finally in 1887, Cullen's life began to regain its equilibrium when he was appointed director of the Irish branch of the Apostleship of Prayer, a devotional society headquartered in France. The group promoted adoration of the Sacred Heart of Jesus and allowed people to join at different levels, depending on their fervor. To promote the society's work, Cullen began publishing a magazine, *The Irish Messenger of the Sacred Heart,* which included regular columns on the virtues of teetotalism.

In 1889 Cullen took an innovative step in his campaign to promote teetotalism. While preaching a mission at St. Peter's Church in Belfast in March, Cullen was asked by the pastor to administer the pledge to all those in attendance. Afraid that many of those present would be unable or unwilling to adhere to a lifetime teetotal pledge, he refused the pastor's request. Believing that the pledges Mathew had administered had been "lightly regarded," he was determined to do things differently.[16] He offered to give the pledge to devout Catholics with no history of intemperance who were willing, in a spirit of sacrificial love for the Sacred Heart, to renounce all alcoholic beverages for life.[17] To Cullen's surprise, three hundred men and women—about one-tenth of the parish—were willing to take the pledge under these conditions, making what Cullen called the "heroic offering." Later in the year, Cullen, ever the organizer, established a teetotal branch of the Apostleship of Prayer. Just like the larger society, the total abstinence branch had varying degrees of membership. Some members agreed to pray for an end to intemperance in society, others took temporary pledges, while the core group took lifelong pledges. By July 1891, 10,103 people had made the heroic offering.[18] Cullen divided these committed abstainers into "pioneer bands" of thirty-three persons. For each band, he appointed a leader who would oversee the other members' behavior, ensuring that each member remained faithful to the pledge.

In 1898 after having returned from mission work in South Africa, Cullen reorganized his teetotal organization. His Pioneer Branch of the Total Abstinence Association of the Sacred Heart—"Pioneers" for short—was henceforth to be independent of the Apostleship of Prayer. The Pioneers catered only to lifelong teetotalers, the core constituency of his previous group. Initially, he limited membership to women, believing they would be instrumental in promoting temperance among the coming generations. Within a year, though, he changed his mind and opened the society to men. From 1900 on, the Pioneers grew dramatically. In 1904, there were 38,000 members; five years later, there were 100,000; and in 1920 there were 280,000.[19]

"IRELAND LOST ALL HER FIGHTS THROUGH DRINK"

Although Cullen and Mathew were both religious-order priests committed to promoting teetotalism among the Irish people, their movements were strikingly dissimilar. Whereas Mathew's movement was de facto Catholic but open to all creeds, Cullen's group was open only to the most devout Catholics. Mathew's society was loosely organized and centered on its charismatic leader, whereas the Pioneers were highly—perhaps rigidly—structured and not dependent on one man for their well-being. Mathew had been out of step with the Irish people on most religious and political questions; Cullen was preeminently a man of his times. He had a deep devotion to the Sacred Heart of Jesus and the Immaculate Heart of Mary, and regularly prayed in front of the Blessed Sacrament and recited the rosary.[20] These practices, which were an integral part of what Emmet Larkin has termed the "Devotional Revolution," had become popular in Ireland over the previous generation.[21] On matters political, Cullen was a cultural nationalist who sympathized with the Gaelic League and like-minded organizations.[22] Elizabeth Malcolm notes that the motto "Ireland sober, Ireland free," which had been coined in the 1880s, perfectly expressed Cullen's attitudes. In a speech to Pioneers at Vinegar Hill in 1911 he linked teetotalism with Catholic nationalism, just as O'Connell had done so often during his Repeal campaign:

> Vinegar Hill, on which we stand, has its warnings for us. In these very fields your fathers fought and fell—fell not so much beneath the fire of the North Cork Militia and the Orange Yeomanry as by the treachery of drink. Drink lost the battle at Ross, lost the battle at Wexford, and helped too the disaster at Vinegar Hill. Ireland lost all her fights through drink . . . The people of Norway and Sweden, contemplating the wreckage of their peoples through drink and the black disgrace brought on them by it, rose up and forced their governments to frame laws which have made them today among the most temperate nations in Europe. . . . Centuries before the so-called Reformation had closed down on these Northern lands, Ireland's missionaries brought the light of the Gospel to them . . . Please God, in the future, Ireland once more will send them apostles, holding in one hand the torch of Faith and in the other the torch of Temperance, and will help them to regain the Faith that has been wrested from them.[23]

Two years later, Cullen laid the blame for Ireland's drinking problems squarely on the English government: "A drunken Ireland, England knew, could never be a free Ireland—then or now! And let us say it, during the last fifty years, since Father Mathew's time, England could never have withheld self-government from Ireland if, by her shameful licensing opportunities and laws, she had not first stupefied, paralysed, degraded and disgraced the people she feared and hated. . . . [L]et the Irish drink and their slavery is secured—make Ireland and keep Ireland a nation of drunkards—then hold its people up to the scorn of the world and our object is gained!"[24]

Since he was in step theologically and politically with most of his coreligionists, Cullen did not have to worry about meeting opposition from the bishops or any other powers in the Church, whereas Mathew's work was hindered considerably by episcopal opposition. Of course, the composition of the hierarchy had changed completely since Mathew's time and the new bishops were much more confident. Thanks in part to Paul Cullen's work, order had been established in the Irish Church in the intervening years. No longer were bishops trying to rein in recalcitrant priests and root out pagan practices among the laity. Mass attendance rates had increased dramatically and vocations had risen so much that bishops were unable to find places for all their priests. At the same time, the bishops themselves were a much more disciplined and unified body than their predecessors. By the 1880s there was no one of John MacHale's ilk to reckon with in the hierarchy. Thus, for a variety of reasons, Cullen encountered a much more cooperative body of bishops than Mathew had dealt with two generations earlier.[25]

The bishops, inspired certainly in part by their favorable opinion of Cullen, took steps to promote teetotalism throughout Ireland. At the same time, they praised and honored Mathew in various ways. In 1890 the hierarchy commemorated the centenary of his birth. Some bishops issued pastorals on temperance and encouraged the establishment of temperance societies in their dioceses. In Dublin a statue of Mathew was commissioned and placed on Sackville Street, the main thoroughfare (now O'Connell Street). The outline of the Franciscan habit is clearly visible on the statue. Perhaps the archbishop of Dublin and the lay sponsors just wanted to make the statue easily identifiable to passersby; on the other hand, the archbishop may have wanted to promote a more orthodox image of Mathew. In Cork, Mathew's church, Holy Trinity, was finally completed in 1890 to mark his anniversary, and the bishop, Thomas O'Callaghan, celebrated a Pontifical High Mass there in his honor.[26]

In 1905 the bishops launched a "National Crusade against Intemperance" and in honor of Mathew entrusted the campaign to the Capuchin friars. The Capuchins dedicated themselves wholeheartedly to the task, preaching dozens of temperance missions each year. In 1912 the Capuchin provincial informed his superior in Rome that the pledge had been given to 1,141,191 persons since 1905. Although this may have been true, the friars' labors were not all that effective. At the end of their missions, they would give the pledge to all comers and then move on to another parish the following week. Without any organizational support or follow-up, many of those who pledged soon fell away.[27]

The work of the Pioneers was to prove more lasting. Their interest in appealing to a Catholic elite rather than the rank and file and their highly organized structure gave them a permanency that the Capuchins were unable to attain. The Pioneers continued to expand in the 1920s and 1930s. Several of Ireland's most revered Catholics from this period were Pioneers: Matt Talbot (1856–1925), a reclaimed alcoholic known for his ascetical piety; Edel Quinn (1907–1944), a lay missionary who spent most of her adult life in Africa; and Father John Sullivan, S.J. (1861–1933), a Dublin priest famed for his sanctity.[28]

When Cullen died in 1921, leadership passed on to another Jesuit, Father Joseph Flinn. Under Flinn, the Pioneers were more overtly political, lobbying the leaders of the fledgling Free State to reduce the pubs' operating hours.[29] In 1924 and 1927, the government enacted licensing acts, which forced pubs to close earlier. Furthermore, in 1927 pubs were ordered to close on St. Patrick's Day to ensure that the Catholic feast day would be celebrated in a reverent manner.[30]

Temperance in Irish America after Mathew

In the United States, just as in Ireland, the temperance movement faded in the 1850s and 1860s. The Maine Laws had proved very controversial and sparked a backlash from distillers, brewers, and saloon keepers, who battled the measures in the courts and the legislatures. By 1860 several of the statutes had been nullified or repealed, and in those states where strict laws remained, temperance advocates were learning that enforcement was difficult and politically unpopular.[31]

Although Catholic temperance leaders had not lobbied for Prohibition—in fact, many of the most vocal Prohibitionists were nativists—their societies nonetheless suffered as the 1850s progressed. Most Catholic temperance groups lost members, and a number became moribund.[32] By 1860 much of what Father Mathew had achieved during his American tour was already undone.

With the onset of the Civil War in 1861, the temperance movement faded still more. As the fighting raged on, most Americans, especially those in uniform, began to view temperance with considerable skepticism. Even so, several Irish chaplains exhorted their soldiers to take the pledge. The most successful was Father James Dillon, C.S.C., who served as a chaplain in General Thomas Meagher's Irish Brigade. In the first year of the war, Dillon administered the pledge to seven hundred of Meagher's troops. Aside from this "Temperance Regiment," Dillon and the other Irish chaplains weren't terribly successful.[33] A contemporary temperance historian, Norman Clark, remarks that the Irish and German regiments in the Union army had "frightful reputations for hard drinking."[34]

TEMPERANCE REVIVAL

As soon as the war ended, Catholic temperance advocates regrouped and tried to revitalize the movement, which had only twenty-two functioning societies at this point. In 1866 the bishops meeting in Baltimore offered their strongest endorsement of teetotalism thus far: "Since the most frightful scandals owe their origin to excess in drinking, . . . We consider most praiseworthy the zeal of those most faithful children of the Church, who, the more surely to avoid all danger of excess, pledge themselves to Total Abstinence."[35]

Over the next five years, priests and laity alike began to respond to the bishops' call. New societies were organized and several older societies were revitalized. Some of the new societies were set up by Paulist, Jesuit, and Passionist preachers during parish missions. Encouraged to some degree by James Roosevelt Bayley, the bishop of Newark, New Jersey, several leaders decided to form a national association of some sort in 1871.[36] On Washington's Birthday in 1872 their idea came to pass with the establishment of the Catholic Total Abstinence Union of America (CTAU).

Representing twenty-eight thousand men, the CTAU delegates chose Father James McDevitt of Washington, D.C., as their president and decided that their emblem would be a cross flanked by shamrocks. Since the union's membership was overwhelmingly Irish, the delegates presumably saw the shamrocks as fitting symbols. In their official statement the delegates expressed hope that the CTAU would help make all the state and local societies "stronger and better" and help do "away with a multitude of aspersions upon [Catholicism]."[37] With nativism on the rise, CTAU leaders clearly hoped that their organization would help make Catholics appear more acceptable to the nation's Protestant majority.

Within a year, a number of temperance bands, reading rooms, and baseball leagues had been established in New York, Massachusetts, Ohio, and Minnesota to provide men with diversions from the saloons. In Boston, Catholic teetotalers staged a large parade on October 10th to commemorate Mathew's birthday.[38] With the movement clearly gaining in size and strength, CTAU leaders became more ambitious. At their 1873 meeting, they discussed the upcoming Centennial Exhibition, which was to be held in Philadelphia's Fairmount Park in 1876. A massive undertaking, the Centennial Exhibition was intended not just to commemorate America's independence but also to serve as America's answer to England's Crystal Palace Exhibit of 1851 and the Paris Exposition of 1867. Its architects planned a six-month-long fair showcasing all of America's latest inventions, along with a sampling of its foods, beverages, artwork, flora, and fauna. Foreign countries were to be invited to display their wares as well.

CTAU leaders decided that their fledgling union should take an active part in the exhibition. Whereas most participating groups were planning to set up booths to promote their concerns, the CTAU planned to erect a large granite and marble water fountain in the middle of the fairground. In the center of the fountain would be a sixteen-foot-high statue of Moses striking a rock with a rod. Water was to gush from the rock into a surrounding pool, recalling the miracle that God worked for Moses in the desert (Exod. 17:1–7). Flanking the pool were to be four statues that would form a Maltese cross. One was to be of Father Mathew, and the others were to be of three American Catholics who played roles in the Revolutionary War: John Carroll, Charles Carroll, and John Barry.

On July 4, 1876, hundreds of CTAU delegates gathered in Fairmount Park to unveil the statues and turn on the water. It wasn't quite finished—one statue was not yet complete—but a great parade and celebration were held nonetheless. The pedestal under each statue carried an inscription that described the subject's life achievements and expressed the CTAU's philosophy. The inscription on John Barry's pedestal stressed the group's enthusiasm for America: "This monument was dedicated to American liberty and republican institutions by the Catholic Total Abstinence Union of America upon July 4, 1876."[39]

TURNING TO THE LAW FOR HELP

In the years following the Centennial Exhibition, the temperance movement grew steadily in size and strength. As the movement expanded, increasing numbers of teetotalers began to doubt—just as they had in the 1840s—whether moral suasion was a sufficient response to the problem. A small Prohibition Party had been formed in 1869 by Protestant teetotal militants and was slowly gaining strength in the 1870s. A more influential force was the Women's Christian Temperance Union (WCTU), which was founded in 1874. Under the leadership of Frances Willard, who took over in 1879, the WCTU came to advocate Prohibition. In 1880 the WCTU and other Prohibitionists scored a victory when Kansas became the first state in twenty-five years to outlaw the manufacture and sale of alcoholic beverages. Shortly thereafter, Maine, Rhode Island, North Dakota, and South Dakota followed suit.[40]

As the Protestant-oriented temperance groups started to favor legislation, so, too, did many members of the CTAU. Few Catholics were ready to champion Prohibition outright, but many, including several bishops, favored restrictive legislation of some sort. Within the hierarchy, the strongest temperance advocates were John Ireland, John Keane, and John Lancaster Spalding. Ireland and Keane were Irish born, and each had taken the pledge from Father Mathew as a child and had remained faithful to it.[41] Keane, who was bishop of Richmond from 1878 until 1887, when he was appointed rector of Catholic University, had lobbied for a

Sunday closing law and urged all Catholic liquor sellers to abandon the trade. Ireland, appointed coadjutor bishop of St. Paul in 1875 and bishop in 1884, regularly denounced saloon keepers as "tools of the Devil" and pressed for high-license laws in Minnesota to reduce their numbers. Spalding, a native Kentuckian appointed bishop of Peoria in 1877, was, for a time at least, an open advocate of Prohibition.[42]

Each of these bishops later became prominent in the liberal movement in the hierarchy known as Americanism because of its enthusiasm for all things American.[43] While a few conservative bishops, such as Michael Corrigan of New York, also championed temperance, most conservatives were unenthusiastic. Temperance was by and large a concern of progressives, promoted in the same breath with American democracy and separation of church and state.

In 1884 the bishops gathered at the Vatican's behest in Baltimore for their Third Plenary Council. Directed by Rome to delineate the rights of priests vis-à-vis their ordinaries and to expand their network of schools, the bishops also found time to discuss temperance. The bishops didn't just decry drunkenness and commend total abstainers, as they had in the past. Prompted by a detailed memorial from the CTAU, they strongly endorsed Sunday closing laws, asking that the laws "not be relaxed but even more rigidly enforced," and called on pastors "to induce all of their flocks that may be engaged in the sale of liquors to abandon as soon as they can the dangerous traffic, and to embrace a more becoming way of making a living." They were sure that these efforts would go "far towards strangling the monstrous evil of intemperance . . . [and] put a powerful check on the desecration of the Lord's Day."[44]

Having received the hierarchy's strong endorsement, the Catholic temperance movement picked up momentum. In 1886 the CTAU held its annual meeting on the campus of Notre Dame. The school's president, Father Thomas Walsh, C.S.C., an ardent teetotaler, was happy to host the gathering. During Walsh's tenure (1881–93), Notre Dame had become such a dry institution that students were forbidden to drink on or off campus even if they were of legal age.[45]

The following year, Catholic teetotalers received another boost: Pope Leo XIII sent a letter to John Ireland expressing his support for temperance groups and singling out the CTAU as an "excellent association" that was helping to "combat the destructive vice of intemperance." He urged all priests to take the pledge so as to "shine before all as models of abstinence."[46]

In 1890 the CTAU had a banner year. Since this was the centennial of Mathew's birth, the CTAU planned special events in his honor that drew Cardinal James Gibbons of Baltimore and several archbishops to its convention.[47] Addressing the conference was Terence Powderly, the Irish American leader of the Knights of Labor. Powderly's union had a progressive membership policy: it admitted blacks as well as whites, women as well as men, Jews as well as Christians. Starting in 1878, though, the union decided that it would not admit saloonkeepers. Since Powderly's election as grand master workman in 1879, the union had become even more clearly identified with temperance principles. A staunch teetotaler, Powderly urged all members to take the total abstinence pledge and exhorted local affiliates to expel any intemperate members.[48]

In Catholic circles Powderly and his union were the subject of considerable controversy. Several conservative bishops were troubled by his union's secrecy and use of Masonic rites and had petitioned the Holy Office to condemn it as a secret society. Although Powderly was at this time a practicing Catholic who opposed labor violence and even strikes, he was still viewed as a radical by key conservative prelates, especially Corrigan.[49] The Americanist bishops were much more sympathetic; Gibbons, Keane and Ireland were well disposed to both Powderly and his union. Learning that a move was afoot to have Rome condemn the union in 1886, Gibbons lobbied strenuously on its behalf. In 1888 the Vatican issued a cautious ruling that satisfied the Americanists: the Knights of Labor could "be allowed for the time being."[50]

At the CTAU conference, Powderly told his listeners that he had helped to organize the first Father Mathew Society in his small hometown, Carbondale, Pennsylvania, in 1868. Over the intervening twenty years, Powderly said, he had become convinced that the intoxicated workingman was a "slave to liquor, and the slave of liquor is now and has always been the slave of man." He concluded his speech with an appeal to workers "to neither touch, taste nor countenance the use of liquor."[51]

The following year, the CTAU again demonstrated its liberal sympathies when it invited Frances Willard to speak at its national convention.[52] Although Willard was known first and foremost for her success with temperance—the 150,000-strong WCTU was America's largest temperance organization—she was also famous for her advocacy of women's suffrage and what she called "Christian Socialism."[53] Willard spoke to the delegates, attended their daily masses and sat on the platform throughout the convention. Perhaps motivated by Miss Willard's presence, the CTAU, which was originally all male, elected its first female vice president, Miss Sallie Moore.[54] Willard's only complaint about the gathering was the "reluctance of our good Catholic friends to declare for prohibitory law."[55]

Relations between the CTAU and the WCTU remained cordial throughout the decade. Willard stressed that her organization was open to Catholic and Jewish as well as Protestant women. To underscore her openness to Catholics, she occasionally invited priests to sit on the platform and offer prayers at the WCTU's annual meetings. Indeed in 1895, two priests attended the WCTU conference: one represented Cardinal Gibbons, and the other was a delegate from the CTAU.[56]

The Catholic temperance movement continued to prosper. By 1895 both the Knights of Columbus and the Saint Vincent de Paul Society had followed the Knights of Labor's lead and expelled liquor dealers from their ranks. In 1902 the Knights of Columbus decided to ban alcoholic beverages from all their functions; the Ancient Order of Hibernians adopted the same policy two years later. The founder of the Knights of Columbus, Father Michael McGivney, who had died in 1890, surely would have approved of these steps, since he had been a total abstainer and served as a chaplain to a total abstinence society before establishing the Knights.[57]

Some Catholic teetotalers also renewed their campaign against the Benedictine monks of St. Vincent's Abbey, who owned and operated a brewery. When a group of Bavarian monks established themselves near Pittsburgh in 1846, the bishop, Michael O' Connor, had tried to prevent them from setting up a brewery, but Rome had overruled him. At the Third Plenary Council, Bishop Keane had proposed a measure that would have forbidden clergy and religious from making any alcoholic beverages (aside from altar wine), but the majority rejected it.[58] In 1892 Martin I. J. Griffin, an Irish American journalist and militant Prohibitionist, revived the issue, charging that the monks belonged not to the Order of Saint Benedict, but rather to the "Order of Sacred Brewers."[59] In 1895 a group of Pittsburgh priests petitioned the newly arrived apostolic delegate, Archbishop Francesco Satolli, to pressure the monks to shut their brewery. Satolli urged them to stop selling their beer to saloons and limit themselves to making beer for their own community, but the archabbot was adamant.[60] The issue was subsequently taken up by Father George Zurcher, a German immigrant and zealous teetotaler, who took aim at the "beer monks" in two pamphlets: *Foreign Ideas in the Catholic Church in America* (1896) and *Monks and their Decline* (1898). In 1899 the monks finally gave in, declaring they would no longer distribute their beer to local taverns.[61]

While Catholic teetotalers were working to get their coreligionists out of the liquor business, some temperance advocates were hoping to put them out of business altogether. In 1895 the Reverend H. H. Russell, a Congregationalist minister, organized the Anti-Saloon League (ASL), which rapidly became the most powerful temperance organization in the nation. Although the ASL had a Protestant orientation, among its founders was John Ireland, who served as a vice president of the group from 1896 to 1901 and was a frequent speaker at its events. ASL leaders would eventually lobby for Prohibition, but in the 1890s they argued only for the suppression of taverns and claimed to have no objections to people's drinking in their homes. Russell and his associates argued that tavernkeepers often promoted drunkenness among their patrons, regularly served alcohol to minors, and allowed prostitution and gambling to occur on their premises.

Some Catholic teetotalers rallied around the semi-Prohibitionist policies of the ASL. As early as 1890 articles had begun appearing in the influential *Catholic World* calling for the prohibition of saloons.[62] The majority, however, remained with the more cautious CTAU. In 1895 the CTAU, whose membership rolls had grown to fifty-five thousand, had another successful convention, drawing both Archbishop Satolli and Theodore Roosevelt, who was then New York City's police commissioner.[63] Satolli celebrated Mass for the CTAU at St. Patrick's Cathedral, while Roosevelt assured the delegates of his support for strict enforcement of Sunday closing laws.

Just as the CTAU seemed to be reaching new heights of influence, the Vatican started to pull its support away from the CTAU's patrons, the Americanist prelates. First, in 1895, Pope Leo XIII issued *Longinqua oceani,* a letter in which he warned American church leaders not to presume that America's system of church–state separation was to be viewed as a model for other countries. The following year, Keane was abruptly removed as the rector of Catholic University at the request of Satolli, who had come to view him as overly ecumenical.[64]

Keane was treated kindly after his dismissal from the rectorship. He was invited to Rome to work for the Vatican's Congregation of Seminaries and Universities and in 1900 was appointed archbishop of Dubuque. Nevertheless, momentum in Rome was still moving strongly against the Americanists. In January 1899 Pope Leo delivered a major blow to liberals when he issued *Testem benevolentiae,* a letter that condemned certain aspects of Americanism. The pope claimed that some Americanists were stressing natural virtues to the exclusion of the supernatural. Although short on specifics, the letter implied that the Americanists were unduly optimistic about the times and insufficiently critical of American society's emphasis on liberty.

Although no Americanist bishop was disciplined as a result of the papal letter, the movement was nevertheless seriously shaken and slowly began to falter. The CTAU was likewise reeling at this time. Its key episcopal patrons, Ireland and Keane, had been rebuffed by the pope and one of the CTAU's regional presidents, Father Zurcher, had resigned in January 1899 after his controversial *Monks and their Decline* had been placed on the Vatican's Index of Forbidden Books. Still, the group pressed on. In the summer of 1899 it sponsored a celebration marking the fiftieth anniversary of Father Mathew's visit to America. In 1903 the CTAU noted that its membership had topped ninety thousand, an all-time high it would never again approach. At this time, the Boston archdiocese alone had seventy-seven Catholic total abstinence societies, a number of which fielded baseball teams that competed against one another in a league. In 1905 the CTAU was able to attract both President Theodore Roosevelt and Cardinal Gibbons to its meeting in Wilkes-Barre, Pennsylvania.[65]

Still, all was not well with the CTAU. Although Gibbons periodically attended CTAU meetings, he was not a total abstainer and was not all that supportive of the group. He liked to describe himself as a "temperate man, but not a temperance man."⁶⁶ The CTAU's strongest episcopal supporters were Ireland and Keane, who remained under a cloud in the wake of *Testem benevolentiae*.⁶⁷ And while the union had an impressive number of members, its leaders could not agree on its aims. As other temperance organizations began to come out for Prohibition, the CTAU was unable to enunciate a clear position.⁶⁸

In 1907, Prohibitionists scored a major victory when Georgia became the first southern state to adopt Prohibition. By 1912, ten states were dry and more than thirty had local option laws that allowed individual towns and counties to ban alcohol. Although pleased with their successes, Prohibitionist leaders were not completely satisfied. They recognized that where a dry state bordered a wet state, saloons and liquor stores would be established just across the state lines. For Prohibition to be effective, it would have to be national in scope. In late 1913 the ASL launched a campaign for a constitutional amendment banning alcohol. While the drive for national Prohibition gained strength, the ASL continued to press for legislation at the state level as well. Success followed success. By the end of 1916, twenty-three states had adopted Prohibition, and bills were pending in several others.⁶⁹

Some Catholic teetotalers, anxious to join this agitation and disappointed by the CTAU's timidity, decided to establish the Catholic Prohibition League of America (CPLA) in 1914. Among the group's leaders were Father J. J. Curran, who at the time was a vice president of the ASL, and Father Zurcher, who was probably the most zealous Catholic Prohibitionist priest of the time. Having discovered that Father Mathew had endorsed restrictive legislation shortly before his death, Zurcher claimed that he was simply carrying on Mathew's work.⁷⁰ A sharp critic of the CTAU, Zurcher led the CPLA and edited a quarterly newsletter, *Catholics and Prohibition*.

A few Catholics followed Zurcher and Curran, but most were much more skeptical about Prohibition. Some prominent Catholics, such as the editors of the fledgling Jesuit journal *America*, wondered whether some extreme Prohibitionists might not want to bar sacramental wine. In 1916 these fears were borne out when Oklahoma added to its existing Prohibition legislation so as to become "bone dry." Under the revised statutes, Oklahoma forbade not only the sale and manufacture of alcoholic beverages but their importation into the state as well. When an Oklahoma City priest was forbidden from shipping two gallons of altar wine into the state, church officials responded by filing a suit claiming that their religious freedom was being infringed upon. After suffering an initial defeat, the plaintiffs were vindicated by the state supreme court, which ruled that the wine was not being used for intoxicating purposes and therefore did not fall under the state's ban.[71]

THE EIGHTEENTH AMENDMENT

In 1917 as the United States was reluctantly entering into World War I, Prohibitionists recognized that the exigencies of the war could redound to their benefit. In May, a month after America entered the war, Congress banned the sale of alcoholic beverages to soldiers in uniform, arguing that their health and effectiveness might otherwise be impaired. In August, congressional leaders, fearing a food shortage, proscribed the distillation of spirits for the duration of the war. In December, President Woodrow Wilson followed up on Congress's actions by imposing strict limits on the amount of grain available for the brewing of beer.

Two weeks later, Congress overwhelmingly approved the Eighteenth Amendment, which outlawed the "manufacture, sale or transportation of intoxicating liquors." In an effort to increase the amendment's popularity, the sponsors used more flexible language than "bone dry" partisans would have wanted. Rather than outlaw all alcoholic beverages, proponents focused on intoxicating liquors. Clearly, sacramental wines were not to be covered under the amendment, and perhaps some types of beer might be exempt as well.

With twenty-seven states already dry, the amendment's chances of being ratified were good. By January 1919 the necessary three-fourths of the state legislatures had voiced their support. Prohibition was set to take effect in January 1920 after a one-year grace period had elapsed. In the meantime, Congress endorsed a proposal by Representative Andrew Volstead that clarified some of the Eighteenth Amendment's ambiguities and provided for its enforcement. The Volstead Act closed one of the amendment's potential loopholes by declaring that all beverages that were more than 0.5% alcohol were to be considered intoxicating. At the same time, several exemptions were specified: alcohol used for medical, sacramental, or industrial purposes was not proscribed, and homemade cider was not subject to legal penalties, provided it was consumed at home.[72]

When Prohibition went into effect, some Catholics cheered. Senators Thomas Walsh of Montana, Henry Ashurst of Arizona, and Joseph Randsdall of Louisiana were Catholic drys. Bishops Thomas Lenihan of Montana and Regis Canevin of Pittsburgh publicly supported Prohibition as well.[73] Father Zurcher was so excited that he discontinued his journal *Catholics and Prohibition,* concluding that the liquor problem had finally been settled once and for all.

Most Catholics were not nearly so enthusiastic. No major American prelate praised the measure. Archbishops Ireland and Keane, the two most likely sympathizers, had both died in 1918. For his part, Gibbons was deeply dismayed by the prospect of Prohibition. In 1917 he had been quoted in the *New York Times* as saying that the passage of Prohibition would be a "national catastrophe, little short of a crime against the spiritual and physical well-being of the American people."[74] He reiterated his opposition in 1918 and again in 1919 after the Volstead Act became law.

A good indicator of the body of bishops' lack of enthusiasm for Prohibition was their publication of the "Program of Social Reconstruction" in 1920. The letter called for government action to ensure that laborers received living wages and the rights of union members were protected. No mention was made in this lengthy document of the need for government action to protect people from the dangers of strong drink. Indeed, alcohol and temperance were not mentioned at all.[75] On the other hand, the bishops were careful not to make any statements denigrating Prohibition.[76] For the fourteen years that Prohibition was in effect, the bishops studiously avoided commenting on it.

Clearly, as the temperance movement became identified with Prohibition, Catholic sympathy for the cause diminished. Since the days of Father Mathew, teetotalism had been a top priority for many assimilation-minded Irish clergy and laity. Over the decades many Irish Catholics had eagerly joined with Protestants to battle the saloons and promote the temperance cause. But by 1920 Catholic enthusiasm for temperance seemed to have run its course; as America's "noble experiment" was getting under way, most Catholics were lining up on the "wet" side behind New York's governor, Al Smith.

The Postwar Pioneers in Ireland

While the Catholic teetotal movement had largely fizzled out in America by the 1930s,[77] the Pioneers continued to prosper in the 1940s and 1950s. In the early forties, the Pioneers were faced with new challenges on two fronts. On one hand, brewers, distillers, and pub owners began to press for a liberalization of the laws on closing hours. In 1941 the government voted to allow bars to open on St. Patrick's Day and extended the hours that bars in Dublin, Cork, Galway, and Limerick could be open on Sundays. Pubs were still to remain closed all day on Sundays in rural areas, however.[78]

The Pioneers faced a challenge of a different order when Alcoholics Anonymous (AA) established its first Irish chapter in 1946. AA focused its energies on problem drinkers, a group from which the Pioneers tended to shy away. AA's organizers argued that alcohol addiction was not a moral failing but a disease that needed to be treated through counseling and group therapy. Although AA leaders acknowledged the important role that spirituality played in healing chronic drinkers, they were considerably more secular in their approach than were the Pioneers. Nonetheless, the Jesuit directors of the Pioneers gave AA a cautious welcome and worked to educate themselves on the medical and pyschological aspects of alcoholism.[79]

As the 1950s dawned, the Pioneers had reason to feel confident. In 1949 eighty thousand of their members filled Dublin's Croke Park for a Mass commemorating their fiftieth anniversary, and by 1952 the Pioneers were picking up one hundred new members every week. New centers were being established in Ireland, England, Scotland, Holland, and the United States.[80]

In 1956 the Pioneers' director claimed they had enrolled their five hundred thousandth member. Considering the Ireland's population had dropped to 2.8 million in the 1950s,[81] the Pioneers had succeeded in drawing almost 20 percent of the Irish people into their elite organization. As the group expanded, it continued to stage triumphal mass rallies and processions. In 1956 at least sixty thousand Pioneers converged on Cork for ceremonies marking the centennial of Mathew's death. At the main event, the Pioneers listened as Cornelius Lucey, the bishop of Cork, hailed Mathew's work: "Of all the great Irishmen of the last century he was the greatest, judged alike by the impact he made on his own generation and the inspiration he has been to the generations since. He could move the nation as neither O'Connell, Parnell nor the rest could; and he did so for a great freedom, namely freedom from the bondage of strong drink." Three years later, ninety thousand Pioneers came back to Croke Park to celebrate their sixtieth anniversary.[82]

Although the Pioneers had much to celebrate in those years, there were disturbing trends as well. Alcohol consumption was rising steadily. In 1950, the per capita consumption of pure alcohol was roughly 0.75 gallons per year; by the end of the decade, it had increased to 1.25 gallons. At the same time, liquor dealers were pressing hard for further liberalization of the licensing laws. In 1960 they got their way: the government repealed what was left of the Sunday closing laws on the grounds that the statutes had discriminated against pub owners in rural areas.[83]

As the 1960s progressed, the Pioneers' problems began to mount. The Second Vatican Council (1962–65) ushered in many changes in Catholic life and led some Pioneers to question whether their devotions to the Sacred Heart were relevant. The issue became more urgent as the decade wore on. Most teenagers were absorbed with television and rock music and not at all inclined to give up alcohol for the rest of their lives.

This decline has accelerated in recent years. Arthur McCrory, the Pioneers' archivist and historian, estimated that there were between 220,000 and 250,000 members in 1990 and acknowledged that many were elderly.[84] He attributed the Pioneers' decline to television, affluence, and the changes associated with Vatican II. Another explanation could be the waning of the Catholic nationalist identity in Ireland. The Pioneers certainly tied themselves to the Church and to nationalism. It should not be surprising that as these forces began to unravel in the 1960s the Pioneers would suffer as well.[85] While the Pioneers have been losing ground, Irish alcohol consumption rates have been climbing. From 1960 to 1980 the per capita consumption of pure alcohol increased from 1.25 gallons annually to 2.5 gallons. Consumption decreased modestly in the 1980s but has risen again in the past decade. A 1993 survey estimated the per capita consumption at 2.2 gallons, but the rate had edged up to 2.4 gallons by 1995.[86] Part of the increase has been attributed to the growing number of women who have taken up social drinking and now frequent pubs, which until recently catered only to men. The economic boom of the 1990s, which has given the average Irish person more disposable income, is another contributing factor.

Nevertheless the effects of Father Theobald Mathew's and Father James Cullen's labors are still evident. While consumption is higher now than it was in the 1950s, Ireland's rates are not out of line with those of other Western nations and its rates of death by cirrhosis are the lowest in the Western world. The editors of the 1991 edition of the *Encyclopedia of Alcoholism* note that out of forty-seven countries surveyed, Ireland ranks thirtieth in alcohol consumption. The French imbibe two-and-a-half times as much alcohol as the Irish and Americans also outdrink them. Irish teenagers drink less than their counterparts in America and England, and there remains an unusually high proportion of adult teetotalers in Ireland.[87] Indeed, teetotal and abstemious Paddies continue to be a presence in Irish society. Surely Mathew and Cullen would take consolation from that knowledge.

Notes

INTRODUCTION

1. James R. Barrett, "Why Paddy Drank: The Social Importance of Whiskey in Pre-Famine Ireland," *Journal of Popular Culture* 11 (Summer 1977): 155; Stephen Birmingham, *Real Lace: America's Irish Rich* (New York, 1973), 52; Elizabeth Malcolm, *"Ireland Sober, Ireland Free": Drink and Temperance in Nineteenth Century Ireland* (Dublin, 1986), 333–34, Robert O'Brien and Morris Chafetz, *The Encyclopedia of Alcoholism*, 2d ed. (New York, 1991), 131–32; Robert O'Brien, Morris Chafetz, and Sidney Cohen, *The Encyclopedia of Understanding Alcohol and Drugs* (New York, 1999), 252; Diarmaid Ferriter, *A Nation of Extremes: The Pioneers in Twentieth Century Ireland* (Dublin, 1999), 249; Phil Davies and Dermot Walsh, *Alcohol Problems and Alcohol Control in Europe* (New York, 1983), 95–96; Gerard E. Sherry, "Irish Temperance Movement Battling Old Problem," *Our Sunday Visitor*, February 21, 1988.

2. Malcolm, x.

3. Robert O'Brien and Morris Chafetz, *The Encyclopedia of Alcoholism*, 1st ed. (New York, 1982), 126 (see also ibid., 332–33); Bruce A. Christiansen and John Teahan, "Cross-Cultural Comparisons of Irish and American Drinking Practices and Beliefs," *Journal of Studies on Alcohol* 48 (1987): 558–60; O'Brien, Chafetz, and Cohen, 252.

4. See Jerome Jaffe, M.D., *Encyclopedia of Drugs and Alcohol* (New York, 1995), 1061.

5. The Capuchins are one of the three branches of the Franciscans. They were established in 1525 in Italy and were first sent to Ireland in 1615. See *Catholic Encyclopedia* (New York, 1909) 3:320–27.

6. Dublin Castle was the headquarters of the British government.

7. For estimates on the Irish population in America in 1850, see Patrick J. Blessing, "Irish," *Harvard Encyclopedia of American Ethnic Groups* (Cambridge, 1980), 528–29.

8. For temperance in England, see Brian Harrison, *Drink and the Victorians: The Temperance Question in England, 1815–1872* (London, 1971); idem, *Dictionary of British Temperance Biography* (Coventry, 1973); Lillian Lewis Shiman, *Crusade against Drink in Victorian England* (New York, 1988). For temperance activity in

America, see Joseph Gusfield, *Symbolic Crusade: Status Politics and the American Temperance Movement*, 2d ed. (Urbana, Ill., 1986); W. J. Rorabaugh, *The Alcoholic Republic: An American Tradition* (New York, 1979); Ian Tyrrell, *Sobering Up: From Temperance to Prohibition in Antebellum America, 1800–1860* (Westport, Conn., 1979); Mark Lender and James Martin, *Drinking in America: A History* (New York, 1987); Jack S. Blocker Jr., *American Temperance Movements: Cycles of Reform* (Boston, 1989).

9. F. S. L. Lyons, *Ireland since the Famine* (London, 1971); Gearóid Ó'Tuathaigh, *Ireland before the Famine, 1798–1848* (Dublin, 1972); R. F. Foster, *Modern Ireland, 1600–1972* (New York, 1988); T. W. Moody and F. X. Martin, O.S.A. eds., *The Course of Irish History*, rev. and enl. ed. (Niwot, Colo., 1995); H. F. Kearney, "Father Mathew: Apostle of Modernisation," in *Studies in Irish History Presented to R. Dudley Edwards*, ed. Art Cosgrove and Donal McCartney (Dublin, 1979), 164.

10. John F. Maguire, *Father Mathew: A Biography* (London, 1863). For the problems with Maguire's claims, see Malcolm, 117.

11. Patrick Rogers, *Father Theobald Mathew: Apostle of Temperance* (Dublin, 1943); Father Augustine, O.F.M. Cap., *Footprints of Father Mathew O.F.M. Cap., Apostle of Temperance* (Dublin, 1947).

12. For example, in describing Mathew's response to the Potato Famine, Augustine writes, "In this awful plight, like the Prophet of old, the man of the people, the priest of God, the son of St. Francis stood before the Government crying aloud on it, in letter after letter, to come to the rescue of the drooping, withering children of our Heavenly Father" (404).

13. George Bretherton, *"The Irish Temperance Movement, 1829–1847"* (Ph.D. diss., Columbia University, 1978). Although Bretherton did not publish his dissertation, he has had an essay and an article published that draw on his research: "Against the Flowing Tide: Whiskey and Temperance in the Making of Modern Ireland," in *Drinking Behavior and Belief in Modern History*, ed. Susanna Barrows and Robin Room (Berkeley, Calif., 1991), 147–64; idem, "The Battle between Carnival and Lent: Temperance and Repeal in Ireland, 1829–1845," *Social History/Histoire Sociale* 27 (1994): 295–320.

14. Colm Kerrigan, "The Social Impact of the Irish Temperance Movement, 1839–1845," *Irish Economic and Social History* 14 (1987): 20–38; idem, "Irish Temperance and U.S. Anti-Slavery: Father Mathew and the Abolitionists," *History Workshop Journal* 31 (Spring 1991): 105–19; idem, "Father Mathew and Teetotalism in London, 1843," *London Journal* 11 (1985): 107–14; idem, *Father Mathew and the Irish Temperance Movement, 1838–1849* (Cork, 1992).

15. The following biographies fail to discuss O'Connell's teetotal sympathies: Sean O'Faolain, *King of the Beggars* (London, 1938; reprint, Dublin, 1986); An-

gus MacIntyre, *The Liberator: Daniel O'Connell and the Irish Party, 1830–1847* (London, 1965); Charles Trevenix Trench, *The Great Dan* (London, 1986).

16. O'Connell wanted to repeal the Act of Union of 1801, which joined Ireland to England. Repeal would have allowed the Irish to have their own legislature in Dublin.

17. Lawrence McCaffrey, *Daniel O'Connell and the Repeal Year* (Lexington, Ky., 1966), 21–23.

18. Mathew receives little or no attention in the following works: Donal Kerr, *Peel, Priests, and Politics: Sir Robert Peel's Administration and the Roman Catholic Church in Ireland, 1846–1852* (Oxford, 1982); idem, *A Nation of Beggars?: Priests, People and Politics in Famine Ireland, 1846–1852* (Oxford, 1994); S. J. Connolly, *Priests and People in Pre-Famine Ireland, 1780–1845* (New York, 1982); Emmet Larkin, *The Making of the Roman Catholic Church in Ireland, 1850–1860* (Chapel Hill, N.C., 1980). One study that pays considerable attention to Mathew is Desmond Keenan, *The Catholic Church in Nineteenth-Century Ireland* (Dublin, 1983).

Chapter One

1. *Alexis de Tocqueville's Journey in Ireland, July–August, 1835*, trans. and ed. Emmet Larkin (Washington, D.C., 1990), 9, 39.

2. Gustave de Beaumont, *Ireland: Social, Political, and Religious*, 2 vols. (London, 1839), 1:264–65, 302–3. Walter Scott was similarly shocked by what he saw during his 1825 trip to Ireland: "Their poverty is not exaggerated—it is on the extreme verge of human misery—their cottages would scarce serve for pig-sties even in Scotland." *The Journal of Sir Walter Scott*, ed. W. E. K. Anderson (Oxford, 1972), 1.

3. For the state of Irish farming in the years before the Famine, see Raymond Crotty, *Irish Agricultural Production: Its Volume and Structure* (Cork, 1966); Foster, 331–44; Cormac Ó'Gráda, *Ireland: A New Economic History, 1789–1939* (Oxford, 1994).

4. *Tocqueville's Journey*, 41, 64, 89, 90, 122–23.

5. Ibid., 48, 72.

6. Beaumont, 2:69.

7. Donal McCartney, *The Dawning of Democracy: Ireland 1800–1870*. (Dublin, 1987), 118–19.

8. The Penal Laws were a series of measures imposed on Irish Catholics after the Revolution of 1688. Catholics were prohibited from practicing their religion openly; purchasing land; voting or holding political office; serving as lawyers, judges, or military officers.

9. *Daniel O'Connell, His Early Life and Journal, 1795–1806,* ed. Arthur Houston (London, 1906), 231–32; Trench, 23–25. O'Connell claimed that he "could never drink more than three glasses of wine without being sick." William O'Neill Daunt, *Personal Recollections of the Late Daniel O'Connell,* 2 vols. (London, 1848), 1:155.

10. Oliver MacDonagh, *The Hereditary Bondsman: Daniel O'Connell, 1775–1829* (New York, 1987), 34–41.

11. *Daniel O'Connell,* 110.

12. Ibid., 138; O'Faolain, 76.

13. At first, O'Connell was a reluctant returnee. Writing to his wife during Lent, he said: "I got your *Sermon* last night and am condemned to eat *fish,* nothing but fish for more than a week." Daniel O'Connell to Mary O'Connell, March 24, 1809, in *The Correspondence of Daniel O'Connell,* ed. Maurice O'Connell 8 vols. (New York, 1972–1980), 1:194 (emphasis in original).

14. Maurice R. O'Connell argues that O'Connell was a consistent defender of religious liberty and church-state separation throughout his life. Indeed, he sees O'Connell as a herald of the Second Vatican Council's Declaration on Religious Freedom. See "Religious Freedom," in *Daniel O'Connell: The Man and His Politics,* (Dublin, 1990), 30–31. Brendan Clifford criticizes an earlier version of this essay for its failure to consider adequately O'Connell's statements in the 1830s and 1840s. See *The Veto Controversy* (Belfast, 1985), 192.

15. Dáire Keogh, *'The French Disease': The Catholic Church and Irish Radicalism, 1790–1800* (Dublin, 1993), 136–58.

16. Foster, 280.

17. Keogh, 215–17.

18. O'Connell, *Daniel O'Connell,* 46.

19. An episcopal veto had been discussed in the 1790s when the Catholic seminary at Maynooth was being established. See Keogh, 78–80.

20. Propaganda Fide was the Congregation in Rome responsible for overseeing the Church's foreign missions.

21. In 1799 the ten bishop trustees of Maynooth declared their willingness to accept a veto in return for Catholic emancipation. By 1808 the bishops decided that it would be "inexpedient" to implement the veto. See Clifford, 19; Keogh 209–13.

22. The Catholic Committee had been suppressed by the government in December 1811; its leaders promptly reestablished the organization, calling it the Catholic Board.

23. W. E. Vaughan, ed., *Ireland under the Union, I: 1801–1870,* vol. 5, *New History of Ireland* (Oxford, 1989), 52.

24. Oliver MacDonagh, "The Politicization of the Irish Bishops, 1800–1850," *Historical Journal* 18 (1975): 39.
25. O'Connell quoted in Trench, 82.
26. "To His Holiness Pius VII: The Humble Address and Remonstrance of the Roman Catholics of Ireland," in John O'Connell, *Life and Speeches of Daniel O'Connell*, 2 vols. (Dublin, 1846), 2:32.
27. On O'Connell's relationship with the secret societies, see Michael Beames, *Peasants and Power: The Whiteboy Movements and Their Control in Pre-Famine Ireland* (Sussex, 1983), 193–97; McCartney, 102–6.
28. There are twelve pence in a shilling and twenty-one shillings in a guinea. Thus wealthy members contributed twenty-one shillings annually, and poorer members contributed one shilling annually.
29. McCartney, 111.
30. Ibid., 113–16.
31. O'Connell quoted in Trench, 147–48.
32. McCartney, 118–19.
33. Asa Briggs, *The Age of Improvement: 1783–1867* (New York, 1959), 265; Douglas Riach, "Daniel O'Connell and American Anti-Slavery," *Irish Historical Studies* 20 (March 1976): 5.
34. Oliver MacDonagh, *The Emancipist: Daniel O'Connell, 1830–1847* (London, 1989), 98–101.
35. Ibid., 127.
36. See Gerard O'Brien, "The New Poor Law in Pre-Famine Ireland: A Case History," *Irish Economic and Social History* 12 (1985): 33–49. For the English Poor Law, see Gertrude Himmelfarb, *The Idea of Poverty: England in the Industrial Age* (New York, 1984), 147–76.
37. MacDonagh, *Emancipist*, 170.
38. Ibid., 158–59.
39. S. J. Connolly estimates the priest to people ratio at 1:2700 in 1800. By 1900 the ratio had dropped to 1:700. See Connolly, 33.
40. R. E. Burns, "Parsons, Priests and the People: The Rise of Irish Anticlericalism, 1785–1789," *Church History* 31 (1962): 157.
41. Connolly, 64; Burns, 159–60; Clifford, 14–17; Keogh, 177 (Keogh claims that 11 out of the 85 priests in Wexford were involved in the rising); Most Rev. James Caulfield to Most Rev. Daniel Troy, September 2, 1798, printed in Joseph McVeigh, *A Wounded Church: Religion, Politics, and Justice in Ireland* (Cork, 1989), 93–94; see Connolly, 65.

42. Keenan, 146.

43. Caitriona Clear, *Nuns in Nineteenth-Century Ireland* (Washington, D.C., 1988), 48–50; Emmet Larkin, "The Devotional Revolution in Ireland, 1850–1875," in *The Historical Dimensions of Irish Catholicism* (Washington, D.C., 1984), 58.

44. For a discussion of the factors contributing to the friars' difficulties, see Hugh Fenning, O.P., *The Undoing of the Friars of Ireland: A Study of the Novitiate Question in the Eighteenth Century* (Louvain, 1972).

45. Keenan, 144–45.

46. For a concise discussion of these three bishops, see J. H. Whyte, "The Appointment of Catholic Bishops in Nineteenth-Century Ireland," *Catholic Historical Review* 48 (1962): 19–20.

47. Kerr, *Peel, Priests, and Politics*, 8.

48. Most Rev. George Plunkett to Cardinal Somaglia, February 6, 1826, quoted in Emmet Larkin, "Church and State in Ireland in the Nineteenth Century," *Church History* 31 (1962): 298–99.

49. Keenan, 119–20; Patrick Corish, *The Irish Catholic Experience* (Dublin, 1985), 160; Kerr, *Peel, Priests, and Politics*, 53; Connolly, 94.

50. Larkin, "Devotional Revolution," 68, 72, 87n. 21; David Miller, "Irish Catholicism and the Great Famine," *Journal of Social History* 9 (September 1975): 81–98.

51. Corish, *Irish Catholic Experience*, 186–87.

52. Kerr, *Peel, Priests, and Politics*, 47–48. Beaumont encountered people who lacked clothes to wear to Church during his visits. Beaumont, 1:268.

53. Keenan, 96–99.

54. Kerr, *A Nation of Beggars?*, 319–20.

55. Connolly, 100–107; Miller 91–92.

56. Connolly, 116–18; Miller, 89. Drunken priests were sometimes thought to have greater powers than their more pious and dutiful brethren. See Lawrence Taylor, "Stories of Power, Powerful Stories: The Drunken Priest in Donegal," in *Religious Orthodoxy and Popular Faith in European Society*, ed. Ellen Badone (Princeton, N.J., 1990), 163–84.

57. Corish, *Irish Catholic Experience*, 190.

58. James S. Donnelly Jr., "Pastorini and Captain Rock: Millenarianism and Sectarianism in the Rockite Movement of 1821–1824," in *Irish Peasants*, ed. Samuel Clark and James S. Donnelly Jr. (Madison, Wis., 1975), 110–35; David Krause, "A Tragic and Comic World of Compassion," *Irish Literary Supplement* 13 (Spring 1994): 32; Connolly, 109–10.

59. Ignatius Murphy, "Some Attitudes to Religious Freedom in Pre-Emancipation Ireland," *Irish Ecclesiastical Record* 105 (1966): 97–98.

60. Quoted in Brian McNamee, O.M.I., "J. K. L.'s Letter on the Union of Churches," *Irish Theological Quarterly* 36 (1969): 59; 56–57.

61. Kerr, *Peel, Priests, and Politics*, 57.

62. Quoted in Brian McNamee, O.M.I., "The 'Second Reformation' in Ireland," *Irish Theological Quarterly* 33 (1966): 39.

63. When the Kildare Place Society was organized in 1811, it was supposed to set up nondenominational schools, but in most parts of Ireland it quickly became associated with Protestantism. See Ó'Tuathaigh, 101; McNamee, "'Second Reformation,'" 51.

64. Connolly, 110.

65. Ibid., 75; Irene Whelan, "The Stigma of Souperism," in *The Great Irish Famine*, ed. Cathal Póirtéir (Cork, 1995), 135–54; McNamee, "'Second Reformation,'" 54–55; Corish, *Irish Catholic Experience*, 156.

66. *Tocqueville's Journey*, 115.

67. O'Connell to a friend in Rome, 1837, in *Correspondence*, 6:2369b.

68. Beaumont, 2:90–91.

69. *Tocqueville's Journey*, 48–49.

70. Connolly contends that the clergy had more affluent backgrounds than Tocqueville was willing to allow. See Connolly, 32–55.

71. Kerr, *Peel, Priests, and Politics*, 38–39. See also John A. Murphy, "Priests and People in Modern Irish History," *Christus Rex* 23 (1969): 240, 244–45, 248–51.

72. Clifford, 23; MacDonagh, *Hereditary Bondsman*, 99–100.

73. MacDonagh, "Politicization," 51.

74. Daniel Murray (1768–1852); John MacHale (1790–1881); William Higgins (1793–1850). John Murphy notes that Maynooth had been set up and funded by the British government, and yet was a center of Irish nationalism. Murphy, "Priests and People," 250. See also Keogh, 79–80.

75. John Foster to Robert Peel, January 20, 1825, quoted in Murphy, "Priests and People," 250.

76. See Donal Kerr's useful table on the bishops' academic training. Kerr, *Peel, Priests, and Politics*, 330–31.

77. MacIntyre, 28–29.

78. Murray accepted one of the seats on the Board. See Emmet Larkin, "The Quarrel among the Roman Catholic Hierarchy over the National System of Education, 1838–1841," in *The Celtic Cross*, ed. Ray B. Browne (Lafayette, Ind., 1964), 122.

79. Larkin, "Quarrel," 122–25. For a complete breakdown of the bishops' views on the national schools, see Kerr, *Peel, Priests, and Politics*, 330–31.

80. Larkin, "Quarrel," 141–42.

81. James Butler, Duke of Ormond (1610–1688), thrice served as viceroy; Christopher Butler, James Butler I, and James Butler II successively served as archbishop of Cashel from 1711 to 1791; George Mathew (d. 1738), Thomas Mathew (d. 1774), Francis Mathew (d. 1806), and Montagu Mathew (d. 1819) each sat in the Irish Parliament. The Duke of Ormond and the Mathews who served in Parliament were Protestants; the Butler bishops were Roman Catholics.

82. David Mathew, "Father Mathew's Family," *Capuchin Annual* 24 (1956): 143–44.

83. Augustine, 6. John F. Maguire was Father Mathew's friend and biographer.

84. Ibid., 2–5; Thomas P. Power, *Land, Politics, and Society in Eighteenth-Century Tipperary* (Oxford, 1993), 116–18, 228–31; idem, "Converts," in *Endurance and Emergence: Catholics in Ireland in the Eighteenth Century*, ed. T. P. Power and Kevin Whelan (Dublin, 1990), 119–24.

85. Power, *Land, Politics*, 99.

86. Mathew, 148. Elizabeth Malcolm speculates that James Mathew may have been the illegitimate son of Thomas Mathew. If that were the case, then Francis and he would have been half-brothers rather than cousins. Malcolm notes that histories of the Mathews are vague about James's origins, and thinks it unlikely that he would have received such favored treatment from Francis Mathew if he were a mere cousin. See Malcolm, 103–4.

87. Rogers, 8.

88. Maguire, 13.

89. Hugh Fenning estimates that there were twenty Capuchins in Ireland in 1775. As most of the regulars suffered losses in the last decades of the eighteenth century, twenty may even be a high estimate for the Capuchins' strength in 1808. See Fenning, 337–38. There is some debate about the date of Mathew's entrance into the Capuchins. Rogers claims he joined in 1808, but Augustine believes he joined in 1810.

90. Rogers, 11.

91. The see was vacant so Mansfield, the vicar capitular, was running the diocese in the interim. The bishops felt that distributing the paschal communion was the prerogative of the parish priests. Regulars were also prohibited from baptizing, marrying, or providing last rites to the faithful without express permission from the bishop. Rogers, 14.

92. Malcolm, 104.

93. Quoted in Rogers, 22.

94. Augustine, 44; Rogers, 20; Rev. Theobald Mathew to Rev. Mr. Devereaux, December 8, 1824, Mathew Papers, Church Street Friary, Dublin, 23:2202 (hereafter abbreviated as MPCSF).

95. Augustine, 85.

96. See William M. Thackeray, *The Irish Sketch-Book of 1842* (London, 1843; reprint, New York, 1923), 72; James Grant, *Impressions of Ireland and the Irish*, 2 vols. (London, 1844), 2:13; Augustine, 80.

97. Mathew to Devereaux, December 8, 1824, MPCSF, 23:2202; see *Journal of the American Temperance Union*, September 1843 (hereafter abbreviated *JATU*); Augustine, 67, 80.

CHAPTER TWO

1. John Carr, *The Stranger in Ireland* (London, 1806), 488; Edward Wakefield, *An Account of Ireland, Statistical and Political,* 2 vols. (London, 1812), 1:151. A dram is a fluid measurement, but "dram" was popularly used to describe a distilled drink.

2. Patrick Lynch and John Vaizey, *Guinness Brewery in the Irish Economy, 1759–1876* (London, 1960), 65–66.

3. Maria Edgeworth quoted in Malcolm, 49; S. C. Hall and A. M. Hall, *Ireland, Its Scenery, Character, Etc.,* 3 vols. (London, 1841–1843), 1:33. Daniel O'Connell had comparable experiences: "In my young days, it was deemed an essential point of hospitality to make guests drink against their will—drink till they were sick." O'Neill Daunt, 1:155.

4. Marianne Elliott, *Wolfe Tone: Prophet of Irish Independence* (New Haven, 1989), 67.

5. Bretherton, "Irish Temperance," 35–36.

6. *Report from the Select Committee on Inquiry into Drunkenness* H.C. 1834 (559) VIII, 228, 71 (hereafter abbreviated as RSCID). The custom of spending Monday in a tavern, or at home inebriated, instead of working was also common in England and the United States. For a discussion of this practice in England, see Douglas Reid, "The Decline of Saint Monday," *Past and Present* 71 (1976): 76–101.

7. John Finch, *Letters to Lord John Russell on Temperance Societies and Church Reform* (Liverpool, [1834]).

8. RSCID, 1–12.

9. Bretherton, "Irish Temperance," 1, 9–10.
10. Ibid., 8; RSCID, 75.
11. Lynch and Vaizey, 39–40.
12. RSCID, 65; Kenneth H. Connell, *The Population of Ireland, 1750–1845* (Oxford, 1950), 97; Bretherton, "Irish Temperance," 2–6.
13. Bretherton, "Irish Temperance," 10–11.
14. Lynch and Vaizey, 80; Malcolm, 323–24.
15. *Oxford English Dictionary;* RSCID, 232.
16. This interpretation is suggested by Barrett, 156.
17. Rev. J. P. Lyons to Mathew, August 5, 1840, MPCSF, 2:194.
18. RSCID, 232; Richard Stivers, *A Hair of the Dog: Irish Drinking and American Stereotypes* (London, 1976), 18; see RSCID, 232; Barrett, 160; Malcolm, 43; on the inadequacies of the Irish medical profession in the early nineteenth century, see John Fleetwood, *The History of Medicine in Ireland* (Dublin, 1983), 132–49.
19. Barrett, 161–62. For the numerous functions played by pubs and publicans in English life, see Brian Harrison, "Pubs," in *The Victorian City,* ed. H. J. Dyos and Michael Wolff, 2 vols. (London, 1973) 1:161–90.
20. In 1830 America's per capita consumption of spirits exceeded five gallons annually; Ireland's per capita consumption of spirits was probably half that. See Rorabaugh, 5–21, 225–39.
21. According to one account, "teetotal" was derived from a stuttering pledge taker who had trouble saying "total abstinence." The term was meant to be pejorative, but the total abstainers promptly adopted it. See Samuel Haughton, *Memoir of James Haughton* (Dublin, 1877), 37.
22. Bretherton, "Irish Temperance," 32.
23. Rorabaugh, 202.
24. Malcolm, 61–62.
25. As discussed later in this chapter, one Irish temperance organization predated both the UTS and Carr's association: a small total abstinence society was established in Skibbereen, County Cork, in 1817.
26. Malcolm, 64–65.
27. Ibid., 57–59.
28. These letters were published as a pamphlet by temperance advocates. See James Doyle, *Two Letters from the Rt. Rev. Doyle . . . on Temperance Societies* (Dublin, 1830).
29. Martin Marty, a leading historian of American Protestantism, describes Pro-

hibition as the "great exception" that brought fundamentalists and liberal Protestants together. He notes that both Billy Sunday, the fire-breathing, baseball player-turned-evangelist, and the leading proponents of the Social Gospel were united in their support for the Eighteenth Amendment. See Marty's *Pilgrims in Their Own Land* (Boston, 1984), 374–78.

30. Malcolm, 80.

31. The Orange Order was founded in 1795 after the Battle of the Diamond, a sectarian skirmish in Armagh. The group named itself after William of Orange, who defeated the Catholic king James II at the Battle of the Boyne in 1690. After the Boyne, King William set about re-establishing the Protestant ascendancy in Ireland, which James II had undone during his brief reign. Parliament began investigating various charges of wrongdoing by the Orange Order in 1836. To prevent the government from taking punitive actions, the leaders of the order dissolved the group for almost a decade. See Ó'Tuathaigh, 183–84.

32. Bretherton, "Irish Temperance," 111–12.

33. Quaker and Unitarian theology helps account for the lay orientation of the DTS. Quakers have no clergy and Unitarian ministers have a relatively circumscribed role. See F. L. Cross, ed., *The Oxford Dictionary of the Christian Church* (London, 1957), 529, 1390–91.

34. Bretherton, "Irish Temperance," 44.

35. Malcolm, 76.

36. Bretherton, 113.

37. Owen's own model community, New Lanark, promoted temperance principles as well. See G. D. H. Cole, *Robert Owen* (Boston, 1925).

38. Malcolm, 77, 87.

39. William Thompson (1785–1833) was a wealthy Cork landlord and political radical. A friend of both Owen and Bentham, Thompson was a committed socialist, feminist, teetotaler, and vegetarian.

40. Bradlaugh was elected to Parliament in 1880 as a radical but was unseated because of his unwillingness to take the oath of office. After a protracted battle in Parliament, Bradlaugh was allowed to take his seat in 1886, becoming the first avowed atheist to sit in the British Parliament.

41. Harrison, *Drink and the Victorians,* 184–86.

42. Bishop Doyle alludes to this double standard in his letters to Carr. See *Two Letters.*

43. Malcolm, 90–91.

44. Bretherton, "Irish Temperance," 134, 139.

45. Malcolm, 88–89.

46. The Manichees were a third-century sect that subscribed to a philosophy that considered all material things evil and all spiritual things good. See *Oxford Dictionary of the Christian Church,* 848–49.

47. Desmond Keenan claims that temperance was "in some ways an anomaly in the Irish Church in the early nineteenth century . . . it did not flow from traditional Catholic theology." Keenan, 152.

48. From the twelfth century until 1850, the Irish bishops never convened a national synod. Consequently there are no statements on any subject by the whole body of bishops. One must rely on the statements of individual bishops and provincial synods of bishops.

49. Connolly, 160–61, 169.

50. Keenan, 216–18.

51. Carr, 489.

52. James Coombes, "Europe's First Total Abstinence Society," *Journal of the Cork Historical and Archeological Society* 72 (January–June 1967): 52. In 1840 the subinspector for Skibbereen estimated that Catholics outnumbered Protestants 17:1. See Report of Inquiry into the Progress of Temperance, National Archives, Dublin, OPMA 131/10 (March 1840), Skibbereen, County Cork (hereafter abbreviated as RIPT).

53. Myles V. Ronan, *An Apostle of Catholic Dublin: Father Henry Young* (Dublin, 1944), 138–39, 142, 189.

54. Doyle, *Two Letters* (emphasis in original). Doyle died in 1834 before teetotalism had become a force in Ireland. Whether he would have favored total abstinence is an open question.

55. Bretherton, "Irish Temperance," 50.

56. Malcolm, 85.

57. See Peter O'Dwyer, O.C.C., "John Francis Spratt, O. Carm., 1796–1871" (Ph.D. diss., Gregorian University, 1968).

58. Bretherton, "Irish Temperance," 114; James Birmingham, *A Memoir of the Very Rev. Theobald Mathew,* 2d ed. (Dublin, 1840), 75; see Lyons to Mathew, August 5, 1840, MPCSF, 2:194.

CHAPTER THREE

1. "Mathew, Theobald," *The Cyclopedia of Temperance and Prohibition* (New York, 1891), 417.

2. Augustine, 92. John O'Connell was not related to Daniel O'Connell.

3. Quoted in Augustine, 97–98.

4. Birmingham, 26; Augustine, 105. George William Frederick Howard, Lord Morpeth, served as chief secretary from 1835 to 1841.

5. For more on Martin's militant attitude, see Maguire, 113–16.

6. Elizabeth Steiner-Scott, "'To Bounce a Boot Off Her Now and Then . . .' : Domestic Violence in Post-Famine Ireland," in *Women and Irish History*, ed. Maryann Gialanella Valiulis and Mary O'Dowd (Dublin, 1997), 139–40.

7. Augustine, 99.

8. *Dublin Weekly Herald*, November 17, 1838 and May 4, 1839 (hereafter abbreviated DWH); M. J. Quin, "The Temperance Movement in Ireland," *Dublin Review* 8 (May 1840):469.

9. Victor Turner and Edith Turner, *Images and Pilgrimages in Christian Culture* (New York, 1978), 128–30.

10. See *DWH*, November 24, December 1, and December 15, 1838; for the Irish Temperance Union, see Malcolm, 93–94. *DWH*, December 1, 1838, September 7, 1839, and February 1, 1840.

11. *DWH*, August 3, 1839.

12. *DWH*, September 28 and October 16 and 19, 1839; Malcolm, 114; Kerrigan, *Father Mathew*, 54; e.g., *Freeman's Journal*, October 3, 1839 (hereafter abbreviated as *FJ*); O'Connell quoted in Augustine, 107; Mother Catherine McAuley to Sr. M. Josephine Warde, October 18, 1839, in *The Letters of Catherine McAuley*, ed. Mary Ignatia Neumann, R.S.M. (Baltimore, 1969), 173.

13. RIPT, Macroom, County Cork; Kinsale, County Cork; Oulart, County Wexford; Waterford, County Waterford; Mathew to James Haughton, [1846], MPCSF, 17:1622.

14. Kerrigan notes that he had changed his mind on this point by 1845. See *Father Mathew*, 113.

15. Augustine, 116, 337–39; for the modified pledge, see W. J. Battersby, ed., *Catholic Directory, Almanac, and Registry* (Dublin, 1841), 256.

16. Augustine, 116; Rogers, 45.

17. "By this sign [the Cross] you shall conquer." The phrase was Constantine's motto before the battle of the Milvian bridge in 312. Victory gave Constantine control over the western half of the Roman Empire and paved the way for the legalization of Christianity.

18. Quoted in Augustine, 153; RIPT, Skibbereen, County Cork; *Dublin Evening Mail*, August 6, 1841 (hereafter abbreviated *DEM*); Rev. James Dowling to Mathew, July 24, 1840, MPCSF, 4:310 (emphasis in original).

19. See, e.g., RIPT, Charleville, County Cork; Arthurstown, County Wexford; Dungarvan, County Waterford; Abbeyleix, County Queens; Malcolm, 295;

Justin McCarthy, *An Irishman's Story* (London, 1904), 37. Another prominent nationalist, A. M. Sullivan, probably took the pledge as a child as well. See his *New Ireland* (Philadelphia, 1878), 73.

20. Ireland quoted in Marvin, R. O'Connell, *John Ireland and the American Catholic Church* (St. Paul, Minn., 1988), 9; Asenath Nicholson, *The Bible in Ireland* (New York, 1927), 100.

21. Maria Luddy, *Women and Philanthropy in Nineteenth-Century Ireland* (London, 1995), 203; Harrison, *Drink and the Victorians*, 192–94.

22. RIPT, Enniscorthy, County Wexford; Arthurstown, County Wexford; see also *Times*, March 11, 1840; ibid., Gort, County Galway. The police inspector from Loughrea, County Galway, reported, however, that "wherever it was perceived by Mister Mathew that they were in this state, he refused to give it to them." RIPT, Loughrea, County Galway.

23. Augustine, 104. If Mathew had engaged in this sort of coercive behavior on a wide scale, no doubt there would have been some mention of it in the police inspectors' accounts.

24. G. H. Fitzgerald to Mathew, September 24, 1839, quoted in Battersby (1841), 246–47.

25. It is not entirely clear who extended the invitation to Mathew. Some writers, including Father Augustine, have claimed that Mathew was invited by the bishop, John Ryan, but it seems that a parish priest, Father Raleigh, invited him with Ryan's approval.

26. W. E. Vaughan and A. J. Fitzpatrick, eds., *Irish Historical Statistics* (Dublin, 1978), 34; Kerrigan, *Father Mathew*, 58.

27. There were some discrepancies about the exact number of people killed and injured during Mathew's stay. See Kerrigan, *Father Mathew*, 58; *Times*, December 5, 1839.

28. *Times*, December 17, 1839, *Dublin Evening Post*, December 5, 1839 (hereafter abbreviated *DEP*); Augustine, 117; *DWH*, December 7, 1839.

29. Murphy was not Rice's immediate successor. Brother Michael Riordan replaced Rice and Murphy succeeded Riordan.

30. Most. Rev. Nicholas Foran to Mathew, November 4, 1839, printed in Battersby (1841), 255.

31. Vaughan and Fitzpatrick, 34.

32. Unfortunately no definitive statistics are available on the number of women who pledged. And none of Mathew's biographers have attempted to answer this question. Some evidence at least can be gleaned from the inspector general's March 1840 survey sent out to police commissioners in twelve counties where

the temperance movement was strongest. Among other things, inspectors were asked whether any women were taking the pledge in their towns. Several reported no women at all or only a small number pledging. The inspector in Charleville, County Cork, claimed: "Several women have taken the pledge but only in the proportion of about 1 to 30." The inspector from Bruff, County Limerick, stated that "it cannot easily be ascertained the number of women who have taken the pledge as they do not wear the medal and don't like to acknowledge it, but I think they are few." In at least some of the larger towns, though, women formed a larger proportion. In Kilkenny 200 of the 600 teetotallers were women and in Waterford there were 1,000 women among the 6,000 pledged. See RIPT, Charleville, County Cork; Bruff, County Limerick; Kilkenny, County Kilkenny; Waterford City, County Waterford.
Perhaps the clearest indication of the male orientation of the society was one of the prayers that Father Mathew would recite after each person had taken the pledge: "May God give you grace and strength to keep the pledge you have taken, and make you be good citizens, subjects, sons and husbands." See Battersby (1841), 256, for the prayer.

33. The editors of the *Dublin Weekly Herald* acknowledged that some prostitutes were among those pledging in Waterford. *DWH*, December 21, 1839.

34. *DWH*, December 28, 1839; Vaughan and Fitzpatrick, 34.

35. *DWH*, January 4, 1840. According to Colm Kerrigan, more than 1,000 taverns closed down in 1839: in 1838, there were 20,399 publicans, and in 1839, there were 19,357. See "Social Impact," 26–27.

36. *DEP*, January 16, 1840. Kilkenny at this time had a population of 20,000.

37. RIPT, Ennis, County Clare.

38. Augustine, 130; Birmingham, 35; Ignatius Murphy, *The Diocese of Killaloe, 1800–1850* (Dublin, 1992), 363.

39. Birmingham, 38.

40. Ibid; Connolly, 117–18. Blindness seems to have been a particularly acute problem in Ireland at this time. Harriet Martineau, an English Unitarian reformer, noted that she saw a great number of cases of blindness and other eye ailments during her travels through Ireland in 1851. See her *Letters from Ireland* (London, 1852), 135–36.

41. There were a number of accounts of miracles performed by Mathew during his temperance travels. John Denvir swore that Mathew healed his brother: "My mother took the whole family [to see Father Mathew in Liverpool].... A younger brother of mine had a running sore which the doctors could not cure.... At St. Patrick's with her children kneeling around her, she asked the good Father to touch her son. He, no doubt thinking it would be presumptuous

on his part to claim any supernatural gift, passed on without complying with her request. [When Mathew appeared at another location] my mother was there again with her afflicted boy and the rest of her children, and again she pleaded in vain. She was a courageous woman, with great force of character—and a *third* time she went to Father Mathew's gathering. . . . Again she besought him to touch the boy's foot. He knew her again, and deeply moved by her importunity and great faith, he, at length to her great joy, put his hand on my brother's foot and gave him his blessing. My mother's faith in the power of God, through his minister, was rewarded for the foot was healed." John Denvir, *Life Story of an Old Rebel* (Dublin, 1910), 13–15, quoted in Roger Swift and Sheridan Gilley, eds., *The Irish in the Victorian City* (London, 1985), 285.

42. Some estimates were as high as 100,000 for Mathew's Galway trip. See Battersby (1841), 251.

43. RIPT, Loughrea, County Galway.

44. This church was also known both as the Metropolitan Church and as the Church of the Conception. Since the Catholic bishops continued to lay claim to St. Patrick's Cathedral—an eleventh-century church controlled by the Church of Ireland—they considered this church to be merely a provisional cathedral (or pro-cathedral).

45. Battersby (1841), 253–54.

46. Andrew O'Connell was not related to Daniel O'Connell.

47. Yore's group, the St. Paul's Total Abstinence Society, claimed 22,000 members, and O'Connell's organization, the Metropolitan Total Abstinence Society, claimed 20,000 members.

48. Quoted in Augustine, 137.

49. Vaughan and Fitzpatrick, 28.

50. Since 1793, Catholics and dissenting Protestants had been allowed to attend Trinity but in 1840 they comprised less than one-tenth of the student body. See John Molony, *A Soul Came into Ireland: Thomas Davis, 1814–1845* (Dublin, 1995), 10–12.

51. Battersby (1841), 255.

52. Bretherton, "Irish Temperance," 94.

53. Among the professors pledging was Charles Russell, a church historian and future president of Maynooth. Russell played an important role in John Henry Newman's conversion to Catholicism (Ambrose Macaulay, *Dr. Russell of Maynooth* [London, 1983], 63). In 1845 Maynooth had eleven professors, eight administrators, and approximately 400 students (John Healy, *Maynooth College: Its Centenary History, 1795–1895* [Dublin, 1895], 425–27). All four of Ireland's

archbishops—Daniel Murray of Dublin, Michael Slattery of Cashel, John MacHale of Tuam, and William Crolly of Armagh—held teaching or administrative positions at Maynooth before being raised to the episcopate.

54. Battersby (1841), 390. For a more conservative estimate, see Augustine, 176.

55. Battersby (1841), 255.

56. Kerrigan, *Father Mathew,* 88; idem, "Social Impact," 24–26; Lynch and Vaizey, 80.

57. Battersby (1841), 255 (emphasis in original); Hall and Hall, 1:37–38.

58. Augustine, 336; RIPT, Newport, County Tipperary; Waterford City, County Waterford; Ennis, County Clare; Dunmore, County Galway; Abbeyleix, County Queens.

59. For references to Ribbonmen in temperance societies, see RIPT, Enniscorthy, County Wexford.

60. RIPT, Kenmare, County Kerry.

61. Ibid. Charleville, County Cork. Vinegar Hill and New Ross were two of the key battles of the 1798 Rising. The English victory at Vinegar Hill halted the rebel activity in Wexford.

62. Ibid., Skibbereen, County Cork.

63. Lord Ebrington quoted in Augustine, 156. In 1842 the subject of temperance processions was brought before the House of Commons. Colonel Acton, an M.P., asked the Irish chief secretary, Lord Eliot, if he were planning to "introduce any measure for regulating or restricting the parading of vast bodies of men dressed in scarfs, and accompanied by bands of music, for the purpose of promoting teetotalism?" Both Eliot and O'Connell defended the processions, noting that they were both nonviolent and nonpartisan. See *Hansard's* 63 (1842): 1424–25.

64. O'Connell appears to have discovered the temperance movement just a few days before he delivered this speech. Writing to Richard More O'Ferrall on November 29, 1839, he remarked: "The entire country is quite tranquil, to say nothing of the 100, 000 men who have resolutely and perseveringly given up the use of *all* intoxicating liquors." *Correspondence,* 7:287 (emphasis in original).

65. MacDonagh, *Emancipist,* 183.

66. William Lloyd Garrison to Helen E. Garrison, July 23, 1840, in *The Letters of William Lloyd Garrison,* ed. Walter Merrill and Louis Ruchames, 6 vols. (Cambridge, Mass., 1971–1973), 2:669 (hereafter abbreviated as *Letters of WLG*).

67. MacDonagh, *Emancipist,* 1; Malcolm, 129.

68. Rev. Richard Davys to Mathew, August 12, 1840, MPCSF, 1:44.

69. Rev. Martin Browne to Mathew, August 9, 1840, MPCSF, 4:371; Rev. Joseph Burke to Mathew, September 5, 1840, MPCSF, 2:196 (emphasis in original).

70. At least a few observers were aware of the tensions between Mathew and some of his fellow Catholics. Maria Edgeworth remarked to a friend, "[Father Mathew's] Christian charity and liberality are complained of by his Catholic brethren, priests and laity, who now begin to abuse him for giving the pledge to *Protestants,* and say, 'What good our fastings, our temperance, our being of the true faith, if Father Mathew treat *heretics all as one,* as Catholics themselves! and would have them saved in this world and the next too!'" Maria Edgeworth to George Ticknor, November 19, 1840, in *Maria Edgeworth: Life and Letters,* ed. Augustus Hare 2 vols. (Boston, 1895), 2:635–36 (emphasis in original).

CHAPTER FOUR

1. Mathew quoted in Augustine, 182.

2. See Oliver MacDonagh, *States of Mind* (London, 1983), 20; *DEM,* January 20, 1841; O'Neill Daunt, 1:242–43, 248–51.

3. Some associates warned Mathew that he would risk assassination if he were to visit Ulster. See Rogers, 56.

4. *DEP,* February 29, 1840; Ambrose Macaulay, *William Crolly: Archbishop of Armagh, 1835–1849* (Dublin, 1994), 235; idem, *Patrick Dorrian* (Dublin, 1987), 57.

5. *DWH,* March 20, 1841.

6. Augustine, 193–95; *DWH,* June 12, 1841.

7. Rogers, 59; Mathew to Duffy, September 28, 1845, and November 17, 1848, Duffy Papers, National Library of Ireland, Dublin (hereafter abbreviated as NLI). See also C. G. Duffy, *My Life in Two Hemispheres,* 2 vols. (London, 1898).

8. Doctors who prescribed alcohol to their patients were a source of frustration to Mathew throughout the 1840s. See Mathew to James Haughton, [1844], 2:184, MPCSF; Mathew to William Morris, [n.d.], 8:748, MPCSF.

9. Augustine, 218.

10. Daniel O'Connell had nicknamed MacHale the "Lion of the Tribe of Judah"; this messianic title appears in Rev. 5:5. Many clergymen, including Paul Cullen, regularly referred to MacHale as "the Lion." See Desmond Bowen, *Paul Cardinal Cullen and the Shaping of Modern Irish Catholicism* (Dublin, 1983), 72.

11. *Times,* April 10, 1841; Mathew to John Kirwan, February 26, 1841, printed in *DEM,* April 9, 1841; *DWH,* June 19, 1841.

12. *DWH,* July 3, 1841.

13. Ibid.

14. Is. 42:3. The passage in Isaiah to which Mathew alludes is from the first Servant Song: the Servant, thought by Christians to symbolize Christ, "shall bring forth justice to the nations, not crying out, not shouting, not making his voice heard in the street. A bruised reed he shall not break, and a smoldering wick he shall not quench." Thus Mathew was contrasting O'Connell's behavior with that of Christ. Mathew to Rev. Andrew O'Connell, July 5, 1841, quoted in Augustine, 206–7.

15. A. O'Connell to Mathew, July 7, 1841, quoted in Augustine, 207–8; Ulick Bourke, *The Life and Times of the Most Rev. John MacHale* (Dublin, 1882), 137–38.

16. See Maher's letter praising Mathew in *DEP,* March 10, 1840. See also Rev. James Maher to Rev. Paul Cullen, August 25, 1843, Murray Papers, Dublin Diocesan Archives, 58 (hereafter abbreviated as DDA). For the powers and responsibilities of a commissary apostolic, see *Catholic Encyclopedia,* 4:164. Mathew alluded to tensions with his fellow Capuchins in his letter to Cullen requesting the appointment. See Mathew to Cullen, December 12, 1840, Irish College Correspondence Transcripts, Philadelphia Archdiocese Archives, 158 (hereafter abbreviated as ICCT).

17. Mathew to Cullen, September 20, 1841, ICCT, 159 (emphasis in original). A correspondent from the London *Times* offered a similar account of MacHale's comments: "His 'Grace' denounced the Teetotallers from the altar, and spoke in no very measured terms of the 'wandering ecclesiastic' who dared to intrude within his jurisdiction and create in the minds of his people a superstitious veneration for a piece of Birmingham pewter. He would not allow such interference, and threatened the thunders of the church against any of the faithful who should disregard his commands." *Times,* August 6, 1841.

18. Keenan, 70, 144.

19. Cullen to Mathew, October 10, 1841, quoted in (Rev.) Peadar MacSuibhne, *Paul Cullen and His Contemporaries,* 5 vols. (Naas, Ireland, 1961–1977), 2:9–11. Mathew vigorously denied the indifferentist charge in a letter to Father Tobias Kirby, Cullen's assistant and confidant: "With respect to the charge of lulling Protestants into a false peace, I must say that it is utterly groundless. . . . I never made a single concession, and without vanity I assert that I have reconciled more Protestants to the Holy Roman Catholic Church than any other priest in the Kingdom." Mathew to Kirby, February 11, 1842, ICCT, 161.

20. In September 1841 Mathew visited Belmullet, and in December 1842 he went to Ballina. Both towns were within the Tuam Archdiocese. For an account of Mathew's trip to Ballina, see *Nation,* December 10, 1842.

21. Mathew to Kirby, October 6, 1841, ICCT, 160; Mathew to Kirby, May 5, 1842, ICCT, 163.

22. Mathew to Kirby, September 28, 1842, ICCT, 165.

23. Most. Rev. Daniel Murray to Cardinal Giacomo Fransoni, October 14, 1842, printed in *Archivium Hibernium* 38 (1983), 93–94.

24. Peel served as Irish chief secretary from 1812 to 1818. From their first encounter, he and O'Connell loathed each other. O'Connell nicknamed him "Orange Peel," and the two came close to dueling in 1815. See Trench, 84–85, 92–94.

25. MacDonagh, *Emancipist,* 197–198; Trench, 251.

26. MacDonagh, *Emancipist,* 204.

27. *DWH,* May 22, 1841; *DEM,* January 13, 1841; *DWH,* May 22, 1841.

28. *DWH,* January 8, 1842; O'Neill Daunt, 2:52. In 1846 Mathew informed his friend Major Russell that in order "to avoid any connexion with him [O'Connell], I was obliged to give up the procession of last Easter Monday. MPCSF, 2:123.

29. Daniel O'Connell to Cullen, May 9, 1842, in *Correspondence,* 7:160. See also O'Connell to Richard More O'Ferrall, November 29, 1839, in ibid., 6:287.

30. O'Connell to Mathew, July 3, 1842, MPCSF, 4:318; *Nation,* October 29, 1842.

31. For an excellent account of O'Connell's 1843 campaign, see McCaffrey.

32. The other key nationalist newspapers were the *Pilot* and the *Freeman's Journal.* The *Dublin Evening Post* generally sympathized with O'Connell but was not a consistent voice of nationalism.

33. Molony, 83–110.

34. McCaffrey, 52n. 2; Norman Gash, *Sir Robert Peel* (London, 1972), 402–4; Peel quoted in O'Faolain, 298.

35. O'Faolain, 297–98; see *Nation,* May 27, 1843. Donal Kerr claims that only seven of the twenty-seven members of the hierarchy did not support Repeal: Crolly, Murray, Murphy of Cork, Ryan of Limerick, Browne of Kilmore, Haly of Kildare and Leighlin, and Egan of Kerry. Kerr, *Peel, Priests, and Politics,* 330–31. Oliver MacDonagh offers a similar tally. See MacDonagh, "Politicization," 47n. 28.

36. MacIntyre, 121; McCartney, 152.

37. O'Connell quoted in O'Faolain, 300–301. Wellington, a Tory hardliner, had no position in Peel's administration.

38. There is some debate about the size of the crowd. Norman Gash believes that 500,000 were in attendance. See Gash, 407–8; McCaffrey, 52.

39. MacDonagh claims that O'Connell was a pledged teetotaler for about eighteen months. Since he enrolled in October 1840, he probably resigned in the

spring of 1842. The pledge that he had taken would have included a medical exemption, so he could licitly withdraw on those grounds.

40. *Nation,* January 28, 1843.

41. A German traveler, J. G. Kohl, visiting Ireland in 1842, keenly noted that the question of whether Ireland's problems were a result of English tyranny or Irish indolence was a point of contention between Repealers and anglophiles. J. G. Kohl, *Ireland, Dublin, the Shannon, Limerick, Cork* . . . (New York, 1844), 21.

42. O'Connell quoted in Michael MacDonagh, *The Life of Daniel O'Connell* (London, 1903), 325. McCaffrey's account of the speech is somewhat different; see 22–23.

43. Grant, 1:116.

44. McCaffrey, 23, 57; Malcolm, 129–31. In November 1843, Peel told Lord Eliot, the Irish chief secretary, that he viewed Mathew "with suspicion and distrust" after learning of the links between teetotalers and Repealers. Quoted in McCaffrey, 23n. 21.

45. Malcolm, 138.

46. For an account of Mathew's trip to Scotland, see Augustine, 243–46.

47. Harrison, *Drink and the Victorians,* 168.

48. Lynn Lees, *Exiles of Erin* (Ithaca, N.Y. 1979), 42; Harrison, *Drink and the Victorians,* 168; Augustine, 286.

49. In 1850 Pius IX restored the hierarchy in England and appointed Wiseman Cardinal Archbishop of Westminster.

50. Augustine, 280–81. "Old Catholics" refers to those Englishmen and Englishwomen who had remained loyal to Rome since the Reformation. Although long persecuted for their allegiance to the Pope, most old Catholics were fervent gallicanists at this time. Throughout the years of the veto controversy, old Catholics ardently supported the proposed veto. In 1850 some opposed the restoration of the Catholic hierarchy in England, fearing that it might offend Protestants. See Edward R. Norman, *The English Catholic Church in the Nineteenth Century* (Oxford, 1984), 1–28.

51. Mathew quoted in *Tablet,* July 15, 1843, 444, 445.

52. Rev. Dawson Burns, *Temperance History,* 2 vols. (London, 1889), 1:228–30; *Illustrated London News,* July 22, 1843 (hereafter abbreviated as *ILN*). Augustine claims that 100,000 pledged in Liverpool. Augustine, 289.

53. Mathew to Kirby, September 15, 1842, ICCT, 164.

54. For Stanhope, see Harrison, 160–61. Henry Granville Fitzalan Howard, the Earl of Arundel and Surrey, succeeded to the title of the Duke of Norfolk upon

his father's death in 1856. Some years after pledging, Howard excused himself on medical grounds. See D. Burns, 1:229.

55. Jane Welsh Carlyle to Thomas Carlyle, August 9, 1843, printed in *I Too Am Here: Selections from the Letters of Jane Welsh Carlyle*, ed., Alan Simpson and Mary McQueen Simpson (Cambridge, 1977), 62–64.

56. If the census data are accurate, the Irish comprised only about 4 percent of London's population. Lees believes that the Irish were undercounted somewhat in the 1841 census. Lees, 46–47.

57. Colm Kerrigan, "Father Mathew and Teetotalism in London, 1843." *London Journal* 11 (1985): 109.

58. D. Burns, 1:228; *ILN*, August 5, 1843.

59. Kerrigan, "Father Mathew," 111, 112 Shiman; 41; *Nation*, September 2, 1843; Augustine, 296.

60. Handbills and Stanley quoted in Augustine, 304 and 305, and in *JATU*, November 1843.

61. Kerrigan, "Father Mathew," 108, 110.

62. For anti-Catholicism in Victorian England, see John Henry Newman's *Apologia pro Vita Sua* (London, 1864; reprint, New York, 1968), 10. Newman, who became a Catholic in 1845, described himself as a "member of a most un-English communion, whose great aim is considered to be the extinction of Protestants . . . and whose means of attack are popularly supposed to be unscrupulous cunning and deceit." See also E. R. Norman, *Anti-Catholicism in Victorian England* (New York, 1968).

63. Harrison, *Drink and the Victorians*, 167.

64. The Beer Act was supported by a disparate coalition of forces in Parliament: laissez-faire advocates who thought the law would bring an end to smuggling and other corrupt practices, temperance supporters who wanted the English people to drink more beer and less spirits, and populists who wanted to increase the economic opportunities available to working men. For a detailed analysis of the Beer Act, see Harrison, *Drink and the Victorians*, 64–86.

65. Kerrigan, "Father Mathew," 111.

66. Lucas quoted in *Tablet*, September 2, 1843, 547 (emphasis in original).

67. Augustine, 321–27; Malcolm, 137–38.

68. McKenna estimated that 300,000 had pledged, while Maguire claimed six hundred thousand. See Augustine, 302–10. Manning quoted in Augustine, 302. See also Kerrigan, "Father Mathew," 113.

69. Augustine, 307–10; *ILN*, November 18, 1843; Asenath Nicholson, *Annals of*

the Famine in Ireland, ed. Maureen Murphy (New York, 1851; reprint, Dublin, 1998), 154–57.

70. McCaffrey, 191–94.

71. Leon Ó'Broin, "The Trial and Imprisonment of O'Connell, 1843," *Éire-Ireland* 4 (Winter 1973): 47; McCaffrey, 206; Trench, 278–79.

72. Augustine, 347–48.

73. Mathew to John Sheil, M.D., August 26, 1844, printed in *FJ*, September 2, 1844. John Gray (1816–1875) was the editor of the *Freeman's Journal;* Thomas Ray (1801–1881) was secretary of the Repeal Association.

74. Kerrigan claims that O'Brien kept the pledge until at least 1848. *Father Mathew*, 212.

75. Mathew to Clergyman, [1844], MPCSF, 12: 1164.

76. MacDonagh, *Emancipist*, 250–51; MacIntyre, 278–80; O'Neill Daunt, 2:214–17.

77. O'Faolain, 308; Trench, 279.

78. See Bretherton, "Irish Temperance," 279–81.

79. Battersby (1845), 342; Mathew to James Grant, December 6, 1844, MPCSF, 8:729. See also Augustine, 357. When Asenath Nicholson visited Mathew's home in February 1845, however, she was told that "five millions and four thousands" had enrolled. Nicholson, *Annals*, 168.

80. Kerrigan, *Father Mathew*, 87, 88.

81. Kerrigan, "Social Impact," 26; Maurice O'Connell, *Correspondence*, 6:246; Patrick Toole to Mathew, August 4, 1840, MPCSF, 3:284; Mathew to Russell, [1846], MPCSF, 18:1796. Major Russell was not related to Lord John Russell, the Liberal leader.

82. Thackeray, 141; Kerby Miller, *Emigrants and Exiles* (New York, 1985), 250.

83. Nicholson, *Annals*, 68; Kerrigan, "Social Impact," 28–30; idem, *Father Mathew*, 90–95.

84. O'Dwyer, 209; Luddy, 97–105. Mathew claimed that most of the women arrested in Cork for drunkenness were "poor sinful females" who were apprehended dozens of times each year. Thus, a small group of women accounted for the large number of committals. See Mathew to Editor, *Cork Constitution*, May 8, 1846, MPCSF, 12:1143.

85. Maria Edgeworth to Richard Allen, February 28, 1842, printed in *JATU*, May 1842.

86. Thackeray, 85–86. Actually Mathew was fifty-two at this time. Charles Lever, a friend of Thackeray, was a talented Irish Protestant writer with Tory inclina-

tions. Thomas Flanagan considers Lever "the one genuine novelist of Victorian Ireland." See *Ireland under the Union, I: 1801–1870*, Vol. 5 of *A New History of Ireland*, ed. W. E. Vaughan (Oxford, 1989), 493. William Hamilton Maxwell was a Church of Ireland minister and popular novelist. See John S. Crone, ed., *Concise Dictionary of Irish Biography* (Dublin, 1937), 88.

87. Kohl, 58.

88. Grant, 2:15, 231, 249, 297.

89. Maguire, 428.

Chapter Five

1. *DWH*, November 2, 1839; James Downey to Mathew, August 30, 1840, MPCSF, 4:314.

2. Augustine, 359. He would have made a profit of eight pence for each card and medal distributed, and thus one pound for every thirty cards and medals given out.

3. For example, Father J. Kearney of Athlone forwarded four and a half pounds to cover the cost of eighty-five medals. See Kearney to Mathew, March 17, 1840, MPCSF, 3:298.

4. When the Repeal movement was at its height, O'Connell had forty-eight clerks on his payroll. See O'Faolain, 294.

5. Mathew to Richard Allen, October 29, 1844, Friends Library, Morehampton Road, Dublin.

6. "No penny, no Paternoster," was one of the favorite epithets of Mathew's critics in England and Scotland. See William Gregory to Mathew, July 25, 1840, MPCSF, 4:308; Frederick Wheeler to Mathew, July 31, 1840, MPCSF, 3:228; *DWH*, December 4, 1841.

7. *DEM*, April 4, 1841.

8. Augustine, 360–62. Mathew alluded to his expectations regarding his cousin's estate in a letter to S. C. Hall, [1844/1845], MPCSF, 8:779. Father Rogers notes that two of Mathew's sisters received twelve hundred pounds apiece from their cousin; Father Mathew seems to have been one of the only close relatives left out of the will. Rogers, 95.

9. O'Connell to James Haughton, October 26, 1844, printed in *Nation*, November 2, 1844 (emphasis in original).

10. R. D. Webb, a Quaker teetotaler, outlined Haughton's plan to aid Mathew in a letter to an associate in Cork. Webb to Richard Dowden, October 26, 1844, Day Papers, Cork City Archives, 65/49 (hereafter abbreviated as DPCCA).

11. *FJ*, October 30, 1844, and November 5, 1844.

12. Mathew to Rev. John Spratt, [1844], MPCSF, 10:938. See also Mathew's letter to Charles Gavan Duffy thanking him for his contribution: "It was indeed high-minded of you to send it direct to Cork without the hesitation and diffidence displayed by many of my friends in Dublin. *Nolens, volens,* they almost insist upon my surrendering myself into the hands of a self-elected Committee. To unfold to them my most private affairs, allow them to arrange with my creditors, and receive from them whatever pittance they may deem sufficient to supply my daily wants. To this I will never submit." Mathew to Duffy, November 6, 1844, MPCSF, 18:1755.

13. Mathew to Peter Purcell, [1844], MPCSF, 11:1080; *FJ,* October 21, 1844; W. W. Simpson to Mathew, printed in *DEP,* January 2, 1845; *Nation,* December 7, 1844; *FJ,* December 27, 1844.

14. Mathew to Spratt, [1844], MPCSF, 10:935; Mathew to Purcell, [1844], MPCSF, 12:1124.

15. *FJ,* November 28, 1844, and February 13 and 20, 1845.

16. *ILN,* December 21, 1844; Mathew to Rev. John Fitzgerald, May 1845, printed in *DEP,* May 15, 1845.

17. Mathew to Haughton, [1845], MPCSF, 17:1602; Joel Mokyr, *Why Ireland Starved: A Quantitative and Analytical History of the Irish Economy, 1800–1850* (London, 1983), 1. The foreign travelers who visited Ireland in the 1830s and 1840s, such as Alexis de Tocqueville, Gustave de Beaumont, J. G. Kohl, James Grant, and W. M. Thackeray, were all agreed that most Irish people—especially those in rural areas—were impoverished.

18. In 1960 Patrick Lynch and John Vaizey argued that a dual economy existed in pre-famine Ireland: the coastal towns from Belfast to Galway were monetized and modern, while the rural interior regions depended on subsistence farming. Since then, several economic historians have taken issue with certain aspects of their thesis. Mokyr agrees that Ireland had a dual economy, but he claims that the cash and subsistence economies coexisted with one another throughout the island. Thus, some people in the cities relied on bartering, and some people in the most remote rural areas relied on cash. Mokyr, 19–22. See also Joseph Lee, "The Dual Economy in Ireland, 1800–1850," *Historical Studies* 8 (1971): 191–201; Corish, *Irish Catholic Experience,* 151–56.

19. Emmet Larkin estimates that Irish Catholics had an average of £2.8 million per year of discretionary income. This money would have been used among other things to invest in land and property, and to bankroll the Church, O'Connell, and paupers. See Larkin, "Economic Growth, Capital Investment, and the Roman Catholic Church in Nineteenth-Century Ireland," in *The Historical Dimensions of Irish Catholicism,* 17–18, 46–49; MacIntyre, 121.

20. Among the bishops who came to Mathew's assistance were Archbishop Murray, who publicly supported the work of the Mathew Relief Committee, Cornelius Egan of Kerry, Francis Haly of Kildare and Leighlin, Edward Kernan of Clogher, and William Kinsella of Ossory, who served on the board of Purcell's Testimonial Committee.

21. *FJ*, December 5, 1844; *Nation*, December 7, 1844; Augustine, 379.

22. Daniel O'Connell quoted in *FJ*, January 20, 1845.

23. *FJ*, March 18, 1845, April 4, 1845, and June 30, 1845; Mathew to Haughton, [May 1845], MPCSF, 1:84.

24. William Carleton, *Art Maguire: or the Broken Pledge* (Dublin, 1845), 252. Mathew wrote to Carleton to thank him for the dedication. [1845], MPCSF, 10:942.

25. Presumably referring at least in part to the new colleges, Mathew wrote to John Sheil: "That truly great and good man Sir Robert Peel is fulfilling all of the ambitions I formed of his administration." After the schools were established, Mathew tried to use his influence to help friends obtain teaching positions at them. See Mathew to Sheil, April 17, 1845, MPCSF, 11:1041; Mathew to Rev. William Hincks, [1845/1846], MPCSF, 6:539.

26. Kerr, *Peel, Priests, and Politics*, 303–9.

27. The phrase was coined by Robert Inglis, a Tory militant, who felt that Peel's plan conceded too much to Catholics. See Kevin Nowlan, *The Politics of Repeal* (London, 1965), 83–84.

28. William S. McFeely, *Frederick Douglass* (New York, 1991), 116–45; Alan J. Rice and Martin Crawford, eds., *Liberating Sojourn: Frederick Douglass and Transatlantic Reform* (Athens, Ga., 1999).

29. When he first arrived in Ireland, Douglass spent more of his time lecturing on temperance than on slavery: "I have attended several temperance meetings, and given several temperance addresses. Friend Haughton, Buffum and myself spoke today on temperance in the very prison in which O'Connell was put." Frederick Douglass to W. L. Garrison, September 16, 1845, printed in *The Liberator*, October 10, 1845. See also Douglass to Garrison, September 29, 1845, printed in *The Liberator*, October 24, 1845.

30. The address was largely the work of James Haughton, R. D. Webb, and Richard Allen. See Noel Ignatiev, *How the Irish Became White* (New York, 1995), 10.

31. Printed in *The Liberator*, March 25, 1842 (emphasis in original).

32. See Douglass to Garrison, November 10, 1845, printed in *The Liberator*, December 12, 1845.

33. Quoted in *The Frederick Douglass Papers. Series One: Speeches, Debates, Interviews,* ed. John W. Blassingame, 5 vols. (New Haven, 1979), 1:56, 58 (emphasis in original).
34. See ibid., 1:265.
35. Douglass to Garrison, October 28, 1845, printed in *The Liberator,* November 28, 1845. James Buffum was a white abolitionist from Massachusetts who served as Douglass's traveling companion during his tour.
36. Douglass to Garrison, February 26, 1846, printed in *The Liberator,* March 27, 1846.
37. Mokyr, 11–13.
38. Kevin Whelan, "Pre- and Post-Famine Landscape Change," in *The Great Irish Famine,* 21.
39. Mary Daly, *The Famine in Ireland* (Dundalk, 1986), 8.
40. Mary Daly, "The Operation of Famine Relief, 1845–1847," in *The Great Irish Famine,* 123–25; Cecil Woodham-Smith, *The Great Hunger* (New York, 1962), 38.
41. In fact, the commissioners overestimated the extent of the potato losses. See James S. Donnelly Jr., "Famine and Government Response, 1845–1846," in *Ireland under the Union, I: 1801–1870,* 274–76.
42. Ibid., 278. Peter Gray argues that Peel purchased Indian corn in an effort to start weaning the Irish off of potatoes. See "Famine Relief in Comparative Perspective: Ireland, Scotland, and Northwestern Europe, 1845–1849, " *Éire-Ireland* 32 (Spring 1997): 96.
43. Donnelly, "Famine," 283–84.
44. Woodham-Smith, 48–49. Mathew did not support a ban on brewing or distilling; he was still a strict voluntarist at this time. He did not want the government to restrict the production of alcoholic beverages in any fashion. See Augustine, 406–7.

CHAPTER SIX

1. Gash, 584–91; Robert Blake, *Disraeli* (New York, 1967), 228–243; MacIntyre, 287–289. One extreme Tory, Lord Alvaney, declared that Peel "should not be allowed to die a natural death." See Woodham-Smith, 52–53.
2. For Trevelyan's career and personal life, see Jenifer Hart, "Sir Charles Trevelyan at the Treasury," *English Historical Review* 75 (1960): 92–110.
3. O' Connell quoted in MacDonagh, *Emancipist,* 291. The "peace resolutions" were also meant to impress the Whig leaders. See Donnelly, "A famine in Irish politics," in *Ireland under the Union, I: 1801–1870,* 359–61.
4. MacDonagh, *Emancipist,* 295; MacIntyre, 284–89.

5. Richard Davis, *The Young Ireland Movement* (Dublin, 1987), 99–120.
6. Mathew to Russell, [1846], MPCSF, 2:123.
7. Augustine, 394–97.
8. The number of gallons of legal whiskey consumed in Ireland jumped 18 percent from 1844 to 1845. See Kerrigan, *Father Mathew*, 88.
9. Mathew quoted in Murphy, *Diocese of Killaloe*, 363; Augustine, 397.
10. Quoted in Augustine, 399.
11. Rogers, 98. At one point the committee leaders had hoped to raise an £800 annuity for Mathew. An undated broadsheet in the Cork City Archives declares: "A plan being in progress for raising . . . a sum of seven thousand pounds, to procure a life-annuity of £800 for the Rev. Theobald Mathew, in order to enable him to continue during his moral life, the great Temperance Movement."
12. Queen Victoria to Lord John Russell, July 10, 1846, in *The Letters of Queen Victoria*, ed. A. C. Benson and Viscount Esher, 3 vols. (New York, 1908), 2:104–5.
13. Mathew to Major Russell, August 8, 1846, MPCSF, 2:118.
14. Mathew to Major Russell, August 27, 1846, MPCSF, 1:97.
15. Cormac Ó'Gráda, *Black '47 and Beyond: The Great Irish Famine in History, Economy, and Memory* (Princeton, 1999), 6, 82–83; Peter Gray, "Ideology and the Famine," in *The Great Irish Famine*, 95.
16. O'Connell to Lord Russell, August 12, 1846, *Correspondence*, 8:3264 (emphasis in original).
17. Mathew to C. E. Trevelyan, August 8, 1846, MPCSF, 10:927.
18. For a description of Mathew's soup kitchen, see his letter to Randolph Routh, February 5, 1847, MPCSF, 11:1083. Between August and December 1846, Indian corn doubled in price. See Daly, "Operations of Famine Relief," 130; Ó'Gráda, *Black '47*, 143–49; idem, *Ireland*, 199.
19. Mathew to Archbishop J. B. Purcell, March 3, 1847, Purcell Papers, University of Notre Dame Archives, Notre Dame, Indiana (hereafter abbreviated as UNDA).
20. Mathew to Trevelyan, August 25, 1846, in *Correspondence relating to the Measures adopted for the Relief of the Distress in Ireland* (Commissariat Series) 1847 (761) LI; Mathew to Trevelyan, September 30, 1846, printed in *Correspondence*.
21. Quoted in Gray, "Ideology and the Famine," 93.
22. See Peter Gray, "Potatoes and Providence: British Responses to the Great Famine," *Bullán* 1 (Spring 1994): 75–90; Robert Dunlop, "The Famine Crisis:

Theological Interpretations and Implications," in *Fearful Realities': New Perspectives on the Famine,* ed. Chris Morash and Richard Hayes (Dublin, 1996), 166–67.

23. Mathew to James McAdam, October 1, 1846, MPCSF, 8:706; Augustine, 475.

24. County Cork was especially hard hit by the famine. See Ó'Gráda, *Black '47,* 86; Woodham-Smith, 159–60.

25. Mathew to Trevelyan, November 20, 1846, MPCSF, 1:90; Ó'Gráda, *Ireland,* 195–96; Woodham-Smith, 145.

26. Over the course of the famine, roughly 1 million Irish died from famine-related conditions. See James S. Donnelly Jr., "Excess Mortality and Emigration," in *Ireland under the Union, I: 1801–1870,* 350–52; Foster, 324.

27. Mathew to Trevelyan, December 16, 1846, quoted in Augustine, 413–14 (emphasis in original); MacDonagh, *Emancipist,* 306.

28. Daly, *Famine in Ireland,* 115. The Irish agrarian activist James Fintan Lalor claimed that the Famine caused a "deeper social disorganisation than the French Revolution—greater waste of life, wider loss of property—more of the horror with none of the hopes." Quoted in *The Great Irish Famine,* 32.

29. For Spratt's teetotal activities, see O'Dwyer, 167–222.

30. See for example, Mathew to Captain Patrick Duff, October 1, 1846, MPCSF, 11:091; O'Dwyer, 180.

31. Mathew to Duff, June 27, 1846, MPCSF, 11:1090.

32. Mathew to Duff, October 1, 1846, MPCSF, 11:1091. Dundalk was in the Archdiocese of Armagh, which was under the aegis of William Crolly. The attitude of the local ordinary did not always concern Mathew as much. For example, Mathew continued to visit towns in the Tuam archdiocese after MacHale denounced him.

33. Haughton to Mathew, November 21, 1846, MPCSF, 4:331.

34. Brennan quoted in *FJ,* August 28, 1844; Mathew to Purcell, [1844], MPCSF, 8:725.

35. Mathew to Kirby, May 5, 1842, ICCT, 163. In 1846 he made a similar claim in a letter to S. C. Hall. "My whole soul is absorbed in the Temperance Movement, and . . . I am convinced that its success, at present in Ireland, depends upon the continuance of my exertions. I am not influenced by vanity when I make this assertion, but by a knowledge of the prejudice of the Irish People in favor of Father Mathew." MPCSF, 1:83.

36. Kerrigan, *Father Mathew,* 166.

37. For the Quakers' efforts, see Helen E. Hatton, *The Largest Amount of Good: Quaker Relief in Ireland, 1654–1921* (Montreal, 1993), 78–247.

38. James S. Donnelly Jr., "The Soup Kitchens," in *Ireland under the Union, I: 1801–1870,* 307–15; Kerr, *Nation,* 81; Ó'Gráda, *Ireland,* 197.
39. Kerr, *Nation,* 37.
40. Quoted in MacDonagh, *Emancipist,* 313.
41. Ibid., 314–18.
42. Mathew to Mrs. S. C. Hall, January 3, 1847, MPCSF, 9:843.
43. Mathew to Trevelyan, February 4, 1847, MPCSF, 10:924.
44. Mathew to Trevelyan, March 29, 1847, MPCSF, 11:1085.
45. Writing to his friend R. D. Webb, Garrison declared, "The horrid particulars of the famine have made a wide and profound sensation in this country. Contributions are pouring in from every quarter, and the amount of food, money and clothing, that will be contributed, will be very considerable; yet not a fiftieth part that ought to be done." Garrison to Webb, March 1, 1847, in *Letters of WLG* 4: 470.
46. *ILN,* April 24, 1847; Edward Laxton, *The Famine Ships: The Irish Exodus to America* (New York, 1996), 50–52; Kerr, *Nation,* 58.
47. R. B. Forbes, *The Voyage of the Jamestown* (Boston, 1847), 22; *Report of the Select Committee on Colonisation from Ireland* H. C. 1847 (737) VI, query 2359 (hereafter abbreviated as RSCCI).
48. David Fitzpatrick, "Flight from Famine," in *The Great Irish Famine,* 177; Donnelly, "Excess mortality and emigration," 353; Oliver MacDonagh, "Irish Emigration to the United States of America and the British Colonies during the Famine," in *The Great Famine,* ed. R. Dudley Edwards and T. Desmond Williams (Dublin, 1956), 388.
49. See Mathew to Lord Monteagle, June 16, 1847, Mathew Letters, Ms. 5055, NLI.
50. RSCCI, q. 2359–79.
51. Oliver MacDonagh, "The Irish Catholic Clergy and Emigration during the Great Famine," *Irish Historical Studies* 5 (September 1947): 287–302; RSCCI, q. 2400–2492.
52. *Times,* June 28, 1847.
53. For the bitterness felt by many Irish during and after the Famine, see Woodham-Smith, 412–13. Writing in 1849 to Lord Cloncurry, a nationalist-minded Irish nobleman, Father Spratt acknowledged the harmful effects stemming from Mathew's decision: "I am sorry to say the necessities of the good Father Mathew placing him in the category of Government pensioners, has lessened the *prestige* of his respected name." Quoted in O'Dwyer, 207 (emphasis in original).

54. Kerr, *Nation,* 172–73.
55. Most Rev. William Higgins to Pope Gregory XVI, quoted in Kerr, *Nation,* 174; Kerr, *Nation,* 167–95.
56. Mathew to Russell, June 28, 1847, MPCSF, 2:142.
57. "Parish priests" refers to the pastors of the diocesan churches. Therefore, neither curates nor members of religious communities were considered parish priests. The priests' list, known as a *terna,* included three names. The priest who has deemed most worthy—*dignissimus*—was usually chosen as the bishop by Rome.
58. Rev. James Quinlivan to Mathew, June 15, 1847, MPCSF, 4:353; Augustine, 427.
59. Most Rev. Michael Slattery to Cullen, June 25, 1847, quoted in Augustine, 443–44. For Slattery's nationalist sympathies, see MacDonagh, *Emancipist,* 222.
60. Higgins to Cullen, June 30, 1847, quoted in Bowen, 83; Mathew to Cullen, May 10, 1847, ICCT, 166.
61. Technically, the decision was the pope's to make, but he would have relied heavily on Cullen's recommendations for appointments to Irish sees. For Cullen's nationalist attitudes, see E. D. Steele, "Cardinal Cullen and Irish Nationality," *Irish Historical Studies* 19 (March 1975): 239–60; Bowen, 272–81; Patrick Corish, "The Radical Face of Paul Cullen," *Historical Studies* 15 (1985): 171–84; Kerr, *Nation,* 77.
62. Most episcopal elections in nineteenth-century Ireland were very public affairs; secrecy was not imposed until 1911. See Whyte, 13.
63. Mathew to Sr. Basil Lonergan, July 9, 1847, MPCSF, 9:865.
64. Mathew to Cullen, July 2, 1847, ICCT, 168. Mathew's request was never acted upon.
65. Patrick Kennedy was bishop of Killaloe and David Walsh was bishop of Cloyne and Ross. Nicholas Foran was bishop of Waterford and Edmund French was bishop of Kilmacduagh and Kilfenora. Mathew to Maurice Lenihan, July 8, 1847, MPCSF, 12:1169.
66. In comparing the 1847 harvest to that of 1846, James S. Donnelly Jr. says that it was an "equally great catastrophe." Donnelly, "Production, Prices, and Exports, 1846–1851," in *Ireland under the Union, I: 1801–1870,* 287.
67. Gray, "Ideology and the Famine," 99; Ó'Gráda, *Black '47,* 49, 77; idem, *Ireland,* 181.
68. James S. Donnelly Jr., "The Administration of Relief, 1847–1851," in *Ireland under the Union I: 1801–1870,* 316; Ó'Gráda, *Black '47,* 50–52, 69–72; Gray, "Ideology and the Famine," 98. "Outdoor relief" means that they did not have to move to the workhouse to receive food.

69. Augustine, 454–55. Technically, Maginn was the coadjutor to John McLaughlin, but as McLaughlin was mentally ill, Maginn was effectively the bishop.

70. *DWH,* May 8, 1841; Most Rev. F. P. Kenrick to Mathew, April 18, 1843, MPCSF, 2:198.

71. Ignatiev, 148–54.

72. Michael Feldberg, *The Philadelphia Riots of 1844* (Westport, Conn., 1975), ix; (Rev.) Hugh Nolan, *The Most Reverend Francis Patrick Kenrick: Third Bishop of Philadelphia 1830–1851* (Philadelphia, 1948), 288–342.

73. Mathew to Rev. John Marsh, Union, N.Y., [1844], MPCSF, 9: 804.

74. Captain Forbes had tried to persuade Mathew to come to America with him on the *Jamestown,* but Mathew had turned him down. See Forbes, *Voyage,* 25. On nativism, see Robert F. Hueston, *The Catholic Press and Nativism 1840–1860* (New York, 1976), 110–36; Ray Allen Billington, *The Protestant Crusade, 1800–1860* (New York, 1938), 238–61.

75. Senator Henry Clay delivered an address in March 1848 that referred to Mathew's imminent arrival in the United States. See Clay's Speech to the Hibernian Society of Baltimore, March 17, 1848, in *The Papers of Henry Clay,* ed. Melba Porter Hay, 10 vols. (Lexington, Ky., 1991), 10:417–18 (hereafter abbreviated as *PHC*).

76. See Mathew to Sheil, March 6, 1848, MPCSF, 19:1891, and March 18, 1848, MPCSF, 16:1549.

77. *FJ,* April 22, 1848 (emphasis in original).

78. Mathew to Colonel J. H. Sherburne, May 30, 1848, printed in *Boston Pilot,* July 1, 1848 (emphasis in original; hereafter abbreviated as *BP*); Nicholson, *Annals,* 174.

79. Mathew to Sherburne, May 30, 1848.

80. *FJ,* June 1848, reprinted in *BP,* July 15, 1848.

81. S. J. Connolly, "The Great Famine and Irish Politics," in *The Great Irish Famine,* 44; Foster, 314.

82. Kerr, *Nation,* 153; Mitchel quoted in Donnelly, "A Famine in Irish Politics," 369.

83. Mathew to Richard Dowden, August 3, 1848, DPCCA.

84. Duffy's determination to save himself disgusted some nationalists and earned him the nickname "Give-in Duffy." See Steven Knowlton, "The Enigma of Charles Gavan Duffy: Looking for Clues in Australia," *Éire-Ireland* 31 (Fall/Winter 1996): 192.

85. Mathew to Duffy, November 17, 1848, Duffy Papers, NLI.

86. See Kerrigan, *Father Mathew,* 213.

87. O'Brien wasn't so fortunate. He was first sentenced to death, but later was given a life term in Tasmania. In 1856 he was granted an unconditional pardon from the government. See Foster, 314.

88. Mathew to Sherburne, printed in *BP,* October 21, 1848; Murphy, *Diocese of Killaloe,* 363; *BP,* February 24, 1849.

89. Mathew quoted in D. Burns, 1:319; Manners quoted in Andrew Hadfield and John McVeagh eds., *Strangers to that Land: British Perceptions of Ireland from the Reformation to the Famine* (Gerrards Cross, 1994), 142.

90. *Return of the Total Number of Gallons of Spirits distilled and charged with duty* H.C. 1849 (319) L; Malcolm, 145.

Chapter Seven

1. Mathew to Sherburne, April 7, 1849, Ms. 5055, 15, NLI; Mathew quoted in *BP,* June 2, 1849; Augustine, 486; Rogers, 122.

2. Quoted in *BP,* August 4, 1849.

3. In 1836 the American Temperance Society switched from moderationism to teetotalism and changed its name to the American Temperance Union. For the Washingtonians, see Tyrrell, 159–90; J. C. Furnas, *The Americans: A Social History of the United States* (New York, 1969), 501–8.

4. Blocker, 60. Women did not enter the forefront of the American temperance movement until 1874 when the Women's Christian Temperance Union was founded.

5. Beecher quoted in Furnas, 511–12.

6. The following states and territories enacted prohibitionist legislation: Massachusetts, Minnesota, Rhode Island, Vermont, Michigan, Connecticut, New York, Delaware, Indiana, Iowa, Nebraska, New Hampshire. Ohio and Pennsylvania passed restrictive statutes. Tyrrell, 260–61.

7. John P. Marschall, "Francis Patrick Kenrick, 1851–1863: The Baltimore Years" (Ph.D. diss., Catholic University of America, 1965), 53–54; Kenrick quoted in Edith Jeffrey, "Reform, Renewal and Vindication: Irish Immigrants and the Catholic Total Abstinence Movement in Antebellum Philadelphia," *Pennsylvania Magazine of History and Biography* 112 (July 1988): 419; Francis Patrick Kenrick, *Diary and Visitation Record* (Lancaster, Pa., 1916), 191.

8. Joan Bland, S.N.D., *Hibernian Crusade: The Story of the Catholic Total Abstinence Union of America* (Washington, D.C., 1951), 10–13; Jay P. Dolan, *The Immigrant Church: New York's Irish and German Catholics, 1815–1865* (Notre Dame,

Ind., 1983), 129; Thomas Spalding, *The Premier See: A History of the Archdiocese of Baltimore, 1789–1989* (Baltimore, 1989), 144; Morris J. MacGregor, *A Parish for the Federal City: St. Patrick's in Washington, 1794–1994* (Washington, D.C., 1994), 129; Charles Dickens, *American Notes for General Circulation* (London, 1842; reprint, New York, 1985), 207–8. See also Charles Dickens to John Forster, April 15, 1842, in *The Letters of Charles Dickens,* ed. Madeline House and Graham Storey, 6 vols. (Oxford, 1965–1988), 3:192–93.

9. Rev. Joseph Machebeuf to Most Rev. J. B. Purcell, June 3, 1842, Purcell Papers, UNDA. (For German opposition to temperance, see also Bland, 17.) Machebeuf was appointed vicar apostolic of Colorado and Utah in 1868 and became the first bishop of Denver in 1887. See Lynn Bridgers, *Death's Deceiver: The Life of Joseph P. Machebeuf* (Albuquerque, N.M., 1997).

10. Philip Gleason, *The Conservative Reformers: German American Catholics and the Social Order* (Notre Dame, Ind., 1968), 37–38; Jed Dannenbaum, *Drink and Disorder: Temperance Reform in Cincinnati from the Washingtonian Revival to the WCTU* (Urbana, Ill., 1984), 125–26, 151.

11. *Pastoral Letters of the U.S. Catholic Bishops, 1792–1983,* ed. [Rev.] Hugh Nolan, 4 vols. (Washington, D.C., 1983), 1:135–36.

12. Ibid., 1:143, 144.

13. Kenrick to Most. Rev. Peter Kenrick, September 9, 1843, quoted in Nolan, *Most Reverend Francis Patrick Kenrick,* 412–13; Kenrick to Cullen, November 23, 1843, quoted in *Records of the American Catholic Historical Society* 7 (1896): 311–12 (hereafter abbreviated as *RACHS*); Most Rev. Michael O'Connor to Cullen, January 10, 1842, quoted in *RACHS* 7 (1896): 348–49.

14. Hughes had returned to Ireland in 1840 and had been introduced to Mathew during his visit.

15. Richard Shaw, *Dagger John: The Unquiet Life and Times of Archbishop John Hughes of New York* (New York, 1977), 236–38.

16. Mathew to Dowden, July 25, 1849, DPCCA.

17. *BP,* July 21, 1849; Bishop's Journal, July 24, 1849, Archives of Archdiocese of Boston (hereafter abbreviated AABo).

18. Bishop's Journal, July 26, 1849, AABo; *BP,* August 4, 1849; Walter J. Meagher, S.J., and William J. Grattan, *The Spires of Fenwick: A History of the College of the Holy Cross* (New York, 1966), 74–75.

19. Garrison became active in teetotalism before he joined the abolitionist movement and remained interested in the issue all his life. See Walter M. Merrill, *Against Wind and Tide: A Biography of Wm. Lloyd Garrison* (Cambridge, Mass., 1963), 18–20.

20. See *Proceedings of the World's Temperance Convention* (London, 1846); *ILN,* August 15, 1846.

21. Mathew to Richard Webb, [1846], MPCSF, 18:1744.

22. The English government had abolished slavery in the West Indies in 1833 and the last slaves had been freed on August 1, 1840. August 1 then became a holiday of sorts for American anti-slavery activists.

23. In a letter to Richard Allen on February 27, 1842, Garrison remarked: "How mortified, how indignant, how astonished you will be to hear that the noble Address to your countrymen in America, signed by Daniel O'Connell and Father Mathew . . . is spurned and denounced by the Irish papers in Boston!" *Letters of WLG,* 4:51.

24. Gilbert Osofsky, "Abolitionists, Irish Immigrants and the Dilemmas of Romantic Nationalism," *American Historical Review* 80 (October 1975): 901–6.

25. *Liberator,* August 10, 1849; W. P. Garrison and F. J. Garrison, *William Lloyd Garrison,* 4 vols. (New York, 1889), 3:251.

26. O'Connell had had a series of well-publicized confrontations over slavery with Irish American Repealers. See Riach, 10–24; Ignatiev, 9–30.

27. Samuel May Jr. to Douglass, August 4, 1849, printed in *The North Star,* August 10, 1849; *The Liberator,* August 10, 1849, and October 12, 1849.

28. Mathew to John F. Maguire, August 20, 1849, MPCSF, 22:2134; *BP,* September 1, 1849, and October 10, 1849; Robert W. Hayman, *Catholicism in Rhode Island and the Diocese of Providence, 1780–1886* (Providence, 1982), 83–84.

29. Elizur Wright was one abolitionist who supported Mathew against Garrison. See Owen Dudley Edwards, "The American Image of Ireland: A Study of Its Early Phases," in *Perspectives in American History,* ed. Bernard Bailyn, 12 vols. (Cambridge, Mass., 1970), 4:268.

30. *BP,* November 10, 1849.

31. Mathew to Joseph Lumpkin, December 22, 1849, printed in *The North Star,* February 8, 1850. Frederick Douglass characterized Mathew's letter as "servile, cringing and fawning." *North Star,* February 8, 1850.

32. Timothy Huebner, "Joseph Henry Lumpkin and Evangelical Reform in Georgia: Temperance, Education, and Industrialization, 1830–1860," *Georgia Historical Quarterly* 75 (Summer 1991): 262–63.

33. Garrison and Garrison, 3:247; *BP,* September 8, 1849.

34. Fitzpatrick's last diary entry regarding Mathew occurs on November 4, 1849. See Bishop's Journal, November 4, 1849, AABo.

35. Rogers, 129–30; Nolan, 409.

36. Francis Kenrick to Peter Kenrick, November 30, 1849, quoted in Marschall, 55; Nolan, 412–15.
37. "Father Mathew in Baltimore," *United States Catholic Magazine* 8 (December 22, 1849): 805–7.
38. Ryder had banned alcohol on campus when he became president in 1840. Students caught drinking on or off campus were subject to expulsion. See R. Emmet Curran, S.J., *The Bicentennial History of Georgetown University: From Academy to University, 1789–1889* (Washington, D.C., 1993), 180–83.
39. Samuel Lilly, S.J., *Diary,* December 18 and 19, 1849, Catholic Historical Manuscripts Collection, 5:6; and Jesuit Community House Diary, December 18, 1849, Georgetown University Library, Special Collections Division, Washington, D.C. (hereafter abbreviated as GUL-SCD). See also *BP,* December 29, 1849.
40. "Father Mathew in Washington," *United States Catholic Magazine* 8 (December 29, 1849): 823. Senator James Mason of Virginia complained that Mathew "belonged to the priesthood of a church that claimed to be infallible" (*BP,* January 5, 1850).
41. Congress, Senate, Senator Davis of Mississippi, 31st Congress, 1st sess., *Congressional Globe,* 21, pt. 1 (20 December 1849): 52, 56; *BP,* January 5, 1850. All but one of the senators voting against Mathew represented slave states. For the roll call, see *Congressional Globe,* 59.
42. See Daniel Walker Howe, *The Political Culture of American Whigs* (Chicago, 1979), 20, 22, 127–28, 271–72.
43. For the Whigs' interest in the Irish vote at this time, see Hueston, 152–55; Edwards, 249–51, 282.
44. *BP,* January 26, 1850, February 2 and 16, 1850; Mathew to Charles Mathew, March 22, 1850, MPCSF, 22:2132; Most Rev. Michael Portier to Most Rev. Antoine Blanc, March 22, 1850, New Orleans Collection, UNDA.
45. Earl Niehaus, *The Irish in New Orleans, 1800–1860* (Baton Rouge, La., 1965), v, 23; *BP,* October 19, 1850; Niehaus, 103; Mathew to Charles Mathew, June 20, 1850, MPCSF, 22:2131; Mathew to Maguire, August 20, 1849, MPCSF, 22:2134; see *BP,* October 20, 1849, December 29, 1849.
46. Most Rev. John Chanche, S.S., to Blanc, June 1, 1850, New Orleans Collection, UNDA.
47. *BP,* October 5, 1850.
48. *BP,* October 26, 1850, and January 4, 1851; *The North Star,* December 5, 1850.
49. Niehaus, 104; The Sons of Temperance were controversial in Catholic circles because of their secrecy and other Mason-like characteristics; the Holy Office condemned them in 1894.

50. See Most Rev. John Odin, C.M., to Blanc, March 19, 1851, New Orleans Collection, UNDA; Arthur Hope, C.S.C., *Notre Dame—One Hundred Years* (Notre Dame, Ind., 1943), 230; Mathew to Rev. Edward Sorin, C.S.C., June 27, 1851, printed in *St. Joseph Valley Register,* July 17, 1851.

51. *BP,* June 14, 1851. Clay had about sixty slaves at Ashland at this time. See Merrill D. Peterson, *The Great Triumvirate: Webster, Clay, and Calhoun* (New York, 1987), 373.

52. Mathew discusses Clay's appeal in his letters to his brother (see Mathew to Charles Mathew, July 10 and September 25, 1851, MPCSF, 22:2133, 2130). "An Appeal to the American Public, in behalf of the Very Rev. Father Mathew" was printed in *BP,* October 4, 1851.

53. See *BP,* June 28 and July 26, 1851.

54. At some point in the 1840s, O'Connor must have changed his mind about Mathew. Writing to a fellow priest in 1849, O'Connor made clear that he was eagerly anticipating Mathew's visit to Pittsburgh. See Most Rev. Michael O'Connor to Rev. Thomas Heyden, August 9, 1849, Archives of Diocese of Pittsburgh.

55. *BP,* September 6 and 20 and October 11, 1851.

56. *New York Herald,* November 8, 1851, printed in Maguire, 517.

57. Mathew claimed he had pledged 600,000 (*BP,* November 15, 1851). According to the 1850 census there were 1.6 million American Catholics, a majority of whom would have been from Ireland or of Irish descent. See Jay P. Dolan, *Catholic Revivalism: The American Experience, 1830–1900* (Notre Dame, Ind., 1978), 26.

58. For example, Earl Niehaus (104) contends that most of the people who took the pledge in New Orleans were unfaithful to it.

59. Henry Clay to Henry Grinnell, November 5, 1851, *PHC,* 10:929. Clay gave $50 to Mathew's fund, and Grinnell, a shipping magnate, contributed $500.

60. The controversy over what Mathew was doing with contributions is recounted in *BP,* November 8, 1851.

61. Rogers, 143.

62. Mathew to [Dennis?] Mahony, March 8, 1852, CCCM, 2/49, UNDA. The nephew of Napoleon Bonaparte, Louis Napoleon (d. 1873), was elected president of France in 1848. In 1852 he ended the Second Republic and had himself crowned Emperor Napoleon III.

63. Mathew to Cullen, October 1, 1852, Cullen Papers, 325/4, 130, DDA. Cullen had returned to Ireland in January 1850 to succeed the late William Crolly as archbishop of Armagh. He was transferred to Dublin in 1852.

64. Corish, *Irish Catholic Experience,* 197.

65. Mathew to Cullen, October 9, 1852, Cullen Papers, 325/4, 131, DDA. The reference to the Virgin Mary was uncharacteristic for Mathew and may have been included to appeal to Cullen, who was a strong proponent of Marian devotion. Two of Mathew's biographers, Fathers Rogers and Augustine, and the *Dictionary of National Biography* claim that Mathew was offered the Jamaican bishopric in 1851 but declined the appointment because of his failing health. R. F. Foster has repeated this contention in his *Modern Ireland, 1600–1972*. No author has offered any substantive evidence in support of this claim. Given Mathew's interest in obtaining a bishopric and his determination to leave Ireland for a warmer climate, it is extremely unlikely that he would have turned down such an appointment. For these authors' accounts of the issue, see Rogers, 143; Augustine, 523; *Dictionary of National Biography* (1909 ed.) 13:33; Foster, 369.

66. Rogers, 144.

67. Several cures were attributed to Mathew when he was at Lehenagh. See Moira Lysaght, *Fr. Theobald Mathew, OFM Cap.: The Apostle of Temperance* (Dublin, 1983), 43–45.

68. Mathew to Samuel Pope, February 21, 1853, quoted in Augustine, 529. For the United Kingdom Alliance's perspective, see Harrison, 196–218.

69. Mathew to George Pepper, January 14, 1854, quoted in Bland, 41–42. When the temperance movement was in its heyday, though, Mathew was opposed to any coercive legislation. Writing to Dr. Dawson Burns, an English prohibitionist, Mathew remarked: "Trusting in the strength of the Lord, I'm not inclined to appeal to the Law, for aid against intemperance." Mathew to Burns, [n.d.], MPCSF, 5:427.

70. See Mathew to Slattery, July 3, 1854, Slattery Papers, microfilm copy, NLI.

71. Augustine, 556.

Chapter Eight

1. Father James Cullen was not related to Cardinal Paul Cullen.

2. John Forbes, *Memorandums Made in Ireland in the Autumn of 1852* 2 vols. (London, 1853), 1:90, 150, 192–93.

3. Ibid., 1:224, 281–82, 291–92.

4. Ibid., 2:120–21, 191, 220.

5. Ibid., 1:150; 2:26–27.

6. Ibid., 2:271–72.

7. Ken Inglis, "Father Mathew's Statue: The Making of a Monument in Cork." in *Ireland and Irish-Australia: Studies in Cultural and Political History*, ed. Oliver MacDonagh and W. F. Mandle (London, 1986), 121, 122.

8. See James H. Murphy, "The Role of Vincentian Parish Missions in the 'Irish Counter-Reformation' of the Mid-Nineteenth Century," *Irish Historical Studies* 24 (November 1984): 158; Lambert McKenna, S.J., *Father James A. Cullen, S.J.* (London, 1924), 306; Haughton, 169–70; Malcolm, 194–95.

9. Malcolm, 185–87. Leahy, Slattery's successor, was archbishop of Cashel from 1857 to 1875; Furlong was bishop of Ferns from 1857 to 1875; MacEvilly was bishop of Galway from 1856 to 1881 and archbishop of Tuam from 1881 to 1902.

10. A reserved sin is one for which a penitent must seek absolution from the bishop or one of his specially appointed confessors. Ferriter, 10.

11. Malcolm, 217–51. Cullen became Ireland's first cardinal in 1866.

12. McKenna, 308–9; Ferriter, 18.

13. Manning was made a cardinal in 1875.

14. McKenna, 311.

15. Malcolm, 311. Warren was the first bishop since Mathew's day to take the teetotal pledge.

16. Father James Cullen quoted in Ferriter, 32.

17. Ibid., 30.

18. McKenna, 321–22, 324.

19. Ferriter, 80; McKenna, 128, 337.

20. Cullen was also a firm believer in the Lourdes apparitions. McKenna, 161–62, 256–99.

21. Larkin, "Devotional Revolution," 76–80.

22. A number of people were attracted to both the Pioneers and cultural nationalist groups. Patrick Pearse, the leader of the Easter Rising of 1916, was active in both the Pioneers and the Gaelic League as a young man.

23. Malcolm, 319; Cullen quoted in McKenna, 346–47.

24. Cullen quoted in Malcolm, 319.

25. For Cardinal Cullen's achievement, see Larkin, "Devotional Revolution," 57–58; Bowen, *Cullen*, 282–99. MacHale became increasingly senile in the 1870s and died in 1881 in his ninetieth year.

26. "The Temperance Movement and Father Mathew's Visit to the United States, 1849–1851," *Historical Records and Studies* 6 (1911): 114.

27. Ferriter, 56–61.

28. The causes of all three have been sent to Rome for possible beatification. For Quinn and Sullivan, see John J. Dunne, *The Pioneers* (Dublin, 1981); for Talbot, see Mary Purcell, *Remembering Matt Talbot* (Dublin, 1990).

29. The Irish Free State, established in 1922, had jurisdiction over all of Ireland except for the six Ulster counties which comprised Northern Ireland.
30. Ferriter, 116–19.
31. Tyrrell, 282, 290–309.
32. Ibid., 264–69, 303–4; Bland, 42–45.
33. William Corby, C.S.C., *Memoirs of Chaplain Life,* ed. Lawrence Kohl (New York, 1893; reprint, New York, 1992), 291–93. Father Thomas Scully founded a temperance society for soldiers in his Massachusetts regiment. See Maurice Dinneen, *The Catholic Total Abstinence Society in the Archdiocese of Boston* (Boston, 1908), 39–40.
34. Norman H. Clark, *Deliver Us from Evil: An Interpretation of American Prohibition* (New York, 1976), 49.
35. James J. Green, "The Organization of the Catholic Total Abstinence Union of America, 1866–1884," *RACHS* 61 (June 1950): 72; bishops quoted in Bland, 45–46.
36. Bayley was an Episcopalian minister before converting to Catholicism in 1840. He served as bishop of Newark from 1853 to 1872 and archbishop of Baltimore from 1872 to 1877.
37. Delegates quoted in Bland, 60.
38. Dierdre M. Moloney, "Combatting 'Whiskey's Work': The Catholic Temperance Movement in Late Nineteenth-Century America," *U.S. Catholic Historian* 16 (Summer 1998): 17; Green, 82; Dinneen, 112–14.
39. The CTAU ended up spending $60,000 on the fountain. See *Centennial Temperance Volume—A Memorial of the International Temperance Conference* (New York, 1877), 730; Arlene Swidler, "Catholics and the 1876 Centennial," *Catholic Historical Review* 62 (July 1976): 363.
40. Within a decade, however, most of these statutes would be struck down by the courts or repealed, suffering the same fate as the Prohibition laws of the 1850s. Clark, 74.
41. For Ireland, see chapter 3; for Keane, see Patrick H. Ahern, *The Life of John J. Keane, Educator and Archbishop* (Milwaukee, 1954), 19–20.
42. James Reardon, *The Catholic Church in the Diocese of St. Paul* (St. Paul, 1952), 235, 415–16; David Sweeney, O.F.M., *The Life of John Lancaster Spalding 1840–1916* (New York, 1965), 154–55.
43. On Americanism, see the Summer 1993 issue of the *U.S. Catholic Historian,* which is devoted to the subject. Among the issue's seven essays, see especially Margaret Mary Reher, "Phantom Heresy: A Twice-Told Tale," 93–106.
44. *Pastoral Letters,* 232; Green, 95–96.

45. See "No Use for 'Holy Beer' at Notre Dame," *Voice,* May 12, 1898. (The *Voice* was the Prohibition party's newspaper.). Walsh's three successors were teetotalers as well: Fr. Andrew Morrissey, C.S.C. (1893–1905); Fr. John W. Cavanaugh, C.S.C. (1905–1919); and Fr. James Burns, C.S.C. (1919–1922). In 1912 the CTAU returned to Notre Dame for its annual convention.

46. Pope Leo XIII quoted in Reardon, 236.

47. As part of the Mathew centennial observance, John Ireland contributed a hagiographical essay on Mathew for the *Catholic World:* "Theobald Mathew," *Catholic World* 52 (October 1890): 1–8.

48. See Ronald M. Benson, "American Workers and Temperance Reform, 1866–1933" (Ph.D diss., University of Notre Dame, 1974), 150–65.

49. Powderly left the Catholic Church to become a Mason in 1901. See Terence V. Powderly, *The Path I Trod,* ed. Harry J. Carman, Henry David, and Paul N. Guthrie (New York, 1940), 370–75. Powderly devoted sixty-five pages of his autobiography to what he called "Ecclesiastical Opposition."

50. Quoted in Gerald Fogarty, S.J., *The Vatican and the American Hierarchy from 1870 to 1965* (Collegeville, Minn., 1985), 91.

51. Powderly quoted in Benson, 167, 168.

52. Willard had attended a meeting of the Philadelphia branch of the CTAU in 1887. On that occasion she told the members of her prized possession—one of Father Mathew's temperance medals given to her by an Irishwoman. See *Union Signal,* March 3, 1887.

53. Ruth Bordin, *Frances Willard: A Biography* (Chapel Hill, N.C., 1986), 7–11.

54. Women were first allowed to join the CTAU in 1880. See Victor Walsh, "'Drowning the Shamrock': Drink, Teetotalism, and the Irish Catholics of Gilded-Age Pittsburgh," *Journal of American Ethnic History* 10 (Fall 1990–Winter 1991): 74; Moloney, 18–21; Bland, 170.

55. Willard quoted in *Union Signal,* August 27, 1891.

56. See *Writing Out My Heart: Selections from the Journal of Frances E. Willard, 1855–1896,* ed. Carolyn Gifford, (Urbana, Ill., 1995), 397–98; *Union Signal,* November 7, 1895; Bordin, 168–70.

57. Christopher J. Kauffman, *Faith and Fraternalism: The History of the Knights of Columbus, 1882–1982,* rev. ed. (New York, 1992), 136; Moloney, 6; John O'Dea, *History of the Ancient Order of Hibernians and Ladies' Auxiliary,* 3 vols. (1923; reprint, Notre Dame, Ind., 1995), 3: 1302; Kauffman, 11–12.

58. Colman J. Barry, O.S.B., *The Catholic Church and German Americans* (Milwaukee, 1953), 17–18; Bland, 127–28.

59. Griffin quoted in Gleason, 37. For Griffin's Prohibitionist sympathies, see Martin I. J. Griffin Papers, GUL-SCD, boxes 1–2.

60. Omer Kline, O.S.B., "St. Vincent Brewery Once Center of Controversy," *Latrobe Bulletin,* June 25, 1976, 36. I am indebted to John Macey of St. Vincent's College Library for making this reference available to me.

61. Rev. George Zurcher, *Foreign Ideas in the Catholic Church in America* (East Aurora, N.Y., 1896); idem, *Monks and Their Decline* (Buffalo, 1898). The brewery was shut down in 1919 after the passage of Prohibition and was gutted by fire in 1926.

62. See Joseph V. Tracy, "Prohibition and Catholics," *Catholic World* 51 (August 1890): 669–74; and James M. Cleary, "Intemperance: The Evil and the Remedy," *Catholic World* 58 (October 1893): 11–18.

63. Bland, 202, 206.

64. Fogarty, 140–41.

65. Rev. George Zurcher to Martin Griffin, December 1, 1898, Griffin Papers, GUL-SCD, box 5; *Buffalo Evening News,* January 9, 1899; Dinneen, 182, 204–5; Bland, 230–36.

66. Cardinal Gibbons quoted in James Hennesey, S.J., *American Catholics* (New York, 1981), 231. Some Catholic teetotalers were incensed at Gibbons for his detached pose. See, e.g., John Cunneen to Martin Griffin, February 26, 1908, Griffin Papers, GUL-SCD, box 1.

67. Furthermore, Keane's mental and physical health began to fail after 1905. See O'Connell, *John Ireland,* 510–11.

68. By 1909 the CTAU was losing members and running out of money. Writing to Martin Griffin on December 27, 1909, the CTAU's president, Rev. Peter O'Callaghan, C.S.P., remarked: "If we can get over the next few months successfully, we shall be alright." Griffin Papers, GUL-SCD, Box 4.

69. Clark, 112.

70. James Brady, "Father George Zurcher: Prohibitionist Priest," *Catholic Historical Review* 62 (July 1976): 426.

71. Bland, 261; Clark, 126.

72. James Timberlake, *Prohibition and the Progressive Movement, 1900–1920* (Cambridge, Mass., 1963), 183.

73. Clark, 186–87; Benson, 273–74.

74. Cardinal Gibbons quoted in John Tracy Ellis, *The Life of James Cardinal Gibbons: Archbishop of Baltimore, 1834–1921,* 2 vols. (Milwaukee, 1952) 2:537.

75. *Pastoral Letters,* 255–333.

76. At their annual meeting in 1925, the bishops discussed Prohibition but decided not to make any public pronouncement on it. See *Minutes of Administrative Board of the National Catholic Welfare Council* (1925), Archives of the Catholic University of America, Washington, D.C., 95 (hereafter abbreviated as ACUA).

77. The CTAU continued on into the 1950s albeit on a much diminished scale. At the bishops' annual meeting in 1950, one bishop tried to persuade his brethren of the "urgent need of extending the work of the CTAU," but they were not swayed. See *Minutes of the Annual Meetings of the National Catholic Welfare Council* (1950), ACUA, 49.

78. Ferriter, 131.

79. Ibid., 183–84.

80. Ibid., 158–62, 166–79.

81. For census data, see Foster, 616–17.

82. Most. Rev. Cornelius Lucey, "Father Theobald Mathew," *Irish Ecclesiastical Record* 86 (December 1956): 376; Ferriter, 174–75, 195.

83. Ibid., 198–203.

84. Arthur McCrory, interview by author, February 14, 1990, Dublin.

85. For Ireland's recent identity crisis, see Desmond Fennell, *The State of the Nation* (Dublin, 1984), 12–49.

86. Davis and Walsh, 99; *Philadelphia Inquirer,* October 13, 1993, F1; O'Brien, Chafetz, and Cohen, 252.

87. Griffith Edwards, *Alcohol Policy and the Public Good* (Oxford, 1994), 10–12; Ferriter, 248–49; O'Brien and Chafetz (1991 ed.), 131; Christiansen and Teahan, 558–62.

Bibliography

Manuscript Sources

Capuchin Friary, Church Street, Dublin

Mathew Papers. The bulk of Mathew's papers are housed here. The friary has copies of 2,000 of Mathew's letters transcribed by his secretaries and 150 letters written to Mathew.

National Library of Ireland, Kildare Street, Dublin

Charles Gavan Duffy Papers. These papers contain several of Mathew's letters to Duffy.

Mathew Papers. The library has about 30 of Mathew's letters that relate to temperance in the 1841–1849 period.

Slattery Papers. Michael Slattery was archbishop of Cashel from 1833 to 1857. A microfilm copy of his papers is in the National Library along with a calendar describing each letter. The originals are in the Cashel Diocesan Archives at the Archbishop's House in Thurles. Several letters relate to Mathew and a number deal with ecclesiastical politics.

Friends' Library, Morehampton Road, Donnybrook, Dublin

The library has a collection of temperance medals and cards and several letters from Mathew to his Quaker allies in the temperance movement.

Trinity College, Dublin, Manuscript Room

Webb Papers. R. D. Webb was a Quaker who was active in both the temperance and abolitionist movements. There are a number of references to Mathew in the correspondence.

Dublin Diocesan Archives, Holy Cross College, Clonliffe

Murray Papers. Daniel Murray was archbishop of Dublin from 1823 to 1852. He ordained Mathew and remained friendly with him until his death. Several letters relate to Mathew and the temperance movement.

Cullen Papers. Paul Cullen succeeded Murray and remained archbishop of Dublin until his death in 1878. There are several letters between Cullen and Mathew dealing with Mathew's hopes for a bishopric.

NATIONAL ARCHIVES (STATE PAPER OFFICE), DUBLIN CASTLE

Chief Secretary's Office, Registered Papers. The archives houses extensive records from the police investigation of 1840 into Mathew's movement.

CORK CITY ARCHIVES, CORK

Day Papers. The archives has several letters between Mathew and Richard Dowden, the mayor of Cork.

UNIVERSITY OF NOTRE DAME ARCHIVES, NOTRE DAME, IND.

The archives has several letters from Mathew to his American friends and correspondence from American clerics describing the progress of temperance in America.

New Orleans Collection. Correspondence between various southern and southwestern bishops which had originally been housed in the Archives of the New Orleans Archdiocese is now held at Notre Dame. Numerous references are made to Mathew during the time of his tour of the American South.

PHILADELPHIA ARCHDIOCESAN ARCHIVES.

The archives has typescripts of dozens of letters housed in the Irish College in Rome. Included in the Irish College collection is correspondence between Mathew and Cullen.

ARCHIVES OF ARCHDIOCESE OF BOSTON.

The archives has a detailed journal kept throughout the nineteenth century by the successive bishops of Boston.

GEORGETOWN UNIVERSITY LIBRARY, SPECIAL COLLECTIONS DEPARTMENT, WASHINGTON, D.C.

Martin I. J. Griffin Papers. The university has several boxes of materials relating to Griffin, an Irish American active in the temperance movement in the late nineteenth century.

ARCHIVES OF THE CATHOLIC UNIVERSITY OF AMERICA, WASHINGTON, D.C.

NCWC Papers. The university has the records of the meetings of the United States bishops conference from 1919 to 1966.

PARLIAMENTARY PAPERS

Select Committee on Inquiry into Drunkenness, Report and Evidence, 1834 (559) VIII

First Report from His Majesty's Commissioners for Inquiring into the Condition of the Poorer Classes in Ireland, 1835 (369) XXXII
Second Report, 1837 (68) XXXI
Third Report, 1836 (43) XXX
Correspondence relating to the Relief of the Distress in Ireland (Commissariat Series), 1847 (761) LI
Report from the Lords' Select Committee on Colonisation from Ireland, 1847 (737) VI

CONTEMPORARY NEWSPAPERS AND JOURNALS

Catholic World
Dublin Evening Mail
Dublin Evening Post
Dublin Review
Dublin Weekly Herald
Freeman's Journal
Illustrated London News
Irish Temperance and Literary Gazette
Journal of the American Temperance Union
The Liberator
The Nation
The North Star
The Pilot (Boston)
The Tablet
The Times
Union Signal
United States Catholic Magazine

CONTEMPORARY WORKS

Alexis de Tocqueville's Journey in Ireland, July–August, 1835. Trans. and ed. Emmet Larkin. Washington, D.C.: Catholic University of America Press, 1990.
Anderson, W. E. K., ed. *The Journal of Sir Walter Scott.* Oxford: Clarendon Press, 1972.
Battersby, W. J., ed. *Catholic Directory, Almanac, and Registry.* Dublin, 1836–1860.
Beaumont, Gustave de. *Ireland: Social, Political, and Religious.* 2 vols. London, 1839.
Birmingham, James. *A Memoir of the Very Rev. Theobald Mathew.* 2d ed. Dublin, 1840.

Bourke, Ulick. *The Life and Times of the Most Rev. John MacHale, Archbishop of Tuam.* Dublin, 1882.
Carleton, William. *Art Maguire: or the Broken Pledge.* Dublin, 1845.
Carr, John. *The Stranger in Ireland.* London, 1806.
Centennial Temperance Volume—A Memorial of the International Temperance Conference. New York, 1877.
Cleary, James M. "Intemperance: The Evil and the Remedy." *Catholic World* 58 (October 1893): 11–18.
Corby, William, C.S.C. *Memoirs of Chaplain Life.* Ed. Lawrence Kohl. New York, 1893; reprint, New York: Fordham University Press, 1992.
Dickens, Charles. *American Notes for General Circulation.* London, 1842; reprint, New York: Penguin, 1985.
Doyle, James. *Two Letters from the Rt. Rev. Doyle . . . on Temperance Societies.* Dublin, 1830.
Finch, John. *Letters to Lord John Russell on Temperance Societies and Church Reform.* Liverpool, [1834].
Forbes, John. *Memorandums Made in Ireland in the Autumn of 1852.* 2 vols. London, 1853.
Forbes, R. B. *The Voyage of the Jamestown.* Boston, 1847.
Grant, James. *Impressions of Ireland and the Irish.* 2 vols. London, 1844.
Hall, S. C., and A. M. Hall. *Ireland, Its Scenery, Character, Etc.* 3 vols. London, 1841–1843.
Haughton, Samuel. *Memoir of James Haughton.* Dublin, 1877.
Ireland, John. "Theobald Mathew." *Catholic World* 52 (October 1890): 1–8.
Kenrick, Francis Patrick. *Diary and Visitation Record.* Lancaster, Pa.: Wickersham Publishing, 1916.
Kohl, J. G. *Travels in Ireland.* London, 1844.
Martineau, Harriet. *Letters from Ireland.* London, 1852.
Newman, John Henry. *Apologia Pro Vita Sua.* London, 1864; reprint, New York: Norton, 1968.
Nicholson, Asenath. *Annals of the Famine in Ireland.* Ed. Maureen Murphy. New York, 1851; reprint, Dublin: Lilliput Press, 1998.
———. *The Bible in Ireland.* New York: John Day, 1927.
"No Use for 'Holy Beer' at Notre Dame." *Voice,* May 12, 1898.
O'Neill Daunt, W. J. *Personal Recollections of the Late Daniel O'Connell.* 2 vols. London, 1848.
Proceedings of the World's Temperance Convention. London, 1846.
Quin, M. J. "The Temperance Movement in Ireland." *Dublin Review* 8 (May 1840): 448–84.
Sullivan, A. M. *New Ireland.* Philadelphia, 1878.

Thackeray, William M. *The Irish Sketch-Book of 1842.* London, 1879.
Tracy, Joseph. "Prohibition and Catholics." *Catholic World* 51 (August 1890): 669–74.
Wakefield, Edward. *An Account of Ireland, Statistical and Political.* 2 vols. London, 1812.
Zurcher, George. *Foreign Ideas in the Catholic Church in America.* East Aurora, N.Y., 1896.
———. *Monks and Their Decline.* Buffalo, 1898.

Printed Correspondence, Speeches, Addresses

Blassingame, John W., ed. *The Frederick Douglass Papers. Series One: Speeches, Debates, Interviews.* 5 vols. New Haven: Yale University Press, 1979.
Fitzpatrick, W. J. *The Life, Times, and Correspondence of the Right Rev. Dr. Doyle, Bishop of Kildare and Leighlin.* 2 vols. Dublin, 1880.
Gifford, Carolyn, ed. *Writing Out My Heart: Selections from the Journal of Frances E. Willard, 1855–1896.* Urbana: University of Illinois Press, 1995.
Gooch, G. P., ed. *Later Correspondence of Lord John Russell, 1840–1878.* 2 vols. New York: Longmans, 1925.
Hare, Augustus, ed. *Life and Letters of Maria Edgeworth.* 2 vols. Boston, 1895.
Hay, Melba Porter. *The Papers of Henry Clay.* 10 vols. Lexington, Ky., 1991.
House, Madeline, and Graham Storey, eds. *The Letters of Charles Dickens.* 6 vols. Oxford: Clarendon Press, 1965–1988.
Houston, Arthur, ed. *Daniel O'Connell, His Early Life and Journal, 1795–1806.* London: Sir I. Pitman, 1906.
MacSuibhne, Peadar. *Paul Cullen and His Contemporaries.* 5 vols. Naas, Ireland: Leinster Leader, 1961–1977.
Merrill, Walter, and Louis Ruchames, eds. *The Letters of William Lloyd Garrison.* 6 vols. Cambridge: Belknap Press of Harvard University Press, 1971–1973.
Neumann, Mary Ignatia, R.S.M., ed. *The Letters of Catherine McAuley.* Baltimore: Newman Press, 1969.
Nolan, Hugh, ed. *Pastoral Letters of the U.S. Catholic Bishops, 1792–1983.* 4 vols. Washington, D.C., 1983.
O'Connell, John. *The Life and Speeches of Daniel O'Connell.* 2 vols. Dublin 1846.
O'Connell, Maurice, ed. *The Correspondence of Daniel O'Connell.* 8 vols. New York: Barnes & Noble, 1973–1980.
O'Reilly, Bernard. *John MacHale, Archbishop of Tuam: His Life, Times, and Correspondence.* 2 vols. New York, 1890.
Simpson, Alan, and Mary McQueen Simpson, eds. *I Too Am Here: Selections*

from the Letters of Jane Welsh Carlyle. Cambridge: Cambridge University Press, 1977.

SECONDARY SOURCES

Ahern, Patrick. *The Life of John J. Keane, Educator and Archbishop.* Milwaukee: Bruce, 1954.
Augustine, Fr. *Footprints of Father Mathew O.F.M. Cap., Apostle of Temperance.* Dublin: M. H. Gill & Son, 1947.
Barrett, James R. "Why Paddy Drank: The Social Importance of Whiskey in Pre-Famine Ireland." *Journal of Popular Culture* 11 (Summer 1977): 155–66.
Barry, Colman, O.S.B. *The Catholic Church and German Americans.* Milwaukee: Bruce, 1953.
Beames, Michael. *Peasants and Power: The Whiteboy Movements and Their Control in Pre-Famine Ireland.* Sussex: Harvester Press, 1983.
Benson, Ronald. "American Workers and Temperance Reform, 1866–1933." Ph.D. diss., University of Notre Dame, 1974.
Billington, Ray Allen. *The Protestant Crusade, 1800–1860.* New York: Macmillan, 1938.
Birmingham, Stephen. *Real Lace: America's Irish Rich.* New York: Harper & Row, 1973.
Blake, Robert. *Disraeli.* New York: St. Martin's Press, 1967.
Bland, Joan, S.N.D. *Hibernian Crusade: The Story of the Catholic Total Abstinence Union of America.* Washington, D.C.: Catholic University Press, 1951.
Blocker, Jack S., Jr. *American Temperance Movements: Cycles of Reform.* Boston: Twayne Publishers, 1989.
Bordin, Ruth. *Frances Willard: A Biography.* Chapel Hill: University of North Carolina Press, 1986.
Bowen, Desmond. *Paul Cardinal Cullen and the Shaping of Modern Irish Catholicism.* Dublin: Gill & Macmillan, 1983.
———. *The Protestant Crusade in Ireland, 1800–1870.* Dublin: Gill & Macmillan, 1978.
Brady, James. "Father George Zurcher: Prohibitionist Priest." *Catholic Historical Review* 62 (July 1976): 424–33.
Bretherton, George. "Against the Flowing Tide: Whiskey and Temperance in the Making of Modern Ireland." In *Drinking: Behavior and Belief in Modern History,* ed. Susanna Barrows and Robin Room, 147–63. Berkeley: University of California Press, 1991.
———. "The Battle between Carnival and Lent: Temperance and Repeal in Ireland, 1829–1845." *Social History/Histoire Sociale* 27 (1994): 295–320.

———. "The Irish Temperance Movement, 1829–1847." Ph.D. diss., Columbia University, 1978.
Bridger, Lynn. *Death's Deceiver: The Life of Joseph P. Machebeuf.* Albuquerque: University of New Mexico Press, 1997.
Briggs, Asa. *The Age of Improvement: 1783–1867.* New York: Longmans, Green, 1959.
Brown, Malcolm. *The Politics of Irish Literature.* Seattle: University of Washington Press, 1972.
Burns, Dawson. *Temperance History.* 2 vols. London, 1889.
Burns, R. E. "Parsons, Priests, and the People: The Rise of Irish Anticlericalism, 1785–1789." *Church History* 31 (1962): 151–63.
Christiansen, Bruce A., and John Teahan. "Cross-Cultural Comparisons of Irish and American Drinking Practices and Beliefs." *Journal of Studies on Alcohol* 48 (1987): 558–62.
Clark, Norman. *Deliver Us from Evil: An Interpretation of American Prohibition.* New York: Norton, 1976.
Clark, Samuel, and James S. Donnelly Jr., eds. *Irish Peasants: Violence and Political Unrest, 1780–1914.* Madison: University of Wisconsin Press, 1983.
Clear, Caitriona. *Nuns in Nineteenth-Century Ireland.* Washington, D.C.: Catholic University of America Press, 1988.
Clifford, Brendan. *The Veto Controversy.* Belfast: Athol Books, 1985.
Cole, G. D. H. *Robert Owen.* Boston: Little, Brown, 1925.
Connell, K. H. *Irish Peasant Society: Four Historical Essays.* Oxford: Clarendon Press, 1968.
———. *The Population of Ireland, 1750–1845.* Oxford: Clarendon Press, 1950.
Connolly, S. J. *Priests and People in Pre-Famine Ireland, 1780–1845.* New York: St. Martin's Press, 1982.
———. *Religion and Society in Nineteenth-Century Ireland.* Dundalk: Dundalgan Press, 1985.
Coombes, James. "Europe's First Total Abstinence Society." *Journal of the Cork Historical and Archaeological Society* 72 (January–June 1967): 52–57.
Corish, Patrick. "The Catholic Community in the Nineteenth Century." *Archivium Hibernicum* 38 (1983): 26–33.
———. *The Irish Catholic Experience.* Wilmington, Del.: Michael Glazier, 1985.
———. "The Radical Face of Paul Cardinal Cullen." *Historical Studies* 15 (1985): 171–84.
Crotty, Raymond. *Irish Agricultural Production: Its Volume and Structure.* Cork: Cork University Press, 1966.
Curran, R. Emmet, S.J. *The Bicentennial History of Georgetown University: From Academy to University, 1789–1889.* Washington, D.C.: Georgetown University Press, 1993.

Daly, Mary. *The Famine in Ireland.* Dublin: Dundalgan Press, 1986.
Dannenbaum, Jed. *Drink and Disorder: Temperance Reform in Cincinnati from the Washingtonian Revival to the WCTU.* Urbana: University of Illinois Press, 1984.
Davies, Phil, and Dermot Walsh. *Alcohol Problems and Alcohol Control in Europe.* New York: Gardner Press, 1983.
Davis, Richard. *The Young Ireland Movement.* Dublin: Gill & Macmillan, 1987.
Dinneen, Maurice. *The Catholic Total Abstinence Society in the Archdiocese of Boston.* Boston: Grimes, 1908.
Dolan, Jay P. *Catholic Revivalism: The American Experience, 1830–1900.* Notre Dame, Ind.: University of Notre Dame Press, 1978.
———. *The Immigrant Church: New York's Irish and German Catholics, 1815–1865.* Notre Dame, Ind.: University of Notre Dame Press, 1983.
Duffy, Charles Gavan. *Four Years of Irish History, 1845–1849: A Sequel to 'Young Ireland.'* London, 1883.
———. *My Life in Two Hemispheres.* London, 1898.
———. *Young Ireland: A Fragment of Irish History, 1840–1845.* 2d ed. Dublin, 1880.
Dunne, John J. *The Pioneers.* Dublin: Pioneer Publications, 1981.
Dyos, H. J., and Michael Wolff, eds. *The Victorian City.* 2 vols. London: Routledge & Kegan Paul, 1973.
Edwards, Griffith. *Alcohol Policy and the Public Good.* Oxford: Oxford University Press, 1994.
Edwards, Owen Dudley. "The American Image of Ireland: A Study of Its Early Phases." In *Perspectives in American History,* ed. Bernard Bailyn, vol. 4. Cambridge: Harvard University Press, 1970.
Elliott, Marianne. *Wolfe Tone: Prophet of Irish Independence* New Haven: Yale University Press, 1989.
Ellis, John Tracy. *The Life of James Cardinal Gibbons: Archbishop of Baltimore, 1834–1921.* 2 vols. Milwaukee: Bruce, 1952.
Feldberg, Michael. *The Philadelphia Riots of 1844.* Westport, Conn.: Greenwood Press, 1975.
Fennell, Desmond. *The State of the Nation: Ireland since the Sixties.* Dublin: Ward River Press, 1984.
Fenning, Hugh, O. P. *The Undoing of the Friars of Ireland: A Study of the Novitiate Question in the Eighteenth Century.* Louvain: Publications Universitaires de Louvain, 1972.
Ferriter, Diarmaid. *A Nation of Extremes: The Pioneers in Twentieth-Century Ireland.* Dublin: Irish Academic Press, 1999.
Fleetwood, John. *The History of Medicine in Ireland.* 2d ed. Dublin: Skellig, 1983.

Fogarty, Gerald, S.J. *The Vatican and the American Hierarchy from 1870 to 1965.* Collegeville, Minn.: Liturgical Press, 1985.
Foster, R. F. *Modern Ireland, 1600–1972.* New York: Penguin, 1988.
Furnas, J. C. *The Americans: A Social History of the United States.* New York: Putnam, 1969.
Gash, Norman. *Sir Robert Peel.* New Jersey: Rowman & Littlefield, 1972.
Gleason, Philip. *The Conservative Reformers: German American Catholics and the Social Order.* Notre Dame, Ind.: University of Notre Dame Press, 1968.
Gray, Peter. "Famine Relief in Comparative Perspective: Ireland, Scotland, and Northwestern Europe, 1845–1849." *Éire-Ireland* 32 (Spring 1997): 86–108.
———. "Potatoes and Providence: British Responses to the Great Famine." *Bullán* 1 (Spring 1994): 75–90.
Green, James J. "The Organization of the Catholic Total Abstinence Union of America." *Records of the American Catholic Historical Society* 61 (June 1950): 71–97.
Gusfield, Joseph. *Symbolic Crusade: Status Politics and the American Temperance Movement.* 2d ed. Urbana: University of Illinois Press, 1986.
Hadfield, Andrew, and John McVeagh, eds. *Strangers to That Land: British Perceptions of Ireland from the Reformation to the Famine.* Gerrards Cross: Colin Smythe, 1994.
Harrison, Brian. *Drink and the Victorians: The Temperance Question in England, 1815–1872.* London: Faber, 1971.
Hart, Jennifer. "Sir Charles Trevelyan at the Treasury." *English Historical Review* 75 (January 1960): 92–110.
Hatton, Helen E. *The Largest Amount of Good: Quaker Relief in Ireland, 1654–1921.* Montreal: McGill University Press, 1993.
Hayman, Robert W. *Catholicism in Rhode Island and the Diocese of Providence, 1780–1886.* Providence: Diocese of Providence, 1982.
Healy, John. *Maynooth College: Its Centenary History, 1795–1895.* Dublin, 1895.
Hennesey, James, S.J. *American Catholics.* New York: Oxford University Press, 1981.
Hernon, Joseph M., Jr. "A Victorian Cromwell: Sir Charles Trevelyan, the Famine and the Age of Improvement." *Éire-Ireland* 22 (Fall 1987): 15–29.
Hill, Jacqueline. "Nationalism and the Catholic Church in the 1840s: Views of Dublin Repealers." *Irish Historical Studies* 19 (1975): 371–95.
Himmelfarb, Gertrude. *The Idea of Poverty: England in the Industrial Age.* New York: Knopf, 1984.
Hope, Arthur, C.S.C. *Notre Dame: One Hundred Years.* Notre Dame, Ind.: University of Notre Dame Press, 1943.
Hoppen, K. T. *Elections, Politics, and Society in Ireland, 1832–1885.* Oxford: Clarendon Press, 1984.

Howe, Daniel Walker. *The Political Culture of American Whigs*. Chicago: University of Chicago Press, 1979.

Huebner, Timothy. "Joseph Henry Lumpkin and Evangelical Reform in Georgia: Temperance, Education, and Industrialization, 1830–1860." *Georgia Historical Quarterly* 75 (Summer 1991): 254–74.

Hueston, Robert F. *The Catholic Press and Nativism 1840–1860*. New York: Arno Press, 1976.

Ignatiev, Noel. *How the Irish Became White*. New York: Routledge, 1995.

Inglis, Ken. "Father Mathew's Statue: The Making of a Monument in Cork." In *Ireland and Irish-Australia: Studies in Cultural and Political History*, ed. Oliver MacDonagh and W. F. Mandle, 119–35. London: Croom Helm, 1986.

Jeffrey, Edith. "Reform, Renewal, and Vindication: Irish Immigrants and the Catholic Total Abstinence Movement in Antebellum Philadelphia." *Pennsylvania Magazine of History and Biography* 112 (July 1988): 407–31.

Kauffman, Christopher. *Faith and Fraternalism: The History of the Knights of Columbus, 1882–1982*. Rev. ed. New York: Simon & Schuster, 1992.

Kearney, H. F. "Father Mathew: Apostle of Modernisation." In *Studies in Irish History Presented to R. Dudley Edwards*, ed. Art Cosgrove and Donal McCartney, 164–75. Dublin: University College Dublin, 1979.

Keenan, Desmond. *The Catholic Church in Nineteenth-Century Ireland*. Dublin: Gill & Macmillan, 1983.

Keogh, Dáire. *'The French Disease': The Catholic Church and Irish Radicalism, 1790–1800*. Dublin: Four Courts Press, 1993.

Kerr, Donal. *A Nation of Beggars?: Priests, People, and Politics in Famine Ireland*. Oxford: Oxford University Press, 1994.

———. "Peel, and the Political Involvement of the Priests." *Archivium Hibernicum* 36 (1981): 16–25.

———. *Peel, Priests, and Politics*. Oxford: Clarendon Press, 1982.

Kerrigan, Colm. "Father Mathew and Teetotalism in London, 1843." *London Journal* 11 (1985): 107–14.

———. *Father Mathew and the Irish Temperance Movement, 1838–1849*. Cork: Cork University Press, 1992.

———. "Irish Temperance and U.S. Anti-Slavery: Father Mathew and the Abolitionists." *History Workshop Journal* 31 (Spring 1991): 105–19.

———. "The Social Impact of the Irish Temperance Movement, 1839–1845." *Irish Economic and Social History* 14 (1987): 20–38.

Kinealy, Christine. "Beyond Revisionism: Reassessing the Great Irish Famine." *History Ireland* (Winter 1995): 28–34.

Klaus, Robert. *The Pope, the Protestants, and the Irish: Papal Aggression and Anti-Catholicism in Mid-nineteenth-Century England*. New York: Garland, 1987.

Kline, Omer, O.S.B. "St. Vincent Brewery Once Center of Controversy." *Latrobe Bulletin,* June 25, 1976.
Knowlton, Steven. "The Enigma of Charles Gavan Duffy: Looking for Clues in Australia." *Éire-Ireland* 31 (Fall/Winter 1996): 189–208.
Krause, David. "A Tragic and Comic World of Compassion." *Irish Literary Supplement* 13 (Spring 1994): 32–33.
Larkin, Emmet. "Church and State in Ireland in the Nineteenth Century." *Church History* 31 (1962): 294–306.
———. *The Historical Dimensions of Irish Catholicism.* Washington, D.C.: Catholic University of America Press, 1984.
———. *The Making of the Roman Catholic Church in Ireland, 1850–1860.* Chapel Hill: University of North Carolina Press, 1980.
———. "The Quarrel among the Roman Catholic Hierarchy over the National System of Education in Ireland, 1838–1841." In *The Celtic Cross,* ed. Ray B. Browne, William John Roscelli, and Richard Loftus, 121–46. Lafayette, Ind.: Purdue University Press, 1964.
Laxton, Edward. *The Famine Ships: The Irish Exodus to America.* New York: Henry Holt, 1996.
Lee, Joseph. "The Dual Economy in Ireland, 1800–1850." *Historical Studies* 8 (1971): 191–201.
———. *The Modernisation of Irish Society, 1848–1918.* Dublin: Gill & Macmillan, 1979.
Lees, Lynn. *Exiles of Erin: Irish Migrants in Victorian London.* Ithaca, N.Y.: Cornell University Press, 1979.
Lender, Mark, and James Martin. *Drinking in America: A History.* New York: Free Press, 1987.
Longmate, Norman. *The Waterdrinkers.* London: Hamish Hamilton, 1968.
Lucey, Cornelius. "Father Theobald Mathew." *Irish Ecclesiastical Record* 86 (December 1956): 369–76.
Luddy, Maria. *Women and Philanthropy in Nineteenth-Century Ireland.* London: Cambridge University Press, 1995.
Lynch, Patrick, and John Vaizey. *Guinness's Brewery and the Irish Economy, 1759–1876.* Cambridge: Cambridge University Press, 1960.
Lyons, F. S. L. *Ireland since the Famine.* London: Weidenfeld & Nicolson, 1971.
Lysaght, Moira. *Father Theobald Mathew, OFM Cap., Apostle of Temperance.* Dublin: Four Courts, 1983.
Macaulay, Ambrose. *Dr. Russell of Maynooth.* London: Darton, Longman and Todd, 1983.
———. *Patrick Dorrian.* Dublin: Irish Academic Press, 1987.

———. *William Crolly: Archbishop of Armagh, 1835–1849*. Dublin: Four Courts Press, 1994.
MacDonagh, Michael. *The Life of Daniel O'Connell*. London: Cassell, 1903.
MacDonagh, Oliver. *The Emancipist: Daniel O'Connell, 1830–1847*. London: Weidenfeld & Nicolson, 1989.
———. *The Hereditary Bondsman: Daniel O'Connell, 1775–1829*. New York: St. Martin's Press, 1988.
———. "The Irish Catholic Clergy and Emigration during the Great Famine." *Irish Historical Studies* 5 (September 1947): 287–302.
———. "The Politicization of the Irish Catholic Bishops, 1800–1850." *Historical Journal* 18 (1975): 37–53.
———. *States of Mind: Anglo-Irish Relations, 1780–1980*. London: Pimlico, 1983.
MacGregor, Morris J. *A Parish for the Federal City: St. Patrick's in Washington, 1794–1994*. Washington, D.C.: Catholic University of America Press, 1994.
MacIntyre, Angus. *The Liberator: Daniel O'Connell and the Irish Party, 1830–1847*. London: Hamish and Hamilton, 1965.
Maguire, John F. *Father Mathew: A Biography*. London, 1863.
Malcolm, Elizabeth. "The Catholic Church and the Irish Temperance Movement, 1838–1901." *Irish Historical Studies* 23 (May 1982): 1–16.
———. *"Ireland Sober, Ireland Free": Drink and Temperance in Nineteenth-Century Ireland*. Syracuse, N.Y.: Syracuse University Press, 1986.
———. "Popular Recreation in Nineteenth-Century Ireland." In *Irish Culture and Nationalism, 1750–1950*, ed. Oliver MacDonagh, W. F. Mandle, and Pauric Travers, 40–55. Dublin: Gill & Macmillan, 1983.
———. "Temperance and Irish Nationalism," In *Ireland under the Union*, ed. F. S. L. Lyons and R. A. J. Hawkins, 69–114. Oxford: Clarendon Press, 1980.
Marschall, John P. "Francis Patrick Kenrick, 1851–1863: The Baltimore Years." Ph.D. diss., Catholic University of America, 1965.
Marty, Martin. *Pilgrims in Their Own Land*. Boston: Little, Brown, 1984.
Mathew, David. "Father Mathew's Family." *Capuchin Annual* 24 (1956): 143–52.
McCaffrey, Lawrence. *Daniel O'Connell and the Repeal Year*. Lexington: University of Kentucky Press, 1966.
McCarthy, Justin. *An Irishman's Story*. London: Macmillan, 1904.
McCartney, Donal. *The Dawning of Democracy: Ireland 1800–1870*. Dublin: Helicon, 1987.
———, ed. *The World of Daniel O'Connell*. Dublin: Mercier Press, 1980.
McFeely, William. *Frederick Douglass*. New York: Norton, 1991.
McGuire, E. B. *Irish Whiskey: A History of Distilling, the Spirit Trade, and Excise Controls in Ireland*. Dublin: Gill & Macmillan, 1973.

McKenna, Lambert, S.J. *Life and Work of Rev. James Aloysius Cullen, S.J.*. New York: Longmans, 1924.
McNamee, Brian, O.M.I. "J. K. L.'s Letter on the Union of Churches." *Irish Theological Quarterly* 36 (1969): 46–69.
———. "The 'Second Reformation' in Ireland." *Irish Theological Quarterly* 33 (1966): 39–64.
McVeigh, Joseph. *A Wounded Church: Religion, Politics, and Justice in Ireland.* Cork: Mercier Press, 1989.
Meagher, Walter J., S.J., and William J. Grattan. *The Spires of Fenwick: A History of the College of Holy Cross.* New York: Vantage Press, 1966.
Merrill, Walter. *Against Wind and Tide: A Biography of Wm. Lloyd Garrison.* Cambridge: Harvard University Press, 1963.
Miller, David. "Irish Catholicism and the Great Famine." *Journal of Social History* 9 (September 1975): 81–98.
Miller, Kerby. *Emigrants and Exiles: Ireland and the Irish Exodus to North America.* New York: Oxford University Press, 1985.
Mokyr, Joel. *Why Ireland Starved: A Quantitative and Analytical History of the Irish Economy, 1800–1852.* Boston: George Allen & Unwin, 1983.
Moloney, Dierdre M. "Combatting 'Whiskey's Work': The Catholic Temperance Movement in Late Nineteenth-Century America." *U.S. Catholic Historian* 16 (Summer 1998): 1–23.
Molony, John Neylon. *A Soul Came into Ireland: Thomas Davis, 1814–1845.* Dublin: Geography Publications, 1995.
Moody, T. W., and F. X. Martin, O.S.A. *The Course of Irish History.* Rev. and enl. ed. Niwot, Colo.: Roberts Rinehart in assoc. with Radio Telefís Éireann; dist. by Publishers Group West, 1995.
Morash, Chris, and Richard Hayes, eds. *'Fearful Realities': New Perspectives on the Famine.* Dublin: Irish Academic Press, 1996.
Murphy, Ignatius. *The Diocese of Killaloe, 1800–1850.* Dublin: Four Courts Press, 1992.
———. "Some Attitudes to Religious Freedom and Ecumenism in Pre-Emancipation Ireland." *Irish Ecclesiastical Record* 105 (1966): 93–104.
Murphy, James H. "The Role of Vincentian Parish Missions in the 'Irish Counter-Reformation' of the Mid-Nineteenth Century." *Irish Historical Studies* 24 (November 1984): 152–71.
Murphy, John A. "Priests and People in Modern Irish History." *Christus Rex* 23 (1969): 235–59.
Niehaus, Earl. *The Irish in New Orleans, 1800–1860.* Baton Rouge: Louisiana State University Press, 1965.
Nolan, Hugh. *The Most Reverend Francis Patrick Kenrick: Third Bishop of*

Philadelphia 1830–1851. Philadelphia: American Catholic Historical Society, 1948.
Norman, Edward R. *Anti-Catholicism in Victorian England.* New York: Barnes & Noble, 1968.
———. *The English Catholic Church in the Nineteenth Century.* Oxford: Clarendon Press, 1984.
Nowlan, Kevin. *The Politics of Repeal.* Toronto: University of Toronto Press, 1965.
———. "The Catholic Clergy and Irish Politics in the 1830s and 40s." *Historical Studies* 9 (1974): 119–35.
———. "The Meaning of Repeal in Irish History." *Historical Studies* 4 (1967): 1–17.
Nowlan, Kevin, and Maurice O'Connell, eds. *Daniel O'Connell: Portrait of a Radical.* Belfast: Appletree Press, 1984.
O'Brien, Gerard. "The New Poor Law in Pre-Famine Ireland: A Case History." *Irish Economic and Social History* 12 (1985): 33–49.
O'Brien, Robert, and Morris Chafetz. *The Encyclopedia of Alcoholism.* 2d ed. New York: Facts on File, 1991.
O'Brien, Robert, Morris Chafetz, and Sidney Cohen. *The Encyclopedia of Understanding Alcohol and Drugs.* New York: Facts on File, 1999.
Ó'Broin, Leon. "The Trial and Imprisonment of O'Connell, 1843." *Éire-Ireland* 4 (Winter 1973): 39–54.
O'Connell, Marvin R. *John Ireland and the American Catholic Church.* St. Paul: Minnesota Historical Society, 1988.
O'Connell, Maurice. *Daniel O'Connell: The Man and His Politics.* Dublin: Irish Academic Press, 1990.
———. "O'Connell Reconsidered." *Studies* 64 (Summer 1975): 107–19.
———. "Young Ireland and the Catholic Clergy: Contemporary Deceit and Historical Falsehood." *Catholic Historical Review* 74 (April 1988): 199–225.
O'Dea, John. *History of the Ancient Order of Hibernians and Ladies Auxiliary.* 3 vols. New York, 1923; reprint, Notre Dame, Ind.: University of Notre Dame Press, 1995.
O'Dwyer, Peter, O.C.C. "John Francis Spratt, O. Carm, 1796–1871." Ph.D. diss., Gregorian University, 1968.
O'Faolain, Sean. *King of Beggars.* London, 1938; reprint, Dublin: Poolbeg Press, 1986.
O'Farrell, Patrick. "Millenialism, Messianism, and Utopianism in Irish History." *Anglo-Irish Studies* 2 (1976): 45–68.
Ó'Gráda, Cormac. *Black '47 and Beyond: The Great Irish Famine in History, Economy, and Memory.* Princeton, N.J.: Princeton University Press, 1999.

---. *Ireland: A New Economic History, 1789–1939.* (Oxford: Oxford University Press, 1994.
Osofsky, Gilbert. "Abolitionists, Irish Immigrants, and the Dilemmas of Romantic Nationalism." *American Historical Review* 80 (October 1975): 889–912.
Ó'Tuathaigh, Gearóid. *Ireland before the Famine, 1798–1848.* Dublin: Gill & Macmillan, 1972.
Peterson, Merrill D. *The Great Triumvirate: Webster, Clay, and Calhoun.* New York: Oxford University Press, 1987.
Póirtéir, Cathal, ed. *The Great Irish Famine.* Cork: Mercier Press, 1995.
Powderly, Terence. *The Path I Trod.* Ed. Harry J. Carman, Henry David, and Paul N. Guthrie. New York: Columbia University Press, 1940.
Power, Thomas P. *Land, Politics, and Society in Eighteenth-Century Tipperary.* Oxford: Clarendon Press, 1993.
Power, Thomas P., and Kevin Whelan, eds. *Endurance and Emergence: Catholics in Eighteenth-Century Ireland.* Dublin: Irish Academic Press, 1990.
Purcell, Mary. *Remembering Matt Talbot.* Dublin: Veritas Publications, 1990.
Quinn, John F. "Father Mathew's American Tour." *Éire-Ireland* 30 (Spring 1995): 91–104.
---. "Father Mathew's Disciples: Irish American Support for Temperance, 1840–1920." *Church History* 65 (December 1996): 624–40.
---. "Temperance in Tipperary: Father Mathew and Archbishop Slattery, 1839–1854." *Tipperary Historical Journal* 9 (1995): 133–39.
---. "'The Vagabond Friar': Father Mathew's Difficulties with the Irish Bishops, 1840–1856." *Catholic Historical Review* 78 (October 1992): 542–56.
Reardon, James. *The Catholic Church in the Diocese of St. Paul.* St. Paul, Minn.: North Central Publishing, 1952.
Reid, Douglas. "The Decline of Saint Monday." *Past and Present* 71 (1976): 76–101.
Riach, Douglas. "Daniel O'Connell and American Anti-Slavery." *Irish Historical Studies* 20 (March 1976): 3–25.
Rice, Alan J., and Martin Crawford, eds. *Liberating Sojourn: Frederick Douglass and Transatlantic Reform.* Athens: University of Georgia Press, 1999.
Rogers, Patrick. *Father Theobald Mathew: Apostle of Temperance.* New York: Longmans, 1945.
Ronan, Myles V. *An Apostle of Catholic Dublin: Father Henry Young.* Dublin: Browne and Nolan, 1944.
Rorabaugh, W. J. *The Alcoholic Republic: An American Tradition.* New York: Oxford University Press, 1979.

Rushe, Desmond. *Edmund Rice: The Man and His Times.* Dublin: Gill & Macmillan, 1981.
Shaw, Nessan, O.F.M. Cap. "The Total Abstinence Movement." *Capuchin Annual* 24 (1956): 129–37.
Shaw, Richard. *Dagger John: The Unquiet Life and Times of Archbishop John Hughes of New York.* New York: Paulist Press, 1977.
Sherry, Gerard E. "Irish Temperance Movement Battling Old Problem." *Our Sunday Visitor,* February 21, 1988.
Shiman, Lillian Lewis. *The Crusade against Drink in Victorian England.* New York: St. Martin's Press, 1988.
Spalding, Thomas. *The Premier See: A History of the Archdiocese of Baltimore, 1789–1989.* Baltimore: Johns Hopkins University Press, 1989.
Steele, E. D. "Cardinal Cullen and Irish Nationality." *Irish Historical Studies* 19 (1975): 239–60.
Stivers, Richard. *A Hair of the Dog: Irish Drinking and American Stereotype.* University Park: Pennsylvania State University Press, 1976.
Sweeney, David, O.F.M. *The Life of John Lancaster Spalding, First Bishop of Peoria, 1840–1916.* New York: Herder & Herder, 1965.
Swidler, Arlene. "Catholics and the 1876 Centennial." *Catholic Historical Review* 62 (July 1976): 349–65.
Swift, Roger, and Sheridan Gilley, eds. *The Irish in the Victorian City.* London: Croom Helm, 1985.
Taylor, Lawrence. "Stories of Power, Powerful Stories: The Drunken Priest in Donegal." In *Religious Orthodoxy and Popular Faith in European Society,* ed. Ellen Badone, 163–84. Princeton, N.J.: Princeton University Press, 1990.
"The Temperance Movement and Father Mathew's Visit to the United States, 1849–1851." *Historical Records and Studies* 6 (1911): 109–15.
Timberlake, James. *Prohibition and the Progressive Movement, 1900–1920.* Cambridge: Harvard University Press, 1963.
Townend, Paul. "Temperance, Father Mathew, and the Irish Clergy." *New Hibernia Review* 3 (Spring 1999): 111–22.
Trench, Charles Chenevix. *The Great Dan.* London: Grafton Books, 1986.
Turner, Victor, and Edith Turner. *Images and Pilgrimages in Christian Culture.* New York: Columbia University Press; 1978.
Tyrrell, Ian. *Sobering Up: From Temperance to Prohibition in Antebellum America, 1800–1860.* Westport, Conn.: Greenwood Press, 1979.
Valiulis, Maryann Gialanella, and Mary O'Dowd. *Women and Irish History.* Dublin: Wolfhound Press, 1997.
Vaughan, W. E., ed. *Ireland under the Union, I: 1801–1870.* Vol. 5 of *A New History of Ireland.* Oxford: Clarendon Press, 1989.

Vaughan, W. E., and A. J. Fitzpatrick, eds. *Irish Historical Statistics.* Dublin: Royal Irish Academy, 1978.
Walsh, Brendan. *Drinking in Ireland.* Dublin: Brunswick Press, 1980.
Walsh, Victor. "'Drowning the Shamrock': Drink, Teetotalism, and the Irish Catholics of Gilded-Age Pittsburgh." *Journal of American Ethnic History* 10 (Fall 1990-Winter 1991): 60–79.
Whyte, John. "The Appointment of Catholic Bishops in Nineteenth-Century Ireland." *Catholic Historical Review* 48 (1962): 12–32.
———. "Political Problems 1850–1860." In *A History of Irish Catholicism,* ed. Patrick Corish, 1–39. Dublin: Gill & Son, 1967.
Williams, T. D., and R. D. Edwards, eds. *The Great Famine.* Dublin: Browne and Nolan, 1956.
Woodham-Smith, Cecil. *The Great Hunger.* New York: Harper & Row, 1962.

Index

abolitionism. *See* slavery, abolition of
abstinence. *See* teetotalism
Act of Union, 15, 19, 23, 30
alcohol: consumption, 1, 40–44, 78, 112, 153, 192–93, 204n. 20; and crime, 113–14; expenditures on, 1; for medicinal purposes, 37, 45–46, 49, 54, 88–89, 100; production, 43–44, 78, 112, 153; and social uses, 44–46; taxes on, 1, 43, 153
Alcoholics Anonymous, 191–92
Allen, Richard, 114, 117
America, 188
American Temperance Society, 47
American Temperance Union, 148, 155, 158
Americanism, 183–84, 187
Anthony, Susan B., 155
Anti-Saloon League, 186, 188
Art Maguire: or the Broken Pledge, 124
Arundel and Surrey, Earl of, 105, 149, 215n. 54
Augustine, Father, 5, 59, 67, 69, 122, 132, 145

Band of Hope, 66
Barry, James Redmond, 50
Battersby, W. J., 76, 78
Bayley, Bishop James Roosevelt, 180
Beaumont, Gustave de, 10, 12, 31
Beecher, Rev. Lyman, 47, 156, 159
beer, 42–44, 46, 52, 78, 107, 153. *See also* alcohol
Belfast Flax Cultivation Society, 136
Belfast Temperance Advocate, 48
Bentinck, Lord George, 129
Beresford, Lord George, 18
Bianconi, Charles, 76
Birmingham, Father James, 59, 72–73
Blacker, Colonel William, 49, 88
Blake, Bishop Anthony, 24
Blake, Bishop Michael, 55–56, 87–88, 152

Blanc, Bishop Antoine, 165–66
Bloomer, Amelia, 155
Boston Pilot, 155, 161–62
Bradlaugh, Charles, 50, 205n. 40
Brennan, Martin, 138
Bretherton, George, 6, 43–44, 49, 52
breweries. *See* distilleries
Briggs, Bishop John, 103
Browne, Bishop George, 56, 73
Browne, Bishop James, 87–88
Browne, Father Martin, 83
Buckingham, James, 41
Burke, Father Joseph, 83–84
Butler, Elizabeth, 34
Butler, Bishop John, 24
Byrne, Bishop Andrew, 166

Calhoun, John, 164
Cantwell, Bishop John, 98
Capuchins, 36–38, 91, 118, 145, 169, 179, 195n. 5, 202n. 89
Carleton, William, 124, 152
Carlile, Ann, 66
Carlyle, Jane Welsh (Mrs. Thomas Carlyle), 105
Carr, Rev. George, 41, 47–48, 52, 76
Carr, John, 40, 54
Catholic Association, 17–18, 38
Catholic Board, 16–17
Catholic Church: and Prohibition, 190; and Repeal movement, 99, 122; revival of, 23–27; and temperance movement, 9, 53–56, 92–95, 103–4, 157–58, 174–75, 183; and veto controversy, 15–17, 198n. 21
Catholic Committee, 15, 17
Catholic Emancipation, 13, 15, 17–18, 30, 32, 144
Catholic Prohibition League of America, 188
Catholic Relief Bill, 19

Catholic Total Abstinence Union of
  America (CTAU), 4, 9, 181–88
Catholic World, 186
Catholics: and Protestants, 3, 23, 28–30,
  62–63, 106–7
Caulfield, Bishop James, 24
Chanche, Bishop John, 165
Cheyne, John, 49
Church of Ireland, 29, 34, 49, 72
Clarendon, Lord, 150
Clay, Henry, 164, 166, 168
Clogher Statutes, 54
Clontarf Meeting, 109
Coen, Bishop Thomas, 74
Collins, Bishop Michael, 56
Conway, F. W., 61
Corish, Patrick, 26–27
Cork, 36–38, 42, 50, 52, 56–61, 71, 112, 119, 125,
  132, 134, 136, 140–45, 169, 171
Cork House of Industry, 57
Cork Total Abstinence Society (CTAS), 2,
  60–62; and Catholic Church, 92–95; and
  children, 65–66; and founding of, 57–59;
  and membership, 3, 60–62, 66, 69–77,
  86, 88, 104–5, 108, 112, 122, 126, 152, 163,
  165–68, 170; and papal indulgences,
  94–95; and pledge, nature of, 63–65,
  107–8, 158; and pledge-breaking, 123–24;
  and pledge ceremony, 63–67; and temperance medals, 64, 116–18
Cormac, Denis, 112
Corn Laws, 128–29
Crampton, Philip, 49
Crolly, Archbishop William, 28, 87, 99
Cullen, Father James, 4, 9, 172, 175–79
Cullen, Father Paul (later Archbishop),
  33, 91–94, 97, 145–46, 158, 169–70,
  174–75, 178
Curran, Father J. J., 188

Davis, Jefferson, 164
Davis, Thomas Osborne, 97
Davys, Father Richard, 83
Delany, Father John, 76
Delany, Bishop William, 145–46, 171
Denvir, Bishop Cornelius, 87
Denvir, John, 1, 66, 209n. 41

Dickens, Charles, 156
Dillon, John Blake, 97
Disraeli, Benjamin, 129–30
distilleries, 42, 112
Distillery Act, 141
Donahoe, Patrick, 155, 162, 165
Donnybrook Fair, 102
Donovan, Father Daniel, 36–38
Douglas, Stephen, 164
Douglass, Frederick, 125–26, 160, 229n. 31
Dow, Neal, 156
Dowden, Richard, 57, 151, 159
Dowling, Father James, 65
Doyle, Bishop James, 25, 28–29, 48–49, 55
Drummond, Thomas, 79
drunkenness, 40–42, 46, 48, 51, 53–55, 101,
  115, 123, 126, 175
Dublin, 32, 42, 50, 75–76, 87, 97
Dublin Evening Mail, 65, 89, 117
Dublin Evening Post, 28–29, 33, 61, 69
Dublin Juvenile Temperance Society, 66
Dublin Temperance Society, 49
Dublin Weekly Herald, 60–61, 69–71, 96,
  116
Duff, Patrick, 137–38
Duffy, Charles Gavan, 1, 88, 97, 131,
  151–52, 226n. 84
Dunscombe, Rev. Nicholas, 57

Ebrington, Lord, 79, 81
Eccleston, Archbishop Samuel, 163
Edgar, Rev. John, 41, 43, 47–48, 52–53, 173
Edgeworth, Maria, 40, 114, 212n. 70

Fagan, William, 119
Famine, Irish, 3, 30, 127–30, 133–37,
  139–43, 147–48
Ferriter, Diarmaid, 4
Finch, John, 42, 50, 52–53
Fingall, Earl of, 15
Fitzgerald, G. H., 68
Fitzgerald, Father John, 121
Fitzgerald, Vesey, 18, 30
Fitzpatrick, Bishop John, 159–60
Flinn, Father Joseph, 179
Foran, Bishop Nicholas, 70
Forbes, Sir John, 172–74

Forbes, Captain Robert, 142
Foster, John, 32
Foster, R. F., 4, 232n. 65
Freeman's Journal, 61, 91, 120, 123, 149–50
Furlong, Bishop Thomas, 174

Garrison, William Lloyd, 82, 126, 142, 160–62, 164, 224n. 45, 229n. 23
George IV (king of England), 19
Gibbons, Cardinal James, 184–85, 187–88, 190
Grant, James, 102, 112, 115
Grattan, Henry, 15–16, 40
Gregory XVI (pope), 93–94, 144
Gregory, William, 147
Grey, Earl, 19–20, 32
Grey, Lord Lieutenant de, 97
Griffin, Martin, 185–86
Griffiths, Bishop Thomas, 103–4

Hall, S. C., 41, 78, 132
Hall, Mrs. S. C., 41, 78, 140
Harvey, Joshua, 49
Haughton, James, 52, 62, 87, 114, 118–19, 121 123–24, 138, 154, 174
Hibernian Temperance Society, 49–50, 66
Higgins, Bishop William, 8, 25–26, 32–33, 83–84, 98–99, 117, 144–45
Hincks, Rev. Thomas, 118, 120–21
Hockings, John, 51–53
Hughes, Bishop John, 159

Illustrated London News, 105
Ireland, Archbishop John, 9, 66, 172, 182–84, 186–88, 190
"Ireland Sober, Ireland Free," 177
Irish Confederation, 131, 151
Irish Temperance and Literary Gazette, 52
Irish Temperance Union, 60–61

Jebb, Bishop John, 28
Josephian Society, 37

Keane, Bishop John, 182–85, 187–88, 190
Kearney, Hugh, 4–7
Keating, Bishop James, 76
Keenan, Desmond, 26–27

Kennedy, Bishop Patrick, 56
Kenrick, Bishop Francis Patrick, 148, 156, 158, 163
Kenrick, Bishop Peter, 158, 166
Kenyon, Father John, 56
Keogh, John, 15
Kernan, Bishop Edward, 87
Kerr, Father Donal, 26–27, 31, 143–44
Kerrigan, Colm, 6, 106, 113
Kickham, Charles, 1
Kildare Place Society, 29, 33
Kinsella, Bishop William, 12, 27, 72
Kirby, Father Tobias, 94, 139
Kirwan, Father Walter Blake, 24
Kohl, J. G., 114

Landsdowne, Lord, 132
Larkin, Emmet, 26, 121, 219n. 19
Larkin, Jim, 1
League of the Cross, 108
Leahy, Bishop Patrick, 174
Lenihan, Maurice, 147
Leo XIII (pope), 183, 187
Liberator, 161–62
Limerick Reporter, 69
Lonergan, Sister Basil, 146
Lucas, Frederick, 107–8
Lumpkin, Judge Joseph, 162
Lyons, Thomas, 119

McAdam, James, 136
McAuley, Mother Catherine, 24, 61
McCarthy, Justin, 1, 66
McDevitt, Father James, 181
MacDonagh, Oliver, 32, 95
McDowell, Rose, 111
MacEvilly, Bishop John, 174
McGettigan, Bishop Patrick, 87–88
McGivney, Father Michael, 185
McGregor, Duncan, 80
MacHale, Archbishop John, 8, 21, 23, 25–26, 31–34, 36, 39, 83–84, 89–94, 117, 124–25, 173, 178, 213n. 17
Machebeuf, Father Joseph, 156–57
McKenna, James, 58, 60–62, 102, 117
McLeod, Father Denis, 145
Magee, William, 29

Maginn, Bishop Edward, 148
Maguire, John, 5, 62, 120, 162, 165, 174
Maher, Father James, 55–56, 91
Mahony, Cornelius, 154
Maine Law, 156, 179–80
Malcolm, Elizabeth, 1–2, 4–5, 44, 61, 177, 202n. 86
Mallow Defiance, 99, 109
Manners, Lord John, 152
Manning, Archbishop Henry, 108
Mansfield, Father Richard, 36
Marsh, Rev. John, 148–49
Martin, William, 52–53, 57, 59, 62
Mathew, Charles, 169
Mathew, Lady Elizabeth, 35, 118
Mathew, Francis, 35
Mathew, George, 34
Mathew, James, 35
Mathew Liberating Fund, 165
Mathew Relief Committee, 118–19, 122
Mathew Testimonial Committee, 119–20
Mathew, Father Theobald: assessment of, 4–7, 112–15; biographies of, 5–6; birth, 35; and Catholic Church, 8, 79, 82–85; at Cork, 36–39, 57–61, 71, 109, 132, 134, 140; and Cork Total Abstinence Society, 2, 58–77, 108, 177; death, 3, 171; and ecumenism, 9, 34, 38, 53, 62–64, 79, 84, 93, 148, 212n. 70; education of, 35–36; in England, 102–8; family background, 34–35, 113, 118, 169, 202n. 86; and Famine, Irish, 134–36, 140–43, 148; and financial difficulties, 115–22, 131–33, 143–44, 155, 159, 167–68; health of, 149–50, 155, 161, 163, 166, 168–70; at Limerick, 69–70, 86, 88; and MacHale, Archbishop John, 89–94, 173, 213n. 17; memorials to, 4, 109, 174, 178, 182; and miraculous powers, 73–76, 163, 209n. 41; and O'Connell, Daniel, 7–8, 61, 73, 79, 81–82, 85, 96–97, 100–101, 110, 118–23, 131, 135; opposition to, 79–85, 89–94, 144–46, 149–50, 158, 178; ordination of, 36; and pension, 132–33, 143–47, 159; and Prohibition, 170–71, 188, 232n. 69; proposed as bishop of Cork, 144–47; and Repeal movement, 102, 110–12, 131; seeks bishopric in Jamaica, 169–70; and slavery, abolition of, 125, 159–64; joins temperance movement, 57–59; visits United States, 3, 148–49, 152, 154–55, 158–68
Mathew, Thomas, 113
Maude, Sir Thomas, 35
Maynooth College, 24–25, 32, 35–37, 77, 124, 210n. 53
Meagher, Thomas Francis, 131
Melbourne, Lord, 20, 79, 95
Metropolitan Total Abstinence Society, 90–91
Miley, Father John, 140
Miller, Kerby, 114
Mitchel, John, 151
moderationists, 46, 51–52
Moloney, Father Jeremiah, 55
monster meetings, 97, 101–2
Montague, Michael, 77
Monteagle, Lord, 142
Morpeth, Lord, 20–21, 77, 79
Mulgrave, Lord, 20
Municipal Reform Act, 95
Murphy, Father J. J. F., 87
Murphy, Bishop John, 58, 144
Murphy, Brother Patrick Joseph, 70
Murray, Bishop Daniel, 16, 25, 31–34, 36, 38, 75–76, 94, 99, 169

Nagle, Nano, 24
Nation, 98, 102, 151–52
Nenagh Chronicle, 61
Newman, Frank, 50
New Ross Temperance Society, 47–48, 50, 76
New York Herald, 168
Nicholson, Asenath, 66, 113, 150
Nolan, Bishop William, 12

O'Brien, Smith, 110–12, 131, 151
O'Connell, Father Andrew, 75–76, 87, 90–91, 119
O'Connell, Daniel, 12–23, 30, 33, 95, 124–25, 172, 214n. 24; birth, 13; and Catholic Church, 13–18; death, 140; education of, 13–14; and Famine, Irish, 128, 133–34, 136–37, 139–40; and Mathew, Father Theobald, 7–8, 61, 73,

79, 81–82, 85, 96–97, 100–101, 110, 118–23, 131, 135; in Parliament, 19–21; and Repeal movement, 82, 86, 97–102, 109–11, 121–22, 130–31, 177; and slavery, abolition of, 160; and temperance movement, 3, 8–9, 82, 85, 96–97, 100–101, 123, 138
O'Connell, John, 57–58
O'Connell, Maurice, 112, 119, 138
"O'Connell Tribute," 99, 121–22
O'Connor, Feargus, 20, 23
O'Connor, Bishop Michael, 158, 167, 185
O'Connor, William, 109
O'Loghlen, Michael, 21
O'Meara, David, 154
Orange Order, 49, 88, 205n. 31
O'Reilly, Father Jeremiah, 72
O'Shea, Father M. B., 37
O'Sullivan, Father Michael, 56, 58
Owen, Robert, 50

Parliament Whiskey, 42
Pearse, Patrick, 1, 233n. 22
Peel, Sir Robert, 18–20, 95, 97–98, 102, 109, 124–25, 127–29, 133, 214n. 24
Penal Laws, 24, 197n. 8
Penney, Rev. Joseph, 47
Pioneer Total Abstinence Association. *See* Pioneers
Pioneers, 4, 9, 172, 176–77, 179, 191
Pitt, William, 15
Pius VII (pope), 16
Pius IX (pope), 140, 169
pledge, children and, 65–67; nature of, 63–68, 107–8, 158; women and, 71, 208–209n. 32
Plunkett, Bishop George, 25–27
Poor Law, 147
popular religion, 27–28
Portier, Bishop Michael, 165
poteen, 42–44, 112, 153. *See also* alcohol
Powderly, Terence, 184
Prendergast, John, 12
Presentation Sisters, 24, 68, 73
Preston Total Abstinence Society, 52
priests, status in society, 12, 28, 30–31

Prohibition, 9, 46, 170–71, 182, 186, 188–90
Protestants: and Catholics, 3, 23, 28–30, 62–63, 106–7; and temperance movement, 48
pubs, 45–46, 50, 136
Purcell, Archbishop J. B., 134, 156
Purcell, Peter, 119–20, 138
Purgatorian Society, 55, 87

Quakers, 49, 51–52, 60, 139
Queen's Colleges, 124–25, 169–70
Quinlivan, Father James, 144

Rathbone, William, 103, 152
Reform Bill (1832), 19
Repeal Association, 82, 137
"Repeal Martyrs," 110
Repeal movement, 8, 19–20, 79, 82, 95, 97–102, 109–11; and Catholic Church, 99, 122; and Mathew, Father Theobald, 102, 110–12, 131; and O'Connell, Daniel, 82, 86, 97–102, 109–11, 121–22, 130–31; and temperance movement, 7–8, 79, 82, 85, 97, 100–102, 110–12, 131
Repeal pledge, 110–11
"Repeal Rent," 99, 121–22
Rice, Brother Edmund, 2, 24, 70
Rogers, Father Patrick, 5
Roosevelt, Theodore, 186–87
Russell, Lord John, 20, 121, 128, 130, 132–33, 139–41, 143–44, 147
Russell, Major John, 131–33, 144, 149
Ryan, Bishop John, 88
Ryder, Father James, 163

St. Patrick League of the Cross, 175
Satolli, Archbishop Francesco, 186–87
Second Reformation, 29, 53
secret societies, 17, 24, 28, 80–81
Sedwards, Jeffrey, 54–55
Select Committee on Inquiry into Drunkenness, 41, 44
Seward, William, 162, 164
shebeens, 45
Sheehan, Father John, 70
Sheil, John, 110, 149, 152

Sherburne, Colonel J. H., 150, 152, 154
Shrewsbury, Earl of, 149
Simpson, W. W., 120, 132
Slattery, Archbishop Michael, 122, 145–47, 171
slavery, abolition of, 125, 159–64
Smith, Adam, 140
"souperism," 30
Spain, Father John, 72
Spalding, Bishop John Lancaster, 182–83
Spencer, Father George, 103
Spratt, Father John, 52, 56, 87, 119, 124, 137–39, 174
Stanhope, Earl, 105
Stanley, Bishop Edward (Church of England), 106–7
Stanton, Elizabeth Cady, 155
Sunday closing laws: in Ireland, 174–75, 182–83; in the United States, 191–92

Tablet, 107
Taylor, Zachary, 164
teetotalism, 1–2, 4, 9; beginnings of movement, 52–53; and Bible, 52–53, 72, 157; and medicinal purposes, use of alcohol for, 49, 54, 88–89; and moderationists, 51–52
temperance movement: beginnings of, 46–51; and Catholic Church, 9, 53–56, 92–95, 103–4, 157–58, 174–75, 183; and O'Connell, Daniel, 8, 82, 85, 96–97, 100–101, 123, 138; opposition to, 78–85; and Repeal movement, 7–8, 79–82, 85, 97, 100–102, 110–12, 131
Thackeray, William, 113–14
Thompson, William, 50, 205n. 39
Times (London), 69, 89, 97, 143
Tipperary Vindicator, 132
Tocqueville, Alexis de, 10, 12, 27, 30–31, 144
Tories, 20–21, 95, 128–30
Total Abstinence Association of the Sacred Heart. *See* Pioneers
"Tower of Temperance," 109

Trevelyan, Charles, 130, 133–36, 141, 147
Troy, Archbishop John, 25, 31–32
Tuam Statutes, 54
Tuohy, Bishop Charles, 28
Tyrrell, Father Peter, 110

Ulster, 48–49, 86, 173
Ulster Temperance Society, 47–49, 51
United Irishman, 151
United Kingdom Alliance, 170

Victoria (queen of England), 132
Volstead Act, 189–90

Wakefield, Edward, 40
Walmesley, Bishop Charles, 28
Walsh, Father Thomas, 183
Warren, Bishop Michael, 175
Washingtonians, 155, 158
Waterford Chronicle, 61
Wealth of Nations, 140
Webb, Richard, 49, 52, 160
Wellington, Duke of, 13, 19
Westport Total Abstinence Society, 90–92
Whigs, 19–21, 32, 95, 111, 129–30
whiskey, 42–46, 78, 153. *See also* alcohol
Whyte, Ann, 35
Willard, Frances, 184–85, 235n. 52
wine, 51–52. *See also* alcohol
Wiseman, Bishop Nicholas, 103
Women's Christian Temperance Union (WCTU), 182, 185
Woodhull, Caleb, 159
World Temperance Convention, 160
Woulfe, Stephen, 55

Yore, Father John, 75–76, 87
Young, Father Henry, 55
Young Ireland, 98, 124–25, 130–31, 136
Young Men's Total Abstinence Society, 148

Zurcher, Father George, 186–88, 190

John F. Quinn, a native of New Jersey, received his education at Georgetown University (A.B.) and the University of Notre Dame (M.A., Ph.D.). A specialist in Irish history, he is an associate professor of history at Salve Regina University in Newport, Rhode Island, where he has been a faculty member since 1992. He lives in Middletown, Rhode Island, with his wife, Marguerite, and son, Michael.